THE EARLY LIFE
OF
ABRAHAM LINCOLN

THE EARLIEST PORTRAIT OF ABRAHAM LINCOLN.—HITHERTO UNPUBLISHED.

From a carbon enlargement, by Sherman and McHugh, New York, of a daguerreotype in the possession of the Hon. Robert T. Lincoln, and first published in the McClure's Life of Lincoln. It is generally believed that Lincoln was not over thirty-five years old when this daguerreotype was taken, and it is certainly true that it shows the face of Lincoln as a young man. It is probably earlier by six or seven years, at least, than any other existing portrait of Lincoln.

THE EARLY LIFE
OF
ABRAHAM LINCOLN

IDA M. TARBELL

Assisted by

J. McCan Davis

New Introduction by

Paul M. Angle

South Brunswick and New York: A. S. Barnes and Company
London: Thomas Yoseloff Ltd

A. S. Barnes and Co., Inc.
Cranbury, New Jersey 08512

Thomas Yoseloff Ltd
108 New Bond Street
London W1Y OQX, England

ISBN 0-498-01439-8
Printed in the United States of America

PUBLISHER'S NOTE

The prospective reader may certainly be forgiven if he asks why a reissue of this largely obsolete work on the early life of Lincoln at this time. The work (as Dr. Angle suggests in his illuminating Introduction) has been superseded by Miss Tarbell's later complete life of Lincoln, which now is available in all major libraries and on the shelves of many collectors of Lincolniana.

Dr. Angle has provided the answer to this question very ably. The work, written in the white heat of Miss Tarbell's first researches, contains many insights not found in the more formal later work. The comparison itself is rewarding, and few students of Lincoln can come away from the early work without having gained some new nuggets from the mine.

Yet, although many thousands of copies were printed and distributed, the work is something of a rarity today, and is found in few libraries, whose custodians certainly feel that the complete life is sufficient for their needs.

It was through the suggestion of Mr. Robert Marx that the present reissue came about, and it was from his library that a working copy was provided. The Publisher's thanks go also to Dr. Paul Angle for his understanding of the usefulness of a reissue at this time and particularly for his perceptive Introduction to this edition.

NEW INTRODUCTION

When Ida M. Tarbell joined the staff of *McClure's Magazine* in 1894 she had no idea that she would ever write a Lincoln book, let alone several.

S. S. McClure, who had founded the magazine only a year earlier, wanted her for a very different assignment. He had the reproduction rights to a large collection of portraits of Napoleon Bonaparte, and he needed someone to write a supporting text. Moreover, he needed a writer in a hurry. The author originally commissioned had produced a text which the owner of the collection, who had retained the right of approval, refused to accept, yet McClure had already announced a publication date for the series.

In the editor's eyes, Miss Tarbell was ideally qualified for the assignment. She had just returned from three years in Paris, where she had gone to write a biography of Madame Roland, the French revolutionary who, as leader of the Girondists, was executed in 1793. While abroad she had supported herself, somewhat precariously, by free-lance writing, and had sold several articles to the McClure Syndicate. McClure had called on her on one of his trips to Paris, so she was more to him than a name. He may or may not have been aware that she had spent several years on the staff of *The Chautauquan*, the organ of the Chautauqua Literary and Scientific Circle, then in its heyday. But he did know that she could organize a piece of writing and possessed a clear if not elegant style. Besides, she was steeped in the literature of the French Revolution, she handled the French language readily, and was a hard worker. Where could he find a person better suited to his pressing need?

Miss Tarbell had doubts. She was not sure that she wanted to devote her life to journalism. In college—at Allegheny, a small Methodist institution near her home in the oil region of western Pennsylvania—she had decided to become a biologist, but that dream had faded. She had undertaken her study of Madame Roland in the hope that it would throw light on the ways in which women could play influential parts in public affairs. It had not. So here she was, at thirty-seven, at a loose end. After some hesitation she accepted McClure's offer. The salary was a good one and she would have, for a time at least, the security she had not enjoyed for several years.*

She pitched into the Napoleon story with her usual diligence, working for the most part at the Library of Congress. McClure and J. S. Phillips, co-owner of *McClure's*, were pleaesd with what she was producing; so was the owner of the portrait collection. But before she was finished McClure came to her with another idea. She would, of course, complete the Napoleon series, but then McClure wanted her to undertake a study of the life of Abraham Lincoln. The editor believed that an industrious investigator could find a large reservoir of untapped reminiscences of Lincoln. Hundreds of people who had known him well were still living: former members of his Cabinet, members of Congress, residents of Illinois towns who had known him as a practicing lawyer or had heard one or more of the Lincoln-Douglas debates or other speeches which Lincoln had made in the course of the famous campaign of 1858. And there could well be a few survivors from Lincoln's boyhood and youth in Kentucky and Indiana.

Miss Tarbell was skeptical. She knew that soon after Lincoln's death his former law partner, William H. Herndon, and J. G. Holland, former editor of the *Springfield Republican* and a well known man of letters, had both visited Kentucky and Indiana, had assiduously sought out men and women who had known the young Lincoln, and had published their interviews. John G. Nicolay and John Hay had only recently published their monumental biography, and it could be assumed that they had garnered and used all that could be learned from Lincoln's associates during his presidency. What more remained? McClure, following intuition alone, insisted that a further search would be fruitful.

Miss Tarbell, troubled, sought out John G. Nicolay, whom she had come to know while working at the Library of Congress. He

<hr>

* Peter Lyon, in *Success Story: The Life and Times of S. S. McClure* (New York, 1963), tells a somewhat different story. According to Lyon, McClure made a special trip to Paris to hire Miss Tarbell and bring her back to the United States. He even paid her $150 to cover her passage home although he was desperately short of money. I prefer what I have written, which is based on Miss Tarbell's autobiography, *All in the Day's Work* (New York, 1939).

advised her against any venture into the Lincoln field. He and John Hay had already covered all of Lincoln's life that was worth the telling. In a later interview he went further. "You are invading my field," he said. "You write a popular Life of Lincoln and you do just so much to decrease the value of my property."

But Miss Tarbell had a strong streak of stubbornness. Nicolay's opposition, obviously stemming from self-interest, resolved her indecision. She would go ahead with the Lincoln project. In her autobiography she wrote:

"Mr. Nicolay's rebuff settled my plan of campaign. I would not begin at the end of the story with the great and known, but at the start in Kentucky with the humble and unknown; I would follow the trail chronologically, I would see for myself what sort of people and places those were that had known Lincoln, reconstruct the life of his day as far as living men and women backed by published records furnished reliable material. I would gather documents as I went, bits of color, stories, recollections; I would search in courthouses and county histories and newspapers; I would pick up pictures as I went, a picture of everything that directly or indirectly touched on what I was after. I would make sure that if among these people who had known him there might not be letters not in the 'Complete Works [of Nicolay and Hay]' and, if I were lucky, somewhere on the trail I might turn up the important unpublished reminiscences which Mr. McClure was so certain existed. It was a gamble, the greater because I was so profoundly ignorant of American life and history."

Miss Tarbell made her first trip to Kentucky in February, 1895, about the worst possible time of the year, for rain and wet snow could be counted on, and the roads, dirt of course, would be almost impassable. McClure, in a sudden surge of concern, supplied her with warm bed socks to mitigate the cold of the primitive Kentucky hotels. (He was right. Thirty years later, when I made my first trip to Kentucky, the best that could be said of the small town hotels and restaurants was that they were a little better than nothing.)

The results of Miss Tarbell's investigations were disappointing. Originally, McClure had believed she could unearth enough new material so that it could be published with only editorial explanations but the hope did not materialize. She did pick up stray recollections, a few letters that had not been published, some forgotten newspaper paragraphs, and court records that had escaped notice. But it was all too fragmentary to stand by itself, even when supported by editorial comment. McClure, Phillips, and Miss Tarbell put their heads together and decided that what she was finding could be used only to enlarge and retouch the well-known story. So they settled for a new Life of Lincoln, much shorter and more popular than that of Nicolay and Hay, and given additional appeal by the reminiscences, stories, and documents that would be fresh to most readers.

The first installments appeared in *McClure's Magazine* in 1895 and immediately received favorable notice. In spite of the sneering remarks attributed to Richard Watson Gilder, editor of *The Century*, "They got a girl to write a life of Lincoln," the circulation of *McClure's Magazine* jumped by 90,000 in the first month of the Lincoln serial, by 60,000 in the second month. So McClure and Phillips decided to put the first numbers into book form without waiting for the entire Life. Accordingly, *The Early Life of Abraham Lincoln* was published in both cloth and paper by S. S. McClure, New York, in 1896. A book of 240 pages, liberally embellished by illustrations, it carried the story from the advent of the Lincoln family to Massachusetts in 1637 to Abraham Lincoln's departure from New Salem, Illinois, to Springfield two hundred years later. On its title page it bore the name of Ida M. Tarbell and also that of J. McCan Davis, a Springfield newspaperman and lawyer who served as the author's research assistant.

The book had unusal features for its time and still possesses interest for Lincoln students who may have lost sight of it in the deluge of Lincoln books that have come out since it was published. Miss Tarbell did find old men and women in Kentucky, Indiana, and Illinois who remembered the young Lincoln and talked with her at length about him. Their recollections, though a fragile foundation for the historical edifice, are not without importance. Take, for example, the contribution of Christopher Columbus Graham, recorded in his one hundredth year and first published by Miss Tarbell. No wary reader would accept any of Graham's specific statements at face value. He asserted that "Thomas and Nancy [Lincoln] both could read and write"; we know that she could do neither. According to Graham, Tom and Nancy and Sarah Bush Lincoln "were just steeped full of Jesse Head's notions about the wrong of slavery and the rights of man as explained by Thomas Jefferson and Thomas Paine." They may have heard of Jefferson the President, but anyone familiar with the state of knowledge prevailing on the frontier will doubt that any of the three ever heard of Paine. Graham probably attended the wedding and infare of Thomas and Nancy Lincoln, but could he really recall that at the infare the guests were served bear meat, venison, wild turkey and ducks, eggs wild and tame "so common that you could buy them at two bits a bushel," maple sugar, maple syrup, peach-and-honey, a barbecued sheep, and a jug of whiskey? The Lincolns, Graham said, had a cow and a calf, milk and butter, a featherbed, home-woven "kiverlids," big and little pots, and a loom and wheel. Perhaps. Perhaps not. In reality, Graham was not describing the Lincoln establishment, but the state of society in the backwoods of Kentucky. And that is a description worth having.

Or turn to the recollections of Josiah Crawford and his wife, who lived near Gentryville, Indiana. Crawford recalled that Lincoln had borrowed a copy of Weems's Life of Washington from him and carelessly allowed it to get rain-soaked. Crawford permitted him to keep the book on condition that he shuck corn for three days. So far so good. But did the young Lincoln tell Crawford: "I do not always intend to delve, grub, shuck corn, split rails, and the like"? Instead, he planned to prepare himself for a profession. And when Mrs. Crawford would ask him: "What would you like to be?" he would answer: "I'll be President." Austin Gollaher, a boyhood friend of Lincoln's in Kentucky, probably came far closer to the truth when he remembered only that Lincoln was "an unusually bright boy at school, and made splendid progress in his studies. Indeed, he learned faster than any of his schoolmates." Lincoln's later intellectual attainments offer convincing proof of that statement.

In all probability Miss Tarbell presented these recollections for what they were worth, content to have the reader exercise his critical faculties on them. For she was not without scholarly acumen. That she proved when she came to treat one of the most cherished tales of Lincoln's youth, the story of the New Orleans slave auction. Witnessing the public sale of a pretty mulatto girl Lincoln watched prospective buyers paw and pinch to make sure that she was sound and strong. Tortured by the sight, he is reported to have said to his companions: "Boys, let's get away from this. If I ever get a chance to hit that thing, I'll hit it hard." But Miss Tarbell pointed out that the episode rested on the sole authority of John Hanks who, by Lincoln's own statement, started for New Orleans but left the boat at St. Louis on the downriver trip and could have had no first-hand knowledge of the dramatic encounter.

But there were times when Miss Tarbell's critical sense failed her. A case in point is her idealization of Nancy Hanks. At one point in the *Early Life* she had the following to say of Lincoln's mother:

"But it was only in her surroundings and in her family that Nancy Hanks was like Thomas Lincoln. In nature, in education, and in ambition she was, if tradition is to be believed, quite another person. Certainly a fair and delicate woman, who could read and write, who had ideas of refinement, and a desire to get more from life than fortune had allotted her, was hardly enough like Thomas Lincoln to be very happy with him. She was still more unfit to be his wife because of a sensitive nature which made her brood over her situation—a situation made the more hopeless by the fact that she had neither the force of character nor strength of body to do anything to improve it; if, indeed, she had any clear notion of what it lacked. Hers was that pitiful condition where one feels with vague restlessness that life has something better than one has found, something not seen or understood, but without which life will never be complete."

As I have remarked, we know that Nancy Hanks could neither read nor write, and that is about as far as our solid knowledge extends. Not that that was a deficiency to be held against her. By common consent, especially in the South, even a rudimentary education was believed to be of no value for girls, so perhaps two-thirds of the young women of Nancy's age and station on the frontier were illiterate. Nevertheless, illiteracy is a hard fact upon which Miss Tarbell's characterization falls apart. The whole paragraph was spun from her own imagination, and one need only read her own autobiography to surmise that she was putting into the mind of Nancy Hanks what she, Ida Tarbell, would have felt in similar circumstances. In fact, she seems to have come to this conclusion herself, for she omitted this passage in her subsequent *Life of Abraham Lincoln,* in which she incorporated unchanged most of the *Early Life.*

Miss Tarbell's second lapse came in her complete acceptance of the story of Lincoln and Ann Rutledge, but for this she had considerable authority. As early as 1866 William H. Herndon, Lincoln's former law partner, revealed to the world that while living at New Salem Lincoln had fallen in love with Ann Rutledge, a gentle winsome girl previously engaged to a local storekeeper who had gone East but had not returned when he had promised to nor had he written to his fiancée. Believing herself abandoned, Ann fell in love with Lincoln and promised to marry him. But the fact that she was engaged to two men at the same time preyed heavily on the girl's mind. Torn by emotional conflict she fell ill in the summer of 1835 and died, leaving Lincoln so distraught that for weeks he was incapacitated with his mind tottering on the verge of unreason.

This was the story in its classic form, accepted more or less fully by every biographer prior to Miss Tarbell except Nicolay and Hay, who ignored it. (Mrs. Lincoln considered Herndon's revelation of the Ann Rutledge "romance" a personal affront and Robert Lincoln shared her feelings. Since he had the right to pass on everything that Nicolay and Hay wrote, he would have expunged any mention they might have made of Ann Rutledge.)

But in writing of the disastrous effect of Ann's death on Lincoln, Miss Tarbell went further than most. In prose unusually lush for her she wrote that the death of the young woman had plunged Lincoln into the deepest gloom. "The abiding melancholy, that painful sense of the incompleteness of life, which had been his mother's dowry to him, asserted itself." His imagination tortured him with "black pictures." One stormy night, when he was sitting with his friend, William Green, tears streamed from his eyes. Green begged him to control himself. Lincoln moaned: "I cannot; the thought of the snow and rain on her grave fills me with indescribable grief." Friends found him wandering through the woods, muttering to himself, and believed him to be on the verge of madness. Finally Bowling Green, the squire, and his wife took him into their cabin home and kept him there until he mastered his emotions.

"But though he had regained self-control, his grief was deep and bitter. Ann Rutledge was buried in Concord cemetery, a country burying-ground seven miles northwest of New Salem. To this lonely spot Lincoln frequently journeyed to weep over her grave. 'My heart is buried there,' he said to one of his friends."

Thirty years passed before students more critical than Miss Tarbell began to take hard looks at the Ann Rutledge story. Aided by documentary material not available when she wrote, they came to the conclusion that the episode had been blown up out of all proportion. Present-day opinion is best summarized by James G. Randall, who devoted twenty-one pages to a closely reasoned critique of the story:

"Whatever may have been the true situation as to Lincoln and Ann, that situation seems now well nigh unrecoverable. As to a romantic attachment, it has not been *dis*proved. It is more correct to characterize it as *un*proved; as such it has been a famous subject of conjecture. It is a memory which lacks support in any statement recorded in Ann's lifetime. Since it is thus traditional and not reliably established as to its nature and significance, it does not belong in a recital of those Lincoln episodes which one presents as unquestioned reality. . . .

"Assuredly the effect of the episode upon Lincoln's later life has been greatly exaggerated—or rather, fabricated. Nor should one lightly overlook the shabby manner in which the image of Ann has tended to obscure the years of Lincoln's love and devotion for Mary, his wife, and to belittle her love and devotion for him. . . . Evaluation of the evidence, which one seldom finds anywhere but which has been attempted in the preceding pages, is the only answer to the inquiry as to where the pedestrian course of history ends and the limitless soaring of fiction begins."

But these aberrations, long since corrected, pale in importance besides the lasting contributions Miss Tarbell made in unearthing documents relating to Thomas Lincoln and to the early life of his famous son. These included the marriage license of Thomas Lincoln and Nancy Hanks and the certificate of their marriage, laying to rest forever persistent rumors that no marriage had ever taken place. She found the marriage bond given by Thomas Lincoln at the time of his marriage to Sarah Bush Lincoln, his second wife. She came across numerous documents proving that Thomas Lincoln had held positions of responsibility in Kentucky, and that he was a trustworthy citizen who paid his bills. In Illinois she located the record of Abraham Lincoln's first vote, the

---

* James G. Randall, *Lincoln the President* (New York, 1945), Vol. II, pp. 341–42.

election return he made at New Salem in 1832, and various surveys he filed as deputy surveyor of Sangamon County.

The net result of her discoveries was to establish Thomas Lincoln as much more of a person than he had been pictured by earlier writers. He was a landowner whose credit was good and a man who held the respect of his neighbors in both Kentucky and Indiana. He never achieved distinction, but he was far from a shiftless ne'er-do-well. Miss Tarbell herself considered the rehabilitation of Thomas Lincoln her most important contribution to the Lincoln story, and all succeeding biographers have accepted her characterization except Albert J. Beveridge, who, though possessing even more documentary evidence than she had, chose to portray Thomas Lincoln as "a piece of human flotsam thrown forward by the surging tide of immigration."

Miss Tarbell's work on the complete biography of Lincoln was not interrupted by the publication of the *Early Life*. In fact, she devoted four years to the entire project, and in 1900 the full work was published in two volumes with the title, *The Life of Abraham Lincoln*. The book, journalistic in approach, with its emphasis on the personality of Lincoln and its wealth of reminiscences, was one of the most popular Lincoln biographies ever published. It has gone through many editions and still has value.

After the Lincoln biography Miss Tarbell undertook the work on which her reputation will always rest. For five years she investigated the activities of John D. Rockefeller and the practices of the Standard Oil Company. Her findings came out in nineteen articles in *McClure's* and in 1904 were published as *The History of the Standard Oil Company*. The book, with its irrefutable evidence of dishonesty and monopolistic practices, was a sensation, and undoubtedly played an important role in the decision of the federal government to bring its antitrust suit against Standard Oil in 1907.

The History of the Standard Oil Company marked the apex of Miss Tarbell's career. When the McClure firm fell apart in 1906 she joined the staff of the *American Magazine,* on which she remained for nine years. Thereafter she supported herself until her death in 1944 by free-lance writing and lecturing. Her work included a study of the tariff and biographies of Elbert H. Gary and Owen D. Young, but none of these approached the stature of her expose of Standard Oil.

Miss Tarbell never lost interest in the life of Lincoln. In her autobiography she related that for much of her life she had a piece of Lincoln work on her desk. With one exception the results were insubstantial. The exception was *In the Footsteps of the Lincolns*, published in 1924. The book grew out of a pilgrimage which she started at Hingham, Massachusetts, where Samuel Lincoln settled in 1637, and led her through New Jersey, Pennsylvania, Virginia, Kentucky, Indiana, and Illinois, ending at the Lincoln tomb in Springfield. The author hunted again for such records as had survived, copied inscriptions on gravestones, and went into houses in which various Lincolns had lived. She called the book, quite rightly, "the only fresh water" in the "Lincoln stream" in which she had been so long immersed, and summed up her achievement in this sentence: "When I finished my journey I felt that I had quite definitely and finally rescued the Lincolns from the ranks of poor white trash where political enemies had so loved to place them."

She was right.

Paul M. Angle

Chicago, Illinois
October, 1973

INTRODUCTION.

It has been only within the last ten years that the descent of Abraham Lincoln from the Lincolns of Hingham, Massachusetts, has been established with any degree of certainty. The satisfactory proof of his lineage is a matter of great importance. In a way it explains Lincoln. It shows that he came of a family endowed with the spirit of adventure, of daring, of patriotism, and of thrift ; that his ancestors were men who for nearly two hundred years before he was born were active and well-to-do citizens of Massachusetts, New Jersey, Pennsylvania, or Virginia, men who everywhere played their parts well. Abraham Lincoln was but the flowering of generations of upright, honorable men.

The first we learn of the Lincolns in this country is between the years 1635 and 1645, when there came to the town of Hingham, Massachusetts, from the west of England, eight men of that name. Three of these, Samuel, Daniel, and Thomas, were brothers. Their relationship, if any, to the other Lincolns who came over from the same part of the country at about the same time is not clear. Two of these men, Daniel and Thomas, died without heirs ; but Samuel left a large family, including four sons. Among the descendants of Samuel Lincoln's sons were many good citizens and prominent public officers. One was a member of the Boston Tea Party, and served as a captain of artillery in the War of the Revolution. Others were privates in that war. Three served on the brig "Hazard" during the Revolution. Levi Lincoln, a great-great-grandson of Samuel, born in Hingham in 1749, and graduated from Harvard, was one of the minute-men at Cambridge immediately after the battle of Lexington, a delegate to the convention in Cambridge for framing a State Constitution, and in 1781 was elected to the Continental Congress, but declined to serve. He was a member of the House of Representatives and of the Senate of Massachusetts, and was appointed Attorney-General of the United States by Jefferson ; for a few months preceding the arrival of Madison he was Secretary of State, and in 1807 he was elected Lieutenant-Governor of Massachusetts. In 1811 he was appointed Associate Justice of the United States Supreme Court by President Madison, an office which he declined. From the close of the Revolutionary War he was considered the head of the Massachusetts bar.

His eldest son, Levi Lincoln, born in 1782, had also an honorable public career. He was a Harvard graduate, became Governor of the State of Massachusetts, and held other important public offices. He received the degree of LL.D. in 1824 from Williams College, and from Harvard in 1826.

Another son of Levi Lincoln, Enoch Lincoln, served in Congress from 1818 to 1826. He became Governor of Maine in 1827, holding the position until his death in 1829. Enoch Lincoln was a writer of more than ordinary ability.

The fourth son of Samuel Lincoln was called Mordecai (President Lincoln descended from him, being his great-great-great-grandson). Mordecai Lincoln was a rich "blacksmith," as an iron-worker was called in those days, and the proprietor of numerous iron-works, saw-mills, and grist-mills, which with a goodly amount of money he distributed at his death among his children and grandchildren. Two of his children, Mordecai and Abraham, did not remain in Massachusetts, but removed to New Jersey, and thence to Pennsylvania, where both became rich, and dying, left fine estates to their children. Their descendants in Pennsylvania have continued to this day to be well-to-do people, some of them having taken prominent positions in public affairs. Abraham Lincoln, of Berks County, who was born in 1736 and died in 1806, filled many public offices, being a member of the General Assembly of Pennsylvania, of the State Convention of 1787, and of the State Constitutional Convention in 1790.

One of the sons of this second Mordecai, John (the great-grandfather of President Lincoln), received from his father "three hundred acres of land, lying in the Jerseys." But evidently he did not care to cultivate his inheritance, for about 1758 he removed to Virginia. "Virginia" John, as this member of the family was called, had five sons, all of whom he established well. One of these sons, Jacob, entered the Revolutionary Army and served as a lieutenant at Yorktown.

The settlers of western Virginia were all in those days more or less under the fascination of the adventurous spirit which was opening up the West, and three of "Virginia" John's sons decided to try their fortunes in the new country. One went to

Tennessee, two to Kentucky. The first to go to Kentucky was Abraham (the grandfather of the President). He was already a well-to-do man when he decided to leave Virginia, for he sold his estate for some seventeen thousand dollars. A portion of this money he invested in land-office treasury warrants.

On emigrating to Kentucky he bought one thousand seven hundred acres of land. But almost at the beginning of his life in the new country, while still a comparatively young man, he was slain by the Indians. His estate seems to have been inherited by his eldest son, Mordecai, who afterward became prominent in the State ; was a great Indian fighter, a famous story-teller, and, according to the traditions of his descendants, a member of the Kentucky legislature. This last item we have not, however, been able to verify. We have had the fullest collection of journals of the Kentucky legislature which exists, that of Dr. R. T. Durrett of Louisville, Kentucky, carefully searched, but no mention has been found in them of Mordecai Lincoln.

It is with the brother of Mordecai, the youngest son of the pioneer Abraham, we have to do, a boy who was left an orphan at ten years of age, and who in that rude time had to depend upon his own exertions. We find from newly discovered documents that he was the owner of a farm at twenty-five years of age, and from the contemporary evidence that he was a very good carpenter ; from a document we have discovered in Kentucky we learn that he was even appointed a road surveyor, in 1816. We have found his Bible, a very expensive book at that time ; we have also found that he had credit, and was able to purchase on credit a pair of suspenders costing one dollar and fifty cents, and we have learned from the recollections of Christopher Columbus Graham that in marrying the niece of his employer he secured a very good wife. The second child of Thomas Lincoln was Abraham Lincoln, who became the sixteenth President of the United States and the foremost man of his age.

The career of Abraham Lincoln is more easily understood in view of his ancestry. The story of his life, which is here told more fully and consecutively, and in many points, both minor and important, we believe more exactly than ever before, bears out our belief that Abraham Lincoln inherited from his ancestry traits and qualities of mind which made him a remarkable child and a young man of unusual promise and power. So far from his later career being unaccounted for in his origin and early history, it is as fully accounted for as in the case of any man.

So far as possible, the statements in this work are based on original documents. This explains why in several cases the dates differ from those commonly accepted. Thus the year of the death of the grandfather of Abraham Lincoln is made 1788, instead of 1784, because of the recently discovered inventory of his estate. The impression given of Thomas Lincoln is different from that of other biographies, because we believe the new documents we have found and the new contemporary evidence we have unearthed, justify us in it. We have not made it a sign of shiftlessness that Thomas Lincoln dwelt in a log cabin at a date when there was scarcely anything else in the State.

An effort has been made, too, to give what we believe to be a truer color to the fourteen years the Lincolns spent in southern Indiana. The poverty and the wretchedness of their life has been insisted upon until it is popularly supposed that Abraham Lincoln came from a home similar to those of the " poor white trash " of the South. There is no attempt made here to deny the poverty of the Lincoln household, but it is insisted that this poverty was a temporary condition incident to pioneer life and the unfortunate death of Thomas Lincoln's father when he was but a boy. Thomas Lincoln's restless efforts to better his condition by leaving Kentucky for Indiana in 1816, and afterwards, when he had discovered that his farm in Spencer County was barren, by trying his fortunes in Illinois, are sufficient proof that he had none of the indolent acceptance of fate which characterizes the " poor whites."

In telling the story of the six years of Lincoln's life in New Salem, we have attempted to give a consecutive narrative and to show the exact sequence of events, which has never been done before. We have shown, what seems to us very suggestive, the persistency and courage with which he seized every opportunity and carried on simultaneously his business as storekeeper and postmaster and surveyor and at the same time studied law. To establish the order of events in this New Salem period, the records of the county have been carefully examined, and many new documents concerning Lincoln have been found in this search, including his first vote, his first official document (an election return), and several new surveying plats. The latter show Lincoln to have been much more active as a surveyor than has commonly been supposed. We have also brought to light the grammar Lincoln studied, with a sentence written on the title page in Lincoln's own hand.

For the first time, too, we publish documents signed by Lincoln as a postmaster. These two letters are also earlier than any other published letters of Lincoln. Many minor errors have been corrected, such as the real number of votes which he received on his first election to the legislature, and the times and places of his mustering out and into service in the Black Hawk War.

The number of illustrations in the work is many times greater than ever has before appeared in connection with the early life of Lincoln. The scenes of his life in Kentucky, Indiana, and Illinois have been photographed especially for us, and we have collected from various sources numbers of pictures illustrating the primitive surroundings of his boyhood and young manhood, together with portraits of many of his companions in those days. Our object in giving such a profusion of homely scenes and faces has been to make a history of Lincoln's early life *in pictures*. We believe that one examining these prints independently of the text would have a good idea of Lincoln's condition from 1809 to 1836.

By far the most important of the illustrations of the work is the collection of portraits. This is the first systematic effort to make a complete collection of portraits of the great President. Our success so far encourages us in believing that before we end our work on Lincoln we shall have such a collection. Already we have some seventy-five different portraits. Of these, the great majority are photographs, ambrotypes, and daguerreotypes. It was Mr. Lincoln's custom, after the introduction of photography into Illinois, to sit for his picture whenever he visited a town to make a speech. This picture he usually gave to his host; the result was that there now remain, scattered among his old friends, a large number of interesting portraits, of which nobody but the owners knew until we undertook this work. Thus of the twenty portraits which appear in this volume, twelve have never before been published anywhere, so far as we know.

It has been through the generosity and courtesy of collectors and of our correspondents and readers that it has been possible for us to gather so great a number of portraits and documents.

On all sides collections have been put freely at our service, and numbers of our readers have sent us unpublished ambrotypes, daguerreotypes, and photographs, glad, as they have written us, to aid in completing a Lincoln portrait gallery. It is not possible to mention here the names of all those to whom we are indebted, not only for portraits but for documents and manuscripts, but credit is given in inserting the material furnished.

Our effort has been to give in both text and notes as exact and full statements as the information we have been able to gather permitted us to do. If any reader of this volume discovers errors we shall be glad to receive corrections.

CONTENTS.

CHAPTER I.

CHAPTER II.

CHAPTER III.

CHAPTER IV.

CHAPTER V.

CONTENTS.

CHAPTER VI.

CHAPTER VII.

CHAPTER VIII.

CHAPTER IX.

CHAPTER X.

CHAPTER XI.

CONTENTS.

CHAPTER XII.

CHAPTER XIII.

CHAPTER XIV.

CHAPTER XV.

CHAPTER XVI.

CHAPTER XVII.

CONTENTS.

CHAPTER XVIII.

CHAPTER XIX.

APPENDIX.

LINCOLN IN 1854.—HITHERTO UNPUBLISHED.

From a photograph owned by Mr. George Schneider of Chicago, Illinois, former editor of the "Staats Zeitung," the most influential anti-slavery German newspaper of the West. Mr. Schneider first met Mr. Lincoln in 1853, in Springfield. "He was already a man necessary to know," says Mr. Schneider. In 1854 Mr. Lincoln was in Chicago, and Mr. Isaac N. Arnold, a prominent lawyer and politician of Illinois, invited Mr. Schneider to dine with Mr. Lincoln. After dinner, as the gentlemen were going down town, they stopped at an itinerant photograph gallery, and Mr. Lincoln had the above picture taken for Mr. Schneider. The newspaper he holds in his hands is the "Press and Tribune."

LINCOLN IN 1863.

From a photograph by Brady, taken in Washington.

THE EARLY LIFE

OF

ABRAHAM LINCOLN.

CHAPTER I.

THE ORIGIN OF THE LINCOLN FAMILY.—THE LINCOLNS IN KENTUCKY.

HE family from which Abraham Lincoln descended came to America from Norfolk, England, in 1637. A brief table * will show at a glance the line of descent:

> *Samuel Lincoln*, born in 1620. Emigrated from Norfolk County, England, to Hingham, Massachusetts, in 1637. His fourth son was
> *Mordecai Lincoln*, born in 1667. His eldest son was
> *Mordecai Lincoln*, born in 1686. Emigrated to New Jersey and Pennsylvania, 1714. His eldest son was
> *John Lincoln*, born before 1725. In 1758 went to Virginia. His third son was
> *Abraham Lincoln*, date of birth uncertain. In 1780, or thereabouts, emigrated to Kentucky. His third son was
> *Thomas Lincoln*, born in 1778, whose first son was
> ABRAHAM LINCOLN,
> Sixteenth President of the United States.

For our present purpose it is not necessary to examine the lives of these ancestors farther back than the grandfather, Abraham Lincoln, who has been supposed to have been born in Virginia in 1760. A consideration of the few facts we have of his early life shows clearly that this date is wrong. It is known that

---

* This table was prepared especially for this work by the Hon. L. E. Chittenden of New York, Register of the Treasury under Mr. Lincoln. In the Appendix will be found a full memorandum of Lincoln's genealogy, also prepared by Mr. Chittenden.

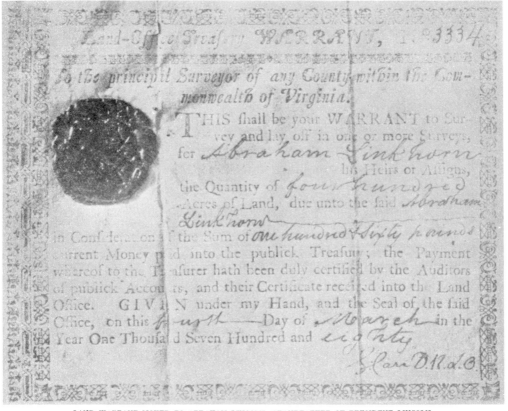

LAND WARRANT ISSUED TO ABRAHAM LINCOLN, GRANDFATHER OF PRESIDENT LINCOLN.

From the original, owned by R. T. Durrett, LL.D., of Louisville, Kentucky. The land records of Kentucky show that Abraham Lincoln entered two tracts of land when in Kentucky in the spring and summer of 1780. These entries, furnished us by Dr. Durrett, are as follows :

MAY 29, 1780.—" Abraham Linkhorn enters four hundred acres of land on Treasury Warrant, laying on Floyd's Fork, about two miles above Tice's Fork, beginning at a Sugar Tree S. B., thence east three hundred poles, then north, to include a small improvement."—*Land Register*, page 107.

JUNE 7, 1780.—" Abraham Linkhorn enters eight hundred acres upon Treasury Warrant, about six miles below Green River Lick, including an improvement made by Jacob Gum and Owen Diver."—Page 126.

The first tract of land was surveyed May 7, 1785 (see page 23), and the second on October 12, 1784. In 1782 he entered a third tract of land, a record of which is found in Daniel Boone's field-book. This entry reads : "Abraham Lincoln enters five hundred acres of land on a Treasury Warrant, No. 5994, beginning opposite Charles Yancey's upper line, on the south side of the river, running south two hundred poles, then up the river for quantity ; December 11, 1782." This is supposed by some authorities to be a tract of five hundred acres of land in Campbell County, surveyed and patented in Abraham Lincoln's name, but after his death. The spelling of the name Linkhorn instead of Lincoln, as it is invariably in other records of the family, has caused some to doubt that the Treasury warrant above was really issued to the grandfather of the President. The family traditions, however, all say that the elder Abraham owned a tract on Floyd's Fork. The misspelling and mis-pronunciation of the name Lincoln is common in Kentucky, Indiana, and Illinois. The writer of this note has frequently heard persons in Illinois speak of " Abe Linkhorn " and " Abe Linkern."

FIELD NOTES OF SURVEY OF FOUR HUNDRED ACRES OF LAND OWNED BY ABRAHAM LINCOLN, GRANDFATHER OF PRESIDENT LINCOLN.

From the record of surveys in the surveyor's office of Jefferson County, Kentucky, Book B., page 60.

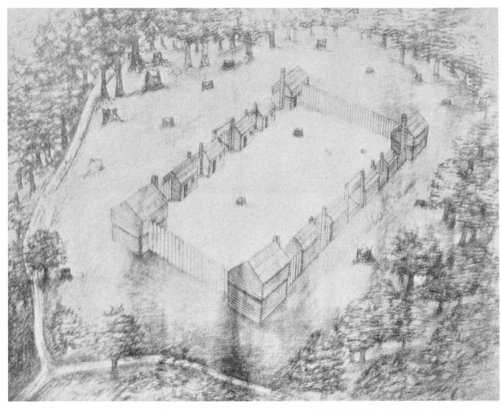

HUGHES STATION, ON FLOYD'S CREEK, JEFFERSON COUNTY, KENTUCKY, WHERE ABRAHAM LINCOLN, GRANDFATHER OF THE PRESIDENT, LIVED.—NOW FIRST PUBLISHED.

From the original, owned by R. T. Durrett, LL.D., of Louisville, Kentucky. "The first inhabitants of Kentucky," says Dr. Durrett, "on account of the hostility of the Indians, lived in what were called forts. They were simple rows of the conventional log cabins of the day, built on four sides of a square or parallelogram, which remained as a court, or open space, between them. This open space served as a playground, a muster field, a corral for domestic animals, and a store-house for implements. The cabins which formed the fort's walls were dwelling-houses for the people." At Hughes Station, on Floyd's Creek, lived Abraham Lincoln and his family. One morning in 1788—the date of the death of Abraham Lincoln is placed in 1784, 1786, and 1788 by different authorities ; the inventory of his estate (page 28) is dated 1788; for this reason we adopt 1788—the pioneer Lincoln and his three sons, Mordecai, Josiah, and Thomas, were in their clearing, when a shot from an Indian killed the father. The two elder sons ran for help, the youngest remaining by the dead body. The Indian ran to the side of his victim, and was just seizing the son Thomas, when Mordecai, who had reached the cabin and secured a rifle, shot through a loophole in the logs and killed the Indian. It was this tragedy, it is said, that made Mordecai Lincoln one of the most relentless Indian haters in Kentucky.

in 1773 Abraham Lincoln's father, John Lincoln, conveyed to his son a tract of two hundred and ten acres of land in Virginia, which he hardly would have done if the boy had been but thirteen years of age. We know, too, that in 1780 Abraham Lincoln had a wife and five children, the youngest of whom was at least

Daniel Boone

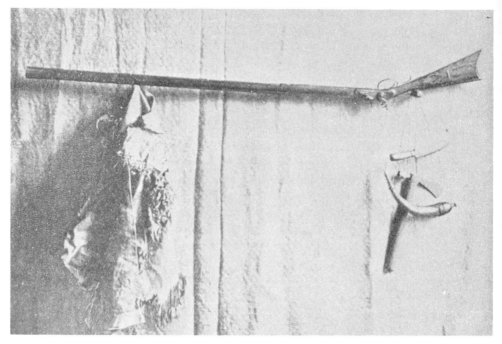

RELICS OF DANIEL BOONE.

Photographed for this work from the originals, in the collection of pioneer relics owned by R. T. Durrett, LL.D., of Louisville, Kentucky. The articles are a rifle, scalping-knife, powder-horn, tomahawk, and hunting-shirt. Dr. Durrett has all the documents needful to establish the authenticity of each of these articles. They unquestionably were used by Boone through a long period of hunting and Indian stalking; all of the articles are well preserved, and even the leather coat is still fit for service. The rifle, says Dr. Durrett, is as true as it ever was. In this same collection are a large number of similar relics of other Kentucky pioneers.

two years old. Evidently he must have been over twenty years of age, and have been born before 1760. Probably, too, his birthplace was Pennsylvania, whence his father moved into Virginia about 1758.

Abraham Lincoln was a farmer, and, by 1780, a rich one for his time. This we know from the fact that in 1780 he sold a tract of two hundred and forty acres of land for "five thousand pounds of current money of Virginia;" a sum equal to about $17.000 at that date. This sale was made, presumably, because the owner wished to move to Kentucky. He and his family had for several generations back been friends of the Boones. The spell the adventurous spirit of Daniel Boone cast over all his friends, Abraham Lincoln felt; and in 1780, soon after selling his Virginia estate, he visited Kentucky, and entered two large tracts of land. Some months later he moved with his family from Virginia into Kentucky.

Abraham Lincoln was ambitious to become a landed proprietor in the new country, and he entered a generous amount of land—four hundred acres on Long Run, in Jefferson County; eight hundred acres on Green River, near Green River Lick; five hundred acres in Campbell County. He settled near the first tract, where he undertook to clear a farm. It was a dangerous task, for the Indians were still troublesome, and the settlers, for protection, were forced to live in or near forts or stations. In 1784, when John Filson published his "History of Kentucky," though there was a population of thirty thousand in the territory, there were but eighteen houses outside of the stations. Of these stations, or stockades, there were but fifty-two. According to the tradition in the Lincoln family, Abraham Lincoln lived in one of these stockades.

All went well with him and his family until 1788. Then, one day, while he and his three sons were at work in their clearing, an unexpected Indian shot killed the father. His death was a terrible blow to the family. The large tracts of land which he had entered were still wild, and his personal property was necessarily small. The difficulty of reaching the country at that date, as well as its wild condition, made it impracticable for even a wealthy pioneer to own more stock or household furniture than was absolutely essential. Abraham Lincoln was probably as well provided with personal property as most of his

LONG RUN BAPTIST MEETING-HOUSE.

From the original drawing, owned by R. T. Durrett, LL.D., of Louisville, Kentucky. This meeting-house was built on the land Abraham Lincoln, grandfather of the President, was clearing when killed by Indians. It was erected about 1797.

neighbors, and much better than many. He had, for a pioneer, an unusual amount of stock, of farming implements, and of tools ; and his cabin contained comforts which were rare at that date. The inventory of his estate, recently found at Bardstown, Kentucky, and here published for the first time, gives a clearer idea of the life of the pioneer Lincoln, and of the condition in which his wife and children were left, than any description could do :

INVENTORY OF ABRAHAM LINCOLN'S ESTATE.*—NOW FIRST
PUBLISHED.

"At the meeting of the Nelson County Court, October 10, 1788, present Benjamin Pope, James Rogers, Gabriel Cox, and James Baird, on the motion of John Coldwell, he was appointed administrator of the goods and chattels of Abraham Lincoln, and gave bond in one thousand pounds, with Richard Parker security.

"At the same time John Alvary, Peter Syburt, Christopher Boston, and William [John (?)] Stuck, or any three of them, were appointed appraisers.

"March 10, 1789, the appraisers made the following return:

	£	s.	d.
1 Sorrel horse .	8		
1 Black horse .	9	10	
1 Red cow and calf .	4	10	
1 Brindle cow and calf .	4	10	
1 Red cow and calf .	5		
1 Brindle bull yearling .	1		
1 Brindle heifer yearling	1		
Bar spear-plough and tackling .	2	5	
3 Weeding hoes .	7	6	
Flax wheel .		6	
Pair smoothing-irons .		15	
1 Dozen pewter plates .	1	10	
2 Pewter dishes .		17	6
Dutch oven and cule, weighing 15 pounds .		15	
Small iron kettle and cule, weighing 12 pounds		12	
Tool adds .		10	
Hand-saw .		5	
One-inch auger .		6	
Three-quarter auger .		4	6
Half-inch auger .		3	
Drawing-knife .		3	
Currying-knife .		10	
Currier's knife and barking-iron .		6	
Old smooth-bar gun .		10	
Rifle gun .		55	
Rifle gun .	3	10	
2 Pott trammels .		14	
1 Feather bed and furniture .	5	10	
Ditto .	8	5	
1 Bed and turkey feathers and furniture .	1	10	
Steeking-iron .		1	6
Candle-stick .		1	6
One axe .		9	
	£68	16s.	6d.

PETER SYBURT,
CHRISTOPHER BOSTON,
JOHN STUCK."

* We owe this interesting document to the courtesy of R. T. Durrett, LL.D., of Louisville, Kentucky, a gentleman who for many years has made a specialty of the pioneer history of his State, and through whose energetic and intelligent researches most of the documents concerning the pioneer Abraham Lincoln have been unearthed.

Soon after the death of Abraham Lincoln, his widow moved from Jefferson County to Washington County. The eldest son, Mordecai, who inherited nearly all of the large estate, became a well-to-do and popular citizen. The deed-book of Washington County still contains a number of records of lands bought and sold by him. At one time he was sheriff of his county, and, again, its representative in the legislature of the State. Mordecai Lincoln is remembered especially for his sporting tastes and his bitter hatred of the Indians. General U. F. Linder of Illinois, who, as a boy, lived near Mordecai Lincoln in Kentucky, says : "I knew him from my boyhood, and he was naturally a man of considerable genius ; he was a man of great drollery, and it would almost make you laugh to look at him. I never saw but one other man whose quiet, droll laugh excited in me the same disposition to laugh, and that was Artemus Ward. He was quite a story-teller. He was an honest man, as tender-hearted as a woman, and, to the last degree, charitable and benevolent.

"Lincoln had a very high opinion of his uncle, and on one occasion said to me : 'Linder, I have often said that Uncle Mord had run off with all the talents of the family.'

THE REV. JESSE HEAD.

From an original drawing in the possession of R. T. Durrett, LL.D., of Louisville, Kentucky. The Rev. Jesse Head was a Methodist preacher of Washington County, Kentucky, who married Thomas Lincoln and Nancy Hanks. Christopher Columbus Graham, who was at the wedding, and who knew Mr. Head well, says : "Jesse Head, the good Methodist preacher who married them, was also a carpenter or cabinet-maker by trade, and, as he was then a neighbor, they were good friends. He had a quarrel with the bishops, and was an itinerant for several years, but an editor and county judge afterwards in Harrodsburg. . . . The preacher, Jesse Head, often talked to me on religion and politics, for I always liked the Methodists. I have thought it might have been as much from his free-spoken opinions as from Henry Clay's American-African colonization scheme, in 1817, that I lost a likely negro man, who was leader of my musicians. . . . But Jesse Head never encouraged any runaway, nor had any 'underground railroad.' He only talked freely and boldly, and had plenty of true Southern men with him, such as Clay."— See Appendix.

"Old Mord, as we sometimes called him, had been in his younger days a very stout man, and was quite fond of playing a game of fisticuffs with any one who was noted as a champion. His sons and daughters were not talented like the old man, but were very sensible people, noted for their honesty and kindness

MARRIAGE BOND OF THOMAS LINCOLN.

From a tracing of the original, made by Henry Whitney Cleveland.

of heart." Mordecai remained in Kentucky until late in life, when he removed to Hancock County, Illinois.

Of Josiah, the second son, we know very little more than that the records show that he owned and sold land. He left Kentucky when a young man, to settle on the Blue River, in Harrison County, Indiana, and there he died. The two daughters married into well-known Kentucky families: the elder, Mary, marrying Ralph Crume; the younger, Nancy, William Brumfield.

THOMAS LINCOLN'S BOYHOOD AND YOUNG MANHOOD.

The death of Abraham Lincoln was saddest for the youngest of the children, a lad of ten years at the time, named Thomas, for

I do hereby certify that by authority of Licence Ised from the Clerks Office of Washington Co I have Solemnized the Rites of Matrimony between Thomas Lincoln and Nancy Hanks, June 12th 1806 A.D. agreeable to the Rites and ceremonies of the Methodist Episcopal Church witness my hand

Jesse Head D.E.M.E.C.

MARRIAGE CERTIFICATE OF THOMAS LINCOLN AND NANCY HANKS.—HITHERTO UNPUBLISHED.

From the original, in the possession of Henry Whitney Cleveland of Louisville, Kentucky. This interesting document, discovered by Mr. Cleveland, and published for the first time in this biography, completes the list of documentary evidence of the marriage of Thomas Lincoln and Nancy Hanks. The bond given by Thomas Lincoln and the returns of Jesse Head, the officiating clergyman, were discovered some years ago, but the marriage certificate was unknown until recently discovered by Mr. Cleveland.

it turned him adrift to become a "wandering laboring-boy" before he had learned even to read. Thomas seems not to have inherited any of the father's estate, and from the first to have been obliged to shift for himself. For several years he supported himself by rough farm work of all kinds, learning, in the meantime, the trade of carpenter and cabinet-maker. According to one of his acquaintances, "Tom had the best set of tools in what was then and now Washington County," and was "a good carpenter for those days, when a cabin was built mainly with the axe, and not a nail or bolt-hinge in it; only leathers and pins to the door, and no glass, except in watches and spectacles and bottles." * Although a skilful craftsman for his day, he never became a thrifty or ambitious man. "He would work energetically enough when a job was brought to him, but he would never seek a job." But if Thomas Lincoln plied his trade spasmodically, he shared the pioneer's love for land, for when but twenty-five years old, and still without the responsibility of a family, he bought a farm in Hardin County, Kentucky. None of his biographers have ever called attention to this fact, if they knew it. A search made for this work in the records of Hardin

* Christopher Columbus Graham, as reported by H. W. Cleveland of Louisville, Ky., in an interview in 1884, in Mr. Graham's hundredth year, and never before published.

Washington Co

    I do hereby certify that the following
is a true list of Marriages Solemnized by me the Subscriber from ~~the~~ ~~June~~ the 28th of April 1806 until
the date hereof
Jun 26th 1806 Joined together in the Holy estate of
Matrimony agreeable to the rules of the M. G. E.

Morris Berry & Peggy Sinnis
Nov 27th 1806 David Mize & Hanah Xter
March 5th 1807 Charles Ridge & Anna Davis
march 24th 1807 John Head & Sally Clark
mach 27th Benjamin Clark & Polly Head
Jan'y 14th David Dyle & Rosanah McMahon
Dec 22nd 1806 Silas Chamberlin & Betsey West
Jun 17th 1806 John Springer & Elizabeth Ingram
Jun 12th 1806 Thomas Lincoln & Nancy Hanks
September 23 1806 John Cambron & Hanah White
October 2nd 1806 Anthony Lypy & Bryah Pattle
October 23rd 1806 Aaron Harding & Hanah Bottot
April 5th 1807 Daniel Payne & Chrishena Peine
July 26th 1806 Benjamin Clark & Polly Clark
May — 1806 Hugh Haskins & Betsey Dyer
September 25th 1806 John Graham & Cathrine Tomi
Given under my hand this 22nd day of April
1807
              Jesse Head D. M. E. Co.

RETURN OF MARRIAGE OF THOMAS LINCOLN AND NANCY HANKS.

From a tracing of the original, made by Henry Whitney Cleveland. This certificate was discovered about 1885 by W. F. Booker, Esq., Clerk of Washington County, Kentucky.

LINCOLN IN FEBRUARY, 1860, AT THE TIME OF THE COOPER INSTITUTE SPEECH.

From a photograph by Brady. The debate with Douglas in 1858 gave Lincoln a national reputation, and the following year he received many invitations to lecture. One came from a young men's Republican club in New York,—which was offering a series of lectures designed for an audience of men and women of the class apt to neglect ordinary political meetings. Lincoln consented, and in February, 1860 (about three months before his nomination for the Presidency), delivered what is known, from the hall in which it was delivered, as the " Cooper Institute speech "—a speech which more than confirmed his reputation. While in New York he was taken by the committee of entertainment to Brady's gallery, and sat for the portrait reproduced above. It was a frequent remark with Lincoln that this portrait and the Cooper Institute speech made him President.

Christopher Columbus Graham

in my 100th year

From a photograph by Klauber of Louisville, Kentucky. Mr. Graham, born in 1784, lived until 1885, and was the only man of our generation who could be called a contemporary of Thomas Lincoln and Nancy Hanks. Long before the documentary evidence of their marriage was found, Mr. Graham gave his reminiscences of that event. Recent discoveries made in the public records of Kentucky regarding the Lincolns, bear out in every particular his recollections. He is, in fact, the most important witness we have as to the character of the parents of President Lincoln and their condition in life. The accuracy of his memory and the trustworthiness of his character are affirmed by the leading citizens of Louisville, Kentucky, of which city he was a resident. In the Appendix will be found a full statement by Mr. Graham of what he knew of Thomas Lincoln and his life.

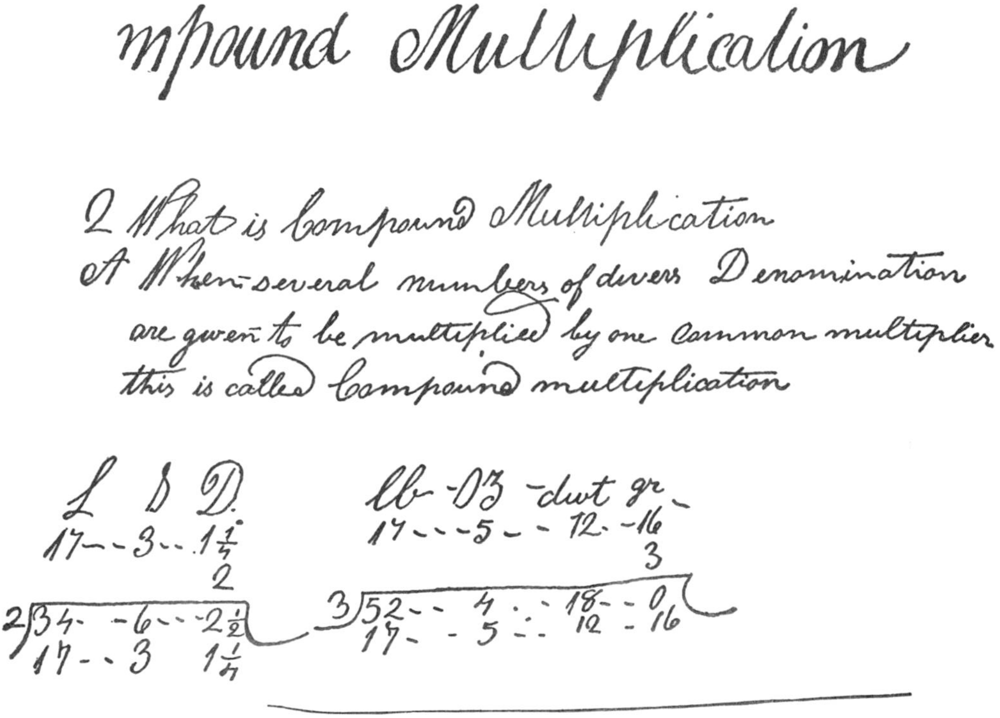

mpound Multiplication

Q What is Compound Multiplication
A When several numbers of divers Denomination are given to be multiplied by one common multiplier this is called Compound multiplication

£ S D.
17 -- 3 -- 1½
        2

2) 34 - 6 -- 2½
   17 -- 3   1¼

lb - oz - dwt gr
17 -- 5 -- 12 -- 16
                3

3) 52 - 4 : 18 - 0
   17 - 5 : 12 - 16

FACSIMILE OF A PASSAGE FROM LINCOLN'S EXERCISE-BOOK.

County first revealed it to us, and we cannot but regard it as of importance, proving as it does that Thomas Lincoln was not the shiftless man he has hitherto been pictured. Certainly he must have been above the grade of the ordinary country boy, to have had the energy and ambition to learn a trade and secure a farm through his own efforts by the time he was twenty-five. He was illiterate, never doing more "in the way of writing than to bunglingly write his own name." Nevertheless, he had the reputation in the country of being good-natured and obliging, and possessing what his neighbors called "good strong horse-sense." Although he was "a very quiet sort of man," he was known to be determined in his opinions, and quite competent to defend his rights by force if they were too flagrantly violated. He was a moral man, and, in the crude way of the pioneer, religious.

Thomas Lincoln learned his trade as carpenter in Elizabeth-town, in the shop of one Joseph Hanks. There he met a niece

HOUSE IN WHICH ABRAHAM LINCOLN WAS BORN.—HITHERTO UNPUBLISHED.

Thomas Lincoln moved into this cabin on the Big South Fork of Nolin Creek, three miles from Hodgensville, in La Rue County, Kentucky, in 1808 ; and here, on February 12, 1809, Abraham Lincoln was born. In 1813 the Lincolns removed to Knob Creek. The Nolin Creek farm has been known as the " Creal Farm " for many years ; recently it was bought by New York people. The cabin was long ago torn down, but the logs were saved. The new owners, in August, 1895, rebuilt the old cabin on the original site. This, the first and only picture which has been taken of it, was made for this biography.

of his employer, Nancy Hanks, whom, when he was twenty-eight years old, he married. Nancy Hanks was, like her husband, a Virginian. Her experience in life had, too, been similar to her husband's, for the Hanks family had been drawn into Kentucky by the fascination of Boone, as had the Lincolns. But it was only in her surroundings and her family that Nancy Hanks was like Thomas Lincoln. In nature, in education, and in ambition she was, if tradition is to be believed, quite another person. Certainly a fair and delicate woman, who could read and write, who had ideas of refinement, and a desire to get more from life than fortune had allotted her, was hardly enough like Thomas Lincoln to be very happy with him. She was still more unfit to be his wife because of a sensitive nature which made her brood over her situation—a situation made the more hope-

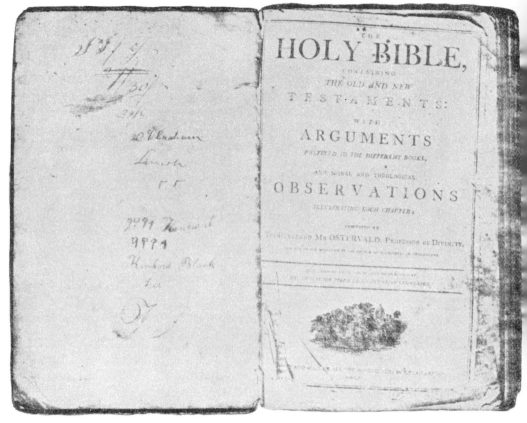

THOMAS LINCOLN'S BIBLE.—NOW FIRST PUBLISHED.

From the original, in the collection of O. H. Oldroyd, Washington, D. C. It is not known when or how Thomas Lincoln obtained this Bible. After his death it passed to his step-children, the Johnstons, and was sold by them to the "Lincoln Log Cabin Company," to be exhibited at the World's Fair. It was purchased from this company for the Oldroyd collection. The family record, reproduced on pages 58 and 59, belongs to this Bible. It was taken out and sold to Mr. C. F. Gunther before the Bible was sold to Mr. Oldroyd.

less by the fact that she had neither the force of character nor strength of body to do anything to improve it; if, indeed, she had any clear notion of what it lacked. Hers was that pitiful condition where one feels with vague restlessness that life has something better than one has found, something not seen or understood, but without which life will never be complete.

Thomas and Nancy Lincoln were married near Beechland, in Washington County, Kentucky, on June 12, 1806. The wedding was celebrated in the boisterous style of one hundred years ago, and was followed by an infare, given by the bride's guardian.

VIEW OF ROCK SPRING FARM, WHERE PRESIDENT LINCOLN WAS BORN.

From a photograph taken in September, 1895, for this biography. The house in which Lincoln was born is seen to the right, in the background. Rock Spring is in a hollow, under a clump of trees, in the left centre of the picture.

ROCK SPRING ON THE FARM WHERE LINCOLN WAS BORN.

From a photograph taken in September, 1895, for this biography. The spring is in a hollow at the foot of the gentle slope on the top of which the house stands.

To this celebration came all the neighbors, and, according to that entertaining Kentucky centenarian, Dr. Christopher Columbus Graham, even those who happened in the neighborhood were made welcome. He tells how he heard of the wedding while "out hunting for roots," and went "just to get a good supper." "I saw Nancy Hanks Lincoln at her wedding," continues Mr. Graham, "a fresh-looking girl, I should say over twenty. I was at the infare, too, given by John H. Parrott, her guardian— and only girls with money had guardians appointed by the court. We had bear-meat; . . . venison; wild turkey and ducks; eggs, wild and tame, so common that you could buy them at two bits a bushel; maple sugar, swung on a string, to bite off for coffee or whiskey; syrup in big gourds; peach-and-honey; a sheep that the two families barbecued whole over coals of wood burned in a pit, and covered with green boughs to keep the juices in; and a race for the whiskey bottle."

After his marriage Thomas Lincoln settled in Elizabethtown. His home was a log cabin, but at that date few people in the State had anything else. Kentucky had been in the Union only fourteen years. When admitted, the few brick structures within its boundaries were easily counted, and there were only log schoolhouses and churches. Fourteen years had brought great improvements, but the majority of the population still lived in log cabins, so that the home of Thomas Lincoln was as good as those of most of his neighbors. Little is known of his position in Elizabethtown, though we have proof that he had credit in the community, for the descendants of two of the early store-keepers of the place still remember seeing on their grandfathers' account books sundry items charged to T. Lincoln. Tools and groceries were the chief purchases he made, though on one of the ledgers a pair of "silk suspenders," worth one dollar and fifty cents, was entered. He not only enjoyed a certain credit with the merchants of Elizabethtown; he was sufficiently respected by the public authorities to be appointed in 1816 a road surveyor, or, as the office is known in some localities, supervisor. It was not, to be sure, a position of great importance, but it proves that he was considered fit to oversee a body of men at a task of considerable value to the community. Indeed, all of the documents which we have been able to discover, mentioning Thomas Lincoln, show him to have had a much better position in Hardin County than he has been credited with.

LINCOLN IN 1858.—HITHERTO UNPUBLISHED.

After a faded ambrotype of Mr. Lincoln, now in the Lincoln Monument collection at Springfield, Illinois. All that is known of it is that it was taken at
Beardstown in 1858. Mr. Lincoln wore a linen coat on the occasion. The picture is regarded as a good likeness of him as he appeared during the Lincoln
Douglas campaign.

Monday 18th May 1816:

Ordered that Thomas Lincoln be and he is hereby appointed surveyor of that part of the road leading from Nolin to Bardstown which lies between the Big hill and the rolling fork in place of George Redman and that all the hands that asisted said Redman do asist said Lincoln in keeping said road in repair

APPOINTMENT OF THOMAS LINCOLN AS ROAD SURVEYOR.—HITHERTO UNPUBLISHED.

From a tracing made by Henry Whitney Cleveland. The original of this document is in the records of Hardin County, at Elizabethtown, Kentucky. It has hitherto been entirely overlooked by the biographers of Lincoln, and was discovered in the course of a search for documents instituted for this work. The appointment was made on May 13, 1816, only a few months before the Lincolns moved to Indiana. It shows that Thomas Lincoln had a standing in the community, which his biographers have always ignored. The appointment, if modest, would not have been made, we have a right to believe, if Lincoln had been the "easy-going" and idle fellow he has been asserted to be.

CHAPTER II.

THE BIRTH OF ABRAHAM LINCOLN.—HIS EARLY EDUCATION AND FRIENDS.

T was at Elizabethtown that the first child of the Lincolns was born, a daughter. Soon after this event Thomas Lincoln decided to combine farming with his trade, and moved to the farm he had bought in 1803 on the Big South Fork of Nolin Creek, in Hardin County, now La Rue County, three miles from Hodgensville, and about fourteen miles from Elizabethtown. Here he was living when, on February 12, 1809, his second child, a boy, was born. The little new-comer was called Abraham, after his grandfather—a name which had persisted through many preceding generations of the Lincolns.

The home into which the child came was the ordinary one of the poorer Western pioneer—a one-roomed cabin with a huge outside chimney, no windows, and only a rude door. The descriptions of its squalor and wretchedness, which are so familiar, have been overdrawn. Dr. Graham, than whom there is no better authority on the life of that day, and who knew Thomas Lincoln well, declares:

"It is all stuff about Tom Lincoln keeping his wife in an open shed in a winter when the wild animals left the woods and stood in the corners next the stick-and-clay chimneys, so as not to freeze to death ; or, if climbers, got on the roof. The Lincolns had a cow and calf, milk and butter, a good feather bed,—for I have slept in it, while they took the buffalo-robes on the floor, because I was a doctor. They had home-woven 'kiverlids,' big and little pots, a loom and wheel ; and William Hardesty, who was there too, can say with me that Tom Lincoln was a man, and took care of his wife.''

The Lincoln home was undoubtedly rude, and in many ways uncomfortable, but it sheltered a happy family, and its poverty affected the new child but little. He was robust and active ; and life is full of interest to the child fortunate enough to be born in the country. He had several companions. There was his sister Nancy, or Sarah—both names are given her—two years his senior ; there was a cousin of his mother's, ten years older, Dennis Hanks, an active and ingenious leader in sports and mischief ; and there were the neighbors' boys. One of the latter, Austin Gollaher, still tells with pleasure of how he

DEED OF SALE SIGNED BY THOMAS LINCOLN AND WIFE.—HITHERTO UNPUBLISHED.

The Book of Deeds in Hardin County, Kentucky, shows that in 1803, three years before his marriage, Thomas Lincoln bought a farm in Hardin County. The same records contain a deed of the sale in 1814 of this same farm, it is supposed, signed by Thomas Lincoln. The deed is evidently written and signed by one person. Nancy Lincoln affixes her mark. This is not proof that she could not write ; it not infrequently happens that people in remote country districts make a mark rather than labor with a pen, to which they are unaccustomed. All accounts of Nancy Lincoln agree that she was well educated for her day.

A KENTUCKY HAND-MILL.

From a photograph of the original, owned by R. T.
Durrett, LL.D., of Louisville, Kentucky. This mill was
formerly the property of Joseph Brooks, a prominent pioneer
of Kentucky. Similar ones were used by all Western pioneers.

played with young Lin-
coln in the shavings of
his father's carpenter
shop, of how he hunted
coons and ran the woods
with him, and once even
saved his life.

"Yes," said Mr. Gol-
laher, "the story that I
once saved Abraham Lin-
coln's life is true, but it
is not correct as gen-
erally related.

"Abraham Lincoln
and I had been going to
school together for a
year or more, and had
become greatly attached
to each o t h e r. Then
school disbanded on ac-
count of there being so
few scholars, and we did
not see each other much
for a long while. One
S u n d a y my m o t h e r
visited the Lincolns, and
I was taken along. Abe
and I played around all
day. Finally, we con-
cluded to cross the creek to hunt for some partridges young
Lincoln had seen the day before. The creek was swollen by a
recent rain, and, in crossing on the narrow footlog, Abe fell in.
Neither of us could swim. I got a long pole and held it out
to Abe, who grabbed it. Then I pulled him ashore. He was
almost dead, and I was badly scared. I rolled and pounded
him in good earnest. Then I got him by the arms and shook
him, the water meanwhile pouring out of his mouth. By this
means I succeeded in bringing him to, and he was soon all right.

"Then a new difficulty confronted us. If our mothers discovered our wet clothes they would whip us. This we dreaded
from experience, and determined to avoid. It was June, the

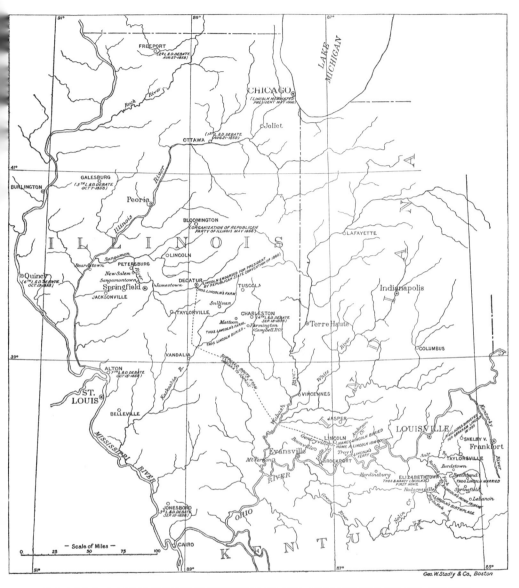

MAP SHOWING POINTS OF INTEREST IN LINCOLN'S EARLY LIFE.—MADE SPECIALLY FOR THIS BIOGRAPHY.

The above map shows where Abraham Lincoln's grandfather first took land in Kentucky, where his father and mother were married, where they first lived, where he was born, and where he lived from 1809 to 1816. It shows the Rolling Fork, Salt River, and the Ohio, which Thomas Lincoln followed in going into Indiana in 1816; the new home in Indiana; the point where Lincoln kept the ferry about 1826; Boonville, where he went to hear trials; the grave of his mother; the route by which it is supposed he went to Illinois in 1830 (see page 87 for note correcting this route); the location of both of Thomas Lincoln's farms in Illinois, and his grave, near Farmington, Coles County. Sangamon, New Salem, Vandalia, Springfield, and the chief places where Mr. Lincoln practised law are shown, as well as the points where the Lincoln and Douglas debates and the important political events of the campaign of 1860 took place.

ABRAHAM LINCOLN'S INDIANA HOME.

After an old photograph showing the cabin as it appeared in 1869. Thomas Lincoln built this house in 1817, and moved into it about a year after he reached his farm. At first it had neither windows, door, nor floor; but after the advent of Sally Bush Lincoln it was greatly improved. When he decided to leave Indiana he was preparing the lumber for a better house.

sun was very warm, and we soon dried our clothing by spreading it on the rocks about us. We promised never to tell the story, and I never did until after Lincoln's tragic end.

"Abraham Lincoln had a sister. Her name was Sallie, and she was a very pretty girl. Sallie Lincoln was about my age; she was my sweetheart. I loved her and claimed her, as boys do. I suppose that was one reason for my warm regard for Abe. When the Lincoln family moved to Indiana, I was prevented by circumstances from bidding good-by to either of the children, and I never saw them again." *

All the young people went to school. At that day the schools in the West were usually accidental, depending upon the coming of some poor and ambitious young man who was willing to teach a few terms while he looked for an opening to something better. The terms were irregular, their length being decided by the time the settlers felt able to board the master and pay his small salary. The chief qualification for a schoolmaster seems to have been enough strength to keep the "big boys" in order, though one high authority affirms that pluck went "for a heap sight more'n sinnoo with boys."

* Unpublished MS. of an interview with Austin Gollaher, by D. J. Thomas.

LINCOLN FARM IN INDIANA.

From a photograph taken for this biography. Present appearance of the quarter section of government land in Spencer County, Indiána, entered by Thomas Lincoln, October 15, 1817, view looking east. Thomas Lincoln selected this tract in 1816, and, to identify it, he blazed the trees, and piled up brush at the corners to establish boundary lines. When he returned with his family he was obliged to cut his way to the spot chosen for his cabin, and to fell trees to find space for the "half-face camp" in which he first lived. This land was entered under the old credit system. Later Mr. Lincoln gave up to the United States the east half, and the amount paid on it was passed to his credit to complete paying for the west half. The patent issued for the latter tract was dated June 6, 1827.

Many of the itinerant masters were Catholics—strolling Irishmen from the colony in Tennessee, or French priests from Kaskaskia. Lincoln's first teacher, Zachariah Riney, was a Catholic. Of his second teacher, Caleb Hazel, we know even less than of Riney. Mr. Gollaher says that Abraham Lincoln, in those days when he was his schoolmate, was "an unusually bright boy at school, and made splendid progress in his studies. Indeed, he learned faster than any of his schoolmates. Though so young, he studied very hard. He would get spice-wood brushes, hack them up on a log, and burn them two or three together, for the purpose of giving light by which he might pursue his studies."

Probably the boy's mother had something to do with the spice-wood illuminations. Tradition has it that Mrs. Lincoln took great pains to teach her children what she knew, and that at her knee they heard all the Bible lore, fairy tales, and country legends that she had been able to gather in her poor life.

Besides the " A B C schools," as Lincoln called them, the only other medium of education in the country districts of Kentucky in those days was " preaching." Itinerants like the schoolmasters, the preachers, of whatever denomination, were generally uncouth and illiterate ; the code of morals they taught was mainly a healthy one, and they, no doubt, did much to keep the consciences of the pioneers awake.   It is difficult to believe that they ever did much for the moral training of young Lincoln, though he certainly got his first notion of public speaking from them ; and for years in his boyhood one of his chief delights was to get his playmates about him, and preach and thump until he had his auditors frightened or in tears.

GRAVE OF NANCY HANKS LINCOLN.

From a photograph loaned by W. W. Admire. The grave of Abraham Lincoln's mother is on a wooded knoll about half a mile southeast of the site of her Indiana home. Near her are buried Thomas and Betsey Sparrow, who followed the Lincolns to Indiana, and who died a few days before Mrs. Lincoln, and of the same disease ; and also Levi Hall and his wife, who died several years later. There are two or three other graves in the vicinity. Until 1879 the only mark about the grave of Nancy Lincoln was the names of visitors to the spot, cut in the bark of the trees which shaded it ; then Mr. P. E. Studebaker of South Bend, Indiana, erected the stone, and soon after a fence was purchased by a few of the leading citizens of Rockport, Indiana. The inscription on the stone runs : " Nancy Hanks Lincoln, Mother of President Lincoln, died October 5, A.D., 1818. Aged thirty-five years. Erected by a friend of her martyred son."

LINCOLN IN 1857.

From a photograph loaned by H. W. Fay of De Kalb, Illinois. The original was taken early in 1857 by Alexander Hesler of Chicago. Mr. Fay writes of the picture : "I have a letter from Mr. Hesler stating that one of the lawyers came in and made arrangements for the sitting, so that the members of the bar could get prints. Lincoln said at the time that he did not know why the boys wanted such a homely face." Mr. Joseph Medill of Chicago went with Mr. Lincoln to have the picture taken. He says that the photographer insisted on smoothing down Lincoln's hair, but Lincoln did not like the result, and ran his fingers through it before sitting. The original negative was burned in the Chicago fire.

State of Kentucky : Hardin County (Set.)

To any authorized Minister of the Gospel (or) an authorized Magistrate these are licence & permit you to join together in the Honourable State of Matrimony according to the rules & customs of the church of Which you are reputed a Member of Mr. Thomas Lincoln and Miss Sarah Johnston — he the said Thomas Lincoln having given bond & security in my office according to law — Given under my hand as clerk of the County Court for the County aforesaid the 2d day of December 1819 and in the 28th year of the Commonwealth.

Sam'l Haycraft Jr. C.H.C.C.

Executed the within by joining in Matrimony the persons therein named December 2nd 1819

Geo. L. Rogers.

MARRIAGE LICENSE OF THOMAS LINCOLN AND SARAH JOHNSTON.—NOW FIRST PUBLISHED.
From a tracing made by Henry Whitney Cleveland.

CHAPTER III.

THE LINCOLNS LEAVE KENTUCKY.—THEY SETTLE IN SOUTHERN
INDIANA.—CONDITIONS OF LIFE IN THEIR NEW HOME.

IN 1816 a great event happened to the little boy. His father emigrated to Indiana from Knob Creek (Thomas Lincoln had removed from the farm on Nolin Creek to one some fifteen miles northeast, on Knob Creek, when Abraham was four years old). "This removal was partly on account of slavery, but chiefly on account of the difficulty in land titles in Kentucky," says his son. It was due, as well, no doubt, to the fascination which an unknown country has always for the adventurous, and to that restless pioneer spirit which drives even

SARAH BUSH LINCOLN.

From a photograph in the possession of her granddaughter, Mrs. Harriet Chapman of Charleston, Illinois. Sarah Bush was born in Kentucky, December 13, 1788. She was a friend of Thomas Lincoln and Nancy Hanks, and it is said that Thomas Lincoln had been her suitor before she married Daniel Johnston. Her husband died in October, 1818. In November, 1819, Thomas Lincoln went to Kentucky to seek her a second time in marriage. An incident of the courtship is told by Mr. J. L. Nall, a cousin of President Lincoln : "Uncle Thomas came back to Kentucky after the death of his first wife, Nancy Hanks, and proposed marriage to the widow Johnston ; she told him that she would be perfectly willing to marry him, as she had known him a long time, and felt that the marriage would be congenial and happy ; but it would be impossible for her even to think of marrying, and leaving the State, as she was considerably in debt. Uncle Thomas told her that need make no difference, as he had plenty of money, and would take care of her financial affairs ; and when he had ascertained the amount of her indebtedness and the names of the parties to whom the money was due, he went around and redeemed all her paper and presented it to her, and told her, when she showed so much honor about debts, he was more fully satisfied than ever that she would make him a good wife. She said, as he had displayed so much generosity in her behalf, she was willing then to marry and go with him to Spencer County, Indiana." Sarah Bush Lincoln changed the character of the Lincoln home completely when she entered it, and there is no question of the importance of her influence upon the development of her step-son Abraham. She was a woman of great natural dignity and kindliness, and highly esteemed by all who knew her. She died on the 10th of December, 1869, at the old homestead in Coles County, Illinois.

THE MARRIAGE BOND GIVEN BY THOMAS LINCOLN AT HIS MARRIAGE WITH SARAH JOHNSTON.—NOW
FIRST PUBLISHED.

From a tracing made by Henry Whitney Cleveland.

men of sober judgment continually towards the frontier, in
search of a place where the conflict with nature is less severe—
some spot farther on, to which a friend or a neighbor has pre-
ceded, and from which he sends back glowing reports. It may
be that Thomas Lincoln was tempted into Indiana by the
reports of his brother Josiah, who had settled on the Big Blue
River in that State. At all events, in the fall of 1816 he started
with wife and children and household stores to journey by horseback and by wagon from Knob Creek to a farm selected on a
previous trip he had made. This farm, located near Little
Pigeon Creek, about fifteen miles north of the Ohio River, and
a mile and a half east of Gentryville, Spencer County, was in a
forest so dense that the road for the travellers had to be hewed
out as they went.

BUCKTHORN VALLEY, WHERE LINCOLN WORKED AND HUNTED.

After a photograph made for this biography. In this valley are located nearly all the farms on which Lincoln worked in his boyhood, including the famous Crawford place, where he and his sister Sarah were both employed as "help." Visitors to the locality have pointed out to them numberless items associated with his early life—fields he helped to clear and till, fences he built, houses he repaired, wells he dug, paths he walked, playgrounds he frequented. Indeed, the inhabitants of Buckthorn Valley take the greatest pride in Lincoln's connection with it.

To a boy of seven years, free from all responsibility, and too vigorous to feel its hardships, such a journey must have been, as William Cooper Howells, the father of the novelist, says of his own trip from Virginia to Ohio, in 1813, "a panorama of delightful novelty." Life suddenly ceased its routine, and every day brought forth new scenes and adventures. Little Abraham saw forests greater than he had ever dreamed of, peopled by strange birds and beasts, and he crossed a river so wide that it must have seemed to him like the sea. To Thomas and Nancy Lincoln the journey was probably a hard and sad one ; but to the children beside them it was a wonderful voyage into the unknown.

A NEW HOME IN INDIANA.

On arriving at the new farm an axe was put into the boy's hands, and he was set to work to aid in clearing a field for corn,

THE OLD SWIMMING-HOLE.

A secluded part of Little Pigeon Creek, not far from Gentryville, where Lincoln, Dennis Hanks, John Johnston, the Gentry boys, and others of the neighborhood used to bathe. It is still pointed out as "the place where Abe went in swimming."

and to help build the "half-face camp" which for a year was the home of the Lincolns. There were few more primitive homes in the wilderness of Indiana in 1816 than this of young Lincoln's, and there were few families, even in that day, who were forced to practise more makeshifts to get a living. The cabin which took the place of the "half-face camp" had but one room, with a loft above. For a long time there was no window, door, or floor; not even the traditional deer-skin hung before the exit; there was no oiled paper over the opening for light; there was no puncheon covering on the ground.

The furniture was of their own manufacture. The table and

BRICK-MOULD USED BY THOMAS LINCOLN.

From a photograph loaned by Jesse W. Weik.

WELL DUG BY LINCOLN.

In a field near the Crawford house is a well which is pointed out to sight-seers as one which Lincoln helped to dig. Many things about the Crawford place—fences, corn-cribs, house, barn—were built in part by Lincoln.

chairs were of the rudest sort—rough slabs of wood in which holes were bored and legs fitted in. Their bedstead, or, rather, bed-frame, was made of poles held up by two outer posts, and the ends made firm by inserting the poles in auger-holes that had been bored in a log which was a part of the wall of the cabin; skins were its chief covering. Little Abraham's bed was even more primitive. He slept on a heap of dry leaves in the corner of the loft, to which he mounted by means of pegs driven into the wall.

Their food, if coarse, was usually abundant; the chief difficulty in supplying the larder was to secure any variety. Of game there was plenty—deer, bear, pheasants, wild turkeys, ducks, birds of all kinds. There were fish in the streams, and wild fruits of many kinds in the woods in the summer, and these were dried for winter use; but the difficulty of raising and milling corn and wheat was very great. Indeed, in many places in the West the first flour cake was an historical

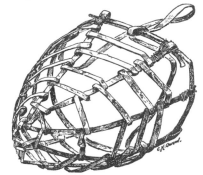

HICKORY-BARK OX-MUZZLE.

After a drawing made from the original, in the collection of pioneer articles in the United States National Museum, at Washington, D. C. Hickory bark was used freely by the Western pioneers. From it and from corn husks they were obliged, in fact, to make most of their harness.

THE CRAWFORD HOUSE, WHERE LINCOLN WAS A FARM-HAND.

The house of Josiah Crawford, near Gentryville, Indiana. Here Lincoln worked by the day for several months, while his sister was a "hired girl" for Mrs. Crawford. In 1829 Lincoln cut down timber and whip-sawed it into planks for a new house which his father proposed to build ; but Thomas Lincoln decided to go to Illinois before the new house was begun, and Abraham sold his planks to Mr. Crawford, who worked them into the southeast room of his house, where relic-seekers have since cut them to pieces to make canes. This picture is made after a photograph taken before the death of Mr. and Mrs. Crawford, both of whom are shown here.

event.* Corn dodger was the every-day bread of the Lincoln household, the wheat cake being a dainty reserved for Sunday mornings.

Potatoes were the only vegetables raised in any quantity, and there were times in the Lincoln family when they were the only food on the table ; a fact proved to posterity by the oft-quoted remark of Abraham to his father after the latter had asked a

---

* The first flour cake made in Louisville, Kentucky, was made in 1779. The records of the city thus describe the event : " It is related that, when the first patch of wheat was raised about this place, after being ground in a rude and laborious hand-mill, it was sifted through a gauze neckerchief, belonging to the mother of the gallant man who gave us the information, as the best bolting-cloth to be had. It was then shortened, as the housewife phrased it, with raccoon fat, and the whole station invited to partake of a sumptuous feast upon a flour cake."—*History of the Ohio Falls Counties*, page 174.

blessing over a dish of roasted potatoes — that they were "mighty poor blessings." Not only were they all the Lincolns had for dinner sometimes; one of their neighbors tells of calling there when raw potatoes, pared and washed, were passed around instead of apples or other fruit.

The food was prepared in the rudest way, for the supply of both groceries and cooking utensils was limited. The former were frequently wanting entirely, and as for the latter, the most important item was the Dutch oven. An indispensable article in the primitive kitchen outfit was the "gritter." It was made by flattening out an old piece of tin, punching it full of holes, and

LINCOLN FAM

Written by Abraham Lincoln
From original in possession of

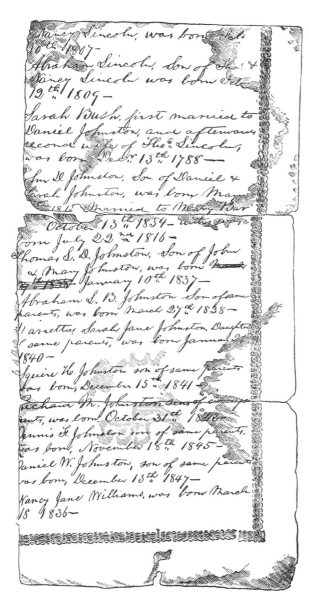

Nancy Lincoln, was born Feb.
10th 1807 —
Abraham Lincoln, Son of Tho.s &
Nancy Lincoln was born Feb.
12th 1809 —
Sarah Bush, first married to
Daniel Johnston, and afterwards
second wife of Tho.s Lincoln,
was born Dec.r 13th 1788 —
Jno H Johnston, Son of Daniel &
Sarah Johnston, was born May
1815 married to Mary Bar
October 13th 1834 — with ...
born July 22nd 1816 —
Thomas S. D. Johnston, Son of John
& Mary Johnston, was born
January 10th 1837 —
Abraham S. B. Johnston Son of same
parents, was born March 27th 1838 —
Harrettas Sarah Jane Johnston, Daughter
of same parents, was born January 2
1840 —
Squire H. Johnston son of same parents
was born, December 15th 1841 —
Richard M. Johnston sons of same
parents, was born October 31st 18..
Jennis F Johnston son of same parents,
was born, November 18th 1845 —
Daniel W. Johnston, son of same parents
was born, December 13th 1847 —
Nancy Jane Williams, was born March
18 1836 —

ILY RECORD.
in his Father's Bible.
C. F. Gunther, Esq., Chicago.

nailing it to a board. Upon this all sorts of things were grated, even ears of corn, in which slow way enough meal was sometimes secured for bread. Old tin was used for many other little contrivances besides the "gritter," and every scrap was carefully saved. Most of the dishes were of pewter; the spoons, iron; the knives and forks, horn-handled.

The Lincolns of course made their own soap and candles, and if they had cotton or wool to wear they had literally to grow it. One of the "old settlers" of Illinois says of her experience in clothing her family:

"As for our clothes, we had to raise, pick, spin, and weave cotton for winter and summer. We also made linsey of wool and flax. The first indigo we had we raised. Besides that we used sumac berries, white-walnut bark,

DENNIS HANKS.

From a photograph in the Libby Prison Museum of Chicago, by permission of Mr. C. F. Gunther. Dennis Hanks, a cousin of Nancy Hanks Lincoln, was born in Kentucky, in 1799, and was brought up by his uncle Thomas Sparrow. The year after Thomas Lincoln moved to Indiana, Thomas Sparrow followed him, but both he and his wife died there in 1818. Dennis then became an inmate of the Lincoln household. He afterwards married one of the daughters of Sally Bush Lincoln. It was largely through his influence that the Lincolns moved into Illinois in 1830. Dennis Hanks has been one of the most prolific contributors to the early period of Mr. Lincoln's life, his letters to Mr. Herndon being full of curious and valuable matter. He died in October, 1892. One of his daughters, Mrs. Harriet Chapman, is still living at Charleston, Illinois.

and other barks for coloring.

"Now for cotton picking. We children had to lie before the fire and pick the seed from the cotton bolls before we could go to bed. The warmer the cotton the better it picked ; so we would take a good sweat. The next day that had to be carded and spun ; so some would soap the cotton, some card, and some spin ; and when we would get enough spun and colored to make a dress apiece we would put it in the loom and weave it. It did not take fifteen or twenty yards to make a dress then ; six or eight yards of linsey were enough for any woman."

It is probable that young Abraham Lincoln wore little cotton or linsey-woolsey. His trousers were of roughly tanned deer-skin, his foot-covering a home-made moccasin, his cap a coonskin ; it was only the material for his shirt or blouse which was woven at home. If this costume had some obvious disadvantages, it was not to be despised. So good an authority as Governor Reynolds says of one of its articles—the linsey-woolsey shirt—"It was an excellent garment. I have never felt so happy and healthy since I put it off."

These "pretty pinching times," as Abraham Lincoln once

MOUTH OF ANDERSON CREEK, WHERE LINCOLN KEPT THE FERRY-BOAT.

From a photograph taken for this biography. This ferry, at the mouth of Anderson Creek, was first established and owned by James McDaniel, and was afterwards kept by his son-in-law James Taylor. It was the latter who hired Abraham Lincoln, about 1826, to attend the ferry-boat. As the boat did not keep him busy all the time, he acted as man-of-all-work around the farm. A son of James Taylor, Captain Green B. Taylor of South Dakota, is still alive, and remembers distinctly the months Lincoln spent in his father's employ. Captain Taylor says that Lincoln "slept up-stairs" with him, and used to read "till near midnight."

described the early days in Indiana, lasted until 1819. The year before, Nancy Lincoln had died, and for many months no more forlorn place could be conceived than this pioneer home bereft of its guiding spirit; but finally Thomas Lincoln went back to Kentucky and returned with a new wife—Sally Bush Johnston, a widow with three children, John, Sarah, and Matilda. The new mother came well provided with household furniture, bringing many things unfamiliar to little Abraham—" one fine bureau, one table, one set of chairs, one large clothes-chest, cooking utensils, knives, forks, bedding, and other articles." She was a woman of energy, thrift, and gentleness, and at once made the cabin home-like, and taught the children habits of cleanliness and comfort.

JOSIAH CRAWFORD.

Among those whom Lincoln served in Indiana as "hired boy" was Josiah Crawford, a well-to-do farmer living near Gentryville. Mr. Crawford owned a copy of Weems's "Life of Washington," a precious book in those days, and Lincoln borrowed it to read. "Late in the night, before going to rest, he placed the borrowed book in his only bookcase, the opening between two logs of the walls of the cabin, and retired to dream of its contents. During the night it rained; the water dripping over the 'mud-daubing' on to the book stained the leaves and warped the binding. Abe valued the book in proportion to the interest he had in the hero, and felt that the owner must value it beyond his ability to pay. It was with the greatest trepidation he took the book home and told the story, and asked how he might hope to make restitution. Mr. Crawford answered: 'Being as it is you, Abe, I won't be hard on you. Come over and shuck corn three days, and the book is yours.' Shuck corn three days and receive a hero's life! He felt that the owner was giving him a magnificent present. After reading the book he used to tell the Crawfords: 'I do not always intend to delve, grub, shuck corn, split rails, and the like.' His whole mind was devoted to books, and he declared he 'was going to fit himself for a profession.' These declarations were often made to Mrs. Crawford, who took almost a mother's interest in him, and she would ask: 'What do you want to be now?' His answer was invariably: "I'll be President.' As he was generally playing a joke on some one, she would answer: 'You'd make a purty President with all your tricks and jokes. Now, wouldn't you?' He would then declare: 'Oh, I'll study and get ready, and then the chance will come.' "*

* Unpublished MS. by A. Hoosier.

ABRAHAM BECOMES A LABORER.

Abraham was ten years old when his new mother came from Kentucky, and he was already an important member of the family. He was remarkably strong for his years, and the work he could do in a day was a decided advantage to Thomas Lincoln. The axe which had been put into his hand to help in making the first clearing, he had never been allowed to drop; indeed, as he says himself, "from that till within his twenty-third year he was almost constantly handling that most useful instrument." Besides, he drove the team, cut the elm and linn brush with which the stock was often fed, learned to handle the old shovel-plough, to wield the sickle, to thresh the wheat with a flail, to fan and clean it with a sheet, to go to mill and turn the hard-earned grist into flour. In short, he learned all the trades the settler's boy must know, and so well that when his father did not need him

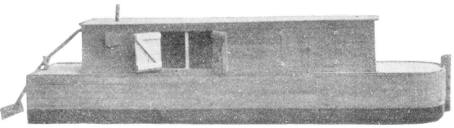

A MISSISSIPPI "BROAD-HORN."

From a model in the exhibit of the United States National Museum at the Atlanta Exposition of 1895. The flatboat which Abraham Lincoln piloted to New Orleans was not, probably, as well built a boat as the above model represents; but it was built on the same general plan. The hold was enclosed to protect the produce, and on the deck was a cabin in which the boatmen lived. In going down the river, rough sails were sometimes rigged up on these broad-horns, though they floated usually, directed by huge paddles. If the boat was brought back, it was warped and poled by hand up the river. More often, however, the boatmen sold both boat and cargo at New Orleans, and came back by the steamers as deck passengers. Boats like the two models on this page are still seen in great numbers on the Ohio and Mississippi Rivers.

he could hire him to the neighbors. Thomas Lincoln also taught him the rudiments of carpentry and cabinet-making, and kept him busy much of the time as his assistant in his trade. There are houses still standing, in and near Gentryville, on which it is said he worked. The families of Lamar, Jones, Crawford, Gentry, Turnham, and Richardson, all claim the honor of having employed him upon their cabins.

As he grew older he became one of the strongest and most popular "hands" in the vicinity, and much of his time was spent as a "hired boy" on some neighbor's farm. For twenty-five cents a day—paid to his father—he was hostler, ploughman, wood-chopper, and carpenter, besides helping the women with the "chores." For them he was ready to carry water, make the fire, even tend the baby. No wonder that a laborer who never refused to do anything asked of him, who could "strike with a mall heavier blows" and "sink an axe deeper into the wood" than anybody else in the community, and who at the same time

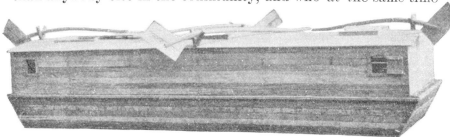

A RIVER PRODUCE BOAT.

From a model in the exhibit of the United States National Museum at the Atlanta Exposition of 1895. The photograph of this model, and of the one above, we owe to the courtesy of the director of the Museum, Mr. G. Brown Goode.

JOSEPH GENTRY.

One of the few companions of Lincoln's youth in Indiana, now living, is Joseph Gentry. He resides on a farm one-fourth mile west from the Lincoln farm, where he has lived about sixty years. When a boy he lived in Gentryville—a town founded by the Gentrys. He was present at the funeral of Nancy Hanks Lincoln, and remembers hearing the minister say it was through the efforts of the little son of the dead woman that his services had been secured.

was general help for the women, never lacked a job in Gentryville.

Of all the tasks his rude life brought him, none seems to have suited him better than going to the mill. It was, perhaps, as much the leisure enforced by this trip as anything else that attracted him. The machinery was primitive, and each man waited his turn, which sometimes was long in coming. A story is told by one of the pioneers of Illinois of going many miles with a grist, and waiting so long for his turn that, when it came, he and his horse had eaten all the corn, and he had none to grind. This waiting with other men and boys on like errands gave an opportunity for talk, story-telling, and games, which were Lincoln's delight.

In 1826 he spent several months as a ferryman at the mouth of Anderson Creek, where it joins the Ohio. This experience suggested new possibilities to him. It was a custom among the farmers of Ohio, Indiana, and Illinois at this date to collect a quantity of produce, and float down to New Orleans on a raft, to sell it. Young Lincoln saw this, and wanted to try his fortune as a produce merchant. An incident of his projected trip he related once to Mr. Seward :

"Seward," he said, "did you ever hear how I earned my first dollar ? "

"No," said Mr. Seward.

"Well," replied he, "I was about eighteen years of age, and belonged, as you know, to what they call down South the 'scrubs;' people who do not own land and slaves are nobody there; but we had succeeded in raising, chiefly by my labor, sufficient produce, as I thought, to justify me in taking it down the river to sell. After much persuasion I had got the consent of my mother to go, and had constructed a flatboat large enough to take the few barrels of things we had gathered to New Orleans. A steamer was going down the river. We have, you know, no wharves on the Western streams, and the custom was, if passengers were at any of the landings, they were to go out in a boat, the steamer stopping, and taking them on board. I was contemplating my new

Carbon enlargement, made by Sherman & McHugh of New York City.

LINCOLN IN 1858.

From a photograph loaned by W. J. Franklin of Macomb, Illinois, and taken in 1866 from an ambrotype made in 1858 in Macomb. This portrait figures in the collection in the Lincoln Home at Springfield, Illinois, and on the back of the photograph is the following inscription : "This likeness of Abraham Lincoln is a faithful copy of an original ambrotype, now in possession of James K. Magie. It was taken August 25, 1858, by Mr. T. P. Pierson, at Macomb, in this State, and is believed to be of anterior date to any other likeness of Mr. Lincoln ever brought before the public. Mr. Magie happened to remain over night at Macomb, at the same hotel with Mr. Lincoln, and the next morning took a walk about town, and upon Mr. Magie's invitation they stepped into Mr. Pierson's establishment, and the ambrotype of which this is a copy was the result. Mr. Lincoln, upon entering, looked at the camera as though he was unfamiliar with such an instrument, and then remarked : ' Well, do you want to take a shot at me with that thing ? ' He was shown to a glass, where he was told to ' fix up,' but declined, saying it would not be much of a likeness if he fixed up any. The old neighbors and acquaintances of Mr. Lincoln in Illinois, upon seeing this picture, are apt to exclaim : ' There ! that's the best likeness of Mr. Lincoln that I ever saw ! ' The dress he wore in this picture is the same in which he made his famous canvass with Senator Douglas." This inscription was written by J. C. Power, now dead, but for many years custodian of the Lincoln monument in Springfield.

boat, and wondering whether I could make it stronger or improve it in any part, when two men with trunks came down to the shore in carriages, and looking at the different boats, singled out mine, and asked, 'Who owns this?' I answered modestly, 'I do.' 'Will you,' said one of them, 'take us and our trunks out to the steamer?' 'Certainly,' said I. I was very glad to have the chance of earning something, and supposed that each of them would give me a couple of bits. The trunks were put in my boat, the passengers seated themselves on them, and I sculled them out to the steamer. They got on board, and I lifted the trunks and put them on the deck. The steamer was about to put on steam again when I called out, 'You have forgotten to pay me.' Each of them took from his pocket a silver half-dollar and threw it on the bottom of my boat. I could scarcely believe my eyes as I picked up the money. You may think it was a very little thing,

S'AMUEL CRAWFORD.

Only living son of Josiah Crawford, who lent Lincoln the Weems's "Life of Washington." To our representative in Indiana, who secured this picture of Mr. Crawford, he said, when asked if he remembered the Lincolns: "Oh, yes; I remember them, although I was not Abraham's age. He was twelve years older than I. One day I ran in, calling out, 'Mother! mother! Aaron Grigsby is sparking Sally Lincoln; I saw him kiss her!' Mother scolded me, and told me I must stop watching Sally, or I wouldn't get to the wedding. [It will be remembered that Sally Lincoln was 'help' in the Crawford family, and that she afterwards married Aaron Grigsby.] Neighbors thought lots more of each other then than now, and it seems like everybody liked the Lincolns. We were well acquainted, for Mr. Thomas Lincoln was a good carpenter, and made the cupboard, mantels, doors, and sashes in our old home that was burned down."

and in these days it seems to me like a trifle, but it was a most important incident in my life. I could scarcely credit that I, the poor boy, had earned a dollar in less than a day; that by honest work I had earned a dollar. I was a more hopeful and thoughtful boy from that time."

Soon after this, while he was working for Mr. Gentry, the leading citizen of Gentryville, his employer decided to send a load of produce to New Orleans, and chose young Lincoln to go as "bow-hand," "to work the front oars." For this trip he received eight dollars a month and his passage back.

ABRAHAM LINCOLN.—NOW FIRST PUBLISHED.
After a photograph in the collection of Mr. J. C. Browne of Philadelphia.

MISSISSIPPI RIVER FLATBOAT.

CHAPTER IV.

EARLY EDUCATION.—BOOKS ABRAHAM READ.—THE JONES GROCERY STORE.—LIFE ON THE RIVER.

ITH all his hard living and hard work, Lincoln was getting, in this period, a desultory kind of education. Not that he received much schooling. He went to school " by littles," he says ; "in all it did not amount to more than a year." And, if we accept his own description of the teachers, it was, perhaps, just as well that it was only "by littles." "No qualification was ever required of a teacher beyond 'readin', writin', and cipherin' to the rule of three.' If a straggler supposed to understand Latin happened to sojourn in the neighborhood, he was looked upon as a wizard." But more or less of the schoolroom is a matter of small importance if a boy has learned to read, and to think of what he reads. And that, this boy had learned. His stock of books was small, but he knew them thoroughly, and they were good books to know : the Bible, "Æsop's Fables," "Robinson

Crusoe," Bunyan's "Pilgrim's Progress," a "History of the United States," Weems's "Life of Washington," and the "Statutes of Indiana." These are the chief ones we know about. He did not own them all, but sometimes had to borrow them from the neighbors: a practice which resulted in at least one casualty, for Weems's "Life of Washington" he allowed to get wet, and to make good the loss he had to pull fodder three days. No matter. The book became his then, and he could read it as he would. Fortunately he took this curious work in profound seriousness, which a wide-awake boy would hardly be expected to do to-day. Washington became an exalted figure in his imagination; and he always contended later, when the question of the real character of the first President was brought up, that it was wiser to regard him as a god-like being, heroic in nature and deeds, as Weems did, than to contend that he was only a man who, if wise and good, still made mistakes and indulged in follies, like other men.

In 1861, addressing the Senate of the State of New Jersey, he said :

"May I be pardoned if, upon this occasion, I mention that away back in my childhood, the earliest days of my being able to read, I got hold of a small book, such a one as few of the younger members have ever seen—Weems's 'Life of Washington.' I remember all the accounts there given of the battle-fields and struggles for the liberties of the country, and none fixed themselves upon my imagination so deeply as the struggle here at Trenton, New Jersey. The crossing of the river, the contest with the Hessians, the great hardships endured at that time, all fixed themselves on my memory more than any single Revolutionary event ; and you all know, for you have all been boys, how these early impressions last longer than any others. I recollect thinking then, boy even though I was, that there must have been something more than common that these men struggled for."

Besides these books he borrowed many. He once told a friend that he "read through every book he had ever heard of in that country, for a circuit of fifty miles." From everything he read he made long extracts, using a turkey-buzzard pen and brier-root ink. When he had no paper he would write on a board, and thus preserve his selections until he secured a copy-book. The wooden fire-shovel was his usual slate, and on its back he ciphered with a charred stick, shaving it off when covered. The logs and boards in his vicinity he filled with his figures and quotations. By night he read and worked as long as there was light, and he kept a book in the crack of the logs in his loft, to have it at hand at peep of day. When acting as ferryman, in his nineteenth year, anxious, no doubt, to get through the books of the house where he boarded, before he left the place, he read every night " till midnight." *

Every lull in his daily labor he used for reading, rarely going to his work without a book. When ploughing or cultivating the rough fields of Spencer County, he found frequently a half hour for reading. At the end of every long row the horse was allowed to rest, and Lincoln had his book out, and was perched on stump or fence, almost as soon as the plough had come to a standstill. One of the few people still left in Gentryville who remembers Lincoln, Captain John Lamar, tells

JOHN HANKS.

The son of Joseph Hanks, with whom Thomas Lincoln learned the carpenter's trade, and a cousin of Nancy Hanks Lincoln. John Hanks lived with Thomas Lincoln in Indiana, from about 1823 to 1827, then returned to Kentucky, and from there emigrated to Illinois. It was largely through his influence that Thomas Lincoln and Dennis Hanks went to the Sangamon country in 1830. When Mr. Lincoln first left home he and John Hanks worked together. In 1831 they made a trip to New Orleans on a flatboat. It was John Hanks who, in 1860, accompanied Governor Oglesby to the old Lincoln farm in Macon County, to select the rails Lincoln had split, and it was he who carried them into the convention of the Republican party of Illinois, which nominated Lincoln as its candidate. John Hanks was an illiterate man, being able neither to read nor write ; but he was honest and kindly, and his reminiscences of Mr. Lincoln's early life, gathered by Mr. Herndon and others, are regarded by all who knew him as trustworthy. After Mr. Lincoln's election to the Presidency, he desired an Indian agency ; but his lack of even a rudimentary education made it impossible to give it to him.

* The first authorized sketch of Lincoln's life was written by the late John L. Scripps of the Chicago "Tribune," who went to Springfield at Mr. Lincoln's request, and by him was furnished the data for a campaign biography. In a letter written to Mr. Herndon after the death of Lincoln, which Herndon turned over to me, Scripps relates that in writing his book he stated that Lincoln as a youth read Plutarch's "Lives." This he did simply because, as a rule, almost every boy in the West in the early days did read Plutarch. When the advance sheets of the book reached Mr. Lincoln, he sent for the author and said, gravely : "That paragraph wherein you state that I read Plutarch's 'Lives' was not true when you wrote it, for up to that moment in my life I had never seen that early contribution to human history ; but I want your book, even if it is nothing more than a campaign sketch, to be faithful to the facts ; and in order that that statement might be literally true, I secured the book a few days ago, and have sent for you to tell you I have just read it through."—JESSE W. WEIK.

JUDGE JOHN PITCHER.

A lawyer of Rockport, Indiana, at the time the Lincolns lived near Gentryville. An essay of Mr. Lincoln's, composed when he was about nineteen, was submitted to Mr. Pitcher, who declared the "world couldn't beat it;" and he seems to have taken a kindly interest in the author from that time forward, lending him books freely from his law office. Mr. Pitcher was still living in 1889, in Mt. Vernon, Indiana, having reached the age of ninety-three years. His reminiscences of the boyhood of Lincoln are embodied in Herndon's "Life."

to this day of riding to mill with his father, and seeing, as they drove along, a boy sitting on the top rail of an old-fashioned stake-and-rider worm fence, reading so intently that he did not notice their approach. His father, turning to him, said : "John, look at that boy yonder, and mark my words, he will make a smart man out of himself. I may not see it, but you'll see if my words don't come true." "That boy was Abraham Lincoln," adds Mr. Lamar, impressively.

In his habits of reading and study the boy had little encouragement from his father, but his step-mother did all she could for him. Indeed, between the two there soon grew up a relation of touching gentleness and confidence. In one of the interviews a biographer of Mr. Lincoln sought with her before her death, Mrs. Lincoln said :

"I induced my husband to permit Abe to read and study at home, as well as at school. At first he was not easily reconciled to it, but finally he too seemed willing to encourage him to a certain extent. Abe was a dutiful son to me always; and we took particular care when he was reading not to disturb him—would let him read on and on till he quit of his own accord."

This consideration of his step-mother won the boy's confidence, and he rarely copied anything that he did not take it to her to read, asking her opinion of it ; and often, when she did not understand it, explaining the meaning in his plain and simple language.

No newspaper ever escaped him. One man in Gentryville, Mr. Jones, the storekeeper, took a Louisville paper, and here Lincoln went regularly to read and discuss its contents. All the men and boys of the neighborhood gathered there, and every-

CORN-HUSK COLLAR.

Drawn from the original, in the United States National Museum, at Washington, D. C. These collars were used in Indiana and Illinois in Lincoln's day.

thing which the paper related was subjected to their keen, shrewd common-sense. It was not long before young Lincoln became the favorite member of the group, the one listened to most respectfully. Politics were warmly discussed by these Gentryville citizens, and it may be that sitting on the counter of Jones's grocery Lincoln even argued on slavery. It certainly was one of the live questions in Indiana at that date.

For several years after the organization of the Territory, and in spite of the Ordinance of 1787, a system of thinly disguised slavery had existed ; and it took a sharp struggle to bring the State in without some form of the institution. So uncertain was the result that, when decided, the word passed from mouth to mouth all over Hoosierdom, " She has come in free, she has come in free ! " Even in 1820, four years after the admission to State-hood, the census showed one hundred and ninety slaves, nearly all of them in the southwest corner, where the Lincolns lived, and it was not, in reality, until 1821 that the State Supreme Court put an end to the question. In Illinois in 1822–1824 there was carried on one of the most violent contests between the friends and opponents of slavery which occurred before the repeal of the Missouri Compromise. The effort to secure slave labor was nearly successful. In the campaign, pamphlets *pro* and *con* literally inundated the State ; the pulpits took it up ; and " almost every stump in every county had its bellowing, indignant orator." So violent a commotion so near their borders could hardly have failed to reach Gentryville.

PUNCHED SHEET-IRON LANTERN.

Drawn from the original, in the United States National Museum, at Washington, D. C. Oiled paper was sometimes used in the lanterns.

There had been other anti-slavery agitation going on within hearing for several years. In 1804 a number of Baptist ministers of Kentucky started a crusade against the institution, which resulted in a hot contest in the denomination, and the organization of the "Baptist Licking-Locust Association Friends of Humanity." The Rev. Jesse Head, the minister who married Thomas Lincoln and Nancy Hanks, talked freely and boldly against slavery ; and one of their old friends, Christopher Columbus Graham, the man who was present at their wedding, says : "Tom and Nancy Lincoln and Sally Bush were just steeped full of Jesse Head's notions about the wrong of slavery and the rights of man as explained by Thomas Jefferson and Thomas Paine." In 1806 Charles Osborn began to preach "immediate emancipation" in Tennessee. Ten years later he started a paper in Ohio, devoted to the same idea, and in 1819 he transferred his crusade to Indiana. In 1821 Benjamin Lundy started, in Tennessee, the famous "Genius," devoted to the same doctrine ; and in 1822, at Shelby-

JOHN W. LAMAR.

Mr. Lamar was a young boy in Spencer County when Lincoln left Indiana, but was old enough to have seen much of him and to have known his characteristics and his reputation in the county. He is still living near his old home.

ville, only about one hundred miles from Gentryville, was started a paper similar in its views, the "Abolition Intelligencer."

At that time there were in Kentucky five or six abolition societies, and in Illinois was an organization called the "Friends of Humanity." Probably young Lincoln heard but vaguely of these movements ; but of some of them he must have heard, and he must have connected them with the "Speech of Mr. Pitt on the Slave Trade ; " with Merry's elegy, "The Slaves ; " and with the discussion given in his "Kentucky Preceptor," "Which has the Most to complain of, the Indian or the Negro ?" all of which tradition declares he was fond of repeating. It is not impossible that,

REV. ALLEN BROONER.

An Indiana acquaintance of Lincoln, still living near Gentryville. "Mr. Brooner's mother was a friend of Nancy Hanks Lincoln. In the fall of 1818 Mrs. Brooner was very sick, and Mrs. Lincoln called to see her. The sick woman was very despondent, and said: 'Mrs. Lincoln, I am going to die. You will not see me again while living.' 'Tut te tut. You must not say that. Why, you will live longer than I. So cheer up,' answered Mrs. Lincoln. Then, after a few parting words, Mrs. Lincoln went home. The next day she was very ill and in a few days she died. A few days later Mrs. Brooner died. When the tombstone was placed at Mrs. Lincoln's grave, no one could state positively which was Mrs. Brooner's and which Mrs. Lincoln's grave. Mr. Allen Brooner gave his opinion, and the stone was placed; but the iron fence encloses both graves, which lie in a half-acre tract of land owned by the United States Government. Mr. Allen Brooner, after his mother's death, became a minister of the United Brethren Church, and moved to Illinois. Like all of the old settlers of Gentryville, he remembers the departure of the Lincolns for Illinois. 'When the Lincolns were getting ready to leave,' says Mr. Brooner, 'Abraham and his step-brother, John Johnston, came over to our house to swap a horse for a yoke of oxen. John did all the talking.' If any one had been asked that day which would make the greatest success in life, I think the answer would have been John Johnston.'" *

* From an unpublished MS. by A. Hoosier.

as Frederick Douglas first realized his own condition in reading a school-speaker, the "Columbian Orator," so Abraham Lincoln first felt the wrong of slavery in reading his "American Preceptor."

Lincoln was not only winning in these days in the Jones grocery store a reputation as a talker and story-teller; he was becoming known as a kind of backwoods orator. He could repeat with effect all the poems and speeches in his various school-readers, he could imitate to perfection the wandering preachers who came to Gentryville, and he could make a political speech so stirring that he drew a crowd about him every time he mounted a stump. The applause he won was sweet; and frequently he indulged his gifts when he ought to have been at work—so thought his employers and Thomas his father. It was trying, no doubt, to the hard-pushed farmers, to see the men who ought to have been cutting grass or chopping wood throw down their sickles or axes and group around a boy, whenever he mounted a stump to develop a pet theory or repeat with variations yesterday's sermon. In his fondness for speechmaking he attended all the trials of the neighborhood, and frequently walked fifteen miles to Boonville to attend court.

Abraham Lincoln
his hand and pen.
he will be good but
god knows When

LINES FROM LINCOLN'S COPY-BOOK.

These lines were written on a leaf of a copy-book in which Lincoln wrote out the tables of weights and measures, and the sums in connection with them. His step-mother, Sarah Bush Lincoln, gave the leaf, with a few others'from the book, to Mr. Herndon. It is now owned by Jesse W. Weik.

He wrote as well as spoke, and some of his productions were even printed, through the influence of his admiring neighbors. Thus a local Baptist preacher was so struck with one of Abraham's essays on temperance that he sent it to Ohio, where it appeared in some paper. Another article, on "National Politics," so pleased a lawyer of the vicinity that he declared the "world couldn't beat it."

INFLUENCE OF THE RIVER LIFE.

In considering the different opportunities for development which the boy had at this time, his months spent on the Ohio as a ferryman and his trips down the Mississippi should not be forgotten. In fact, all that Abraham Lincoln saw of men and the world outside of Gentryville and its neighborhood, until after he was twenty-one years of age, he saw on these rivers. For many years the Ohio and the Mississippi were the Appian Way, the one route to the world for the Western settlers. To preserve it they had been willing in early times to go to war with Spain or with France, to secede from the Union, even to join Spain or France against the United States if either country would insure their right to their highway. In the long years in which the ownership of the great river was unsettled, every man of them had come to feel with Benjamin Franklin, "a neighbor might as well ask me to sell my street-door." In fact, this water-way was their "street-door," and all that many of them ever saw of the world passed here. Up and down the rivers was a continual movement. Odd craft of every kind possible on a river went by: "arks"

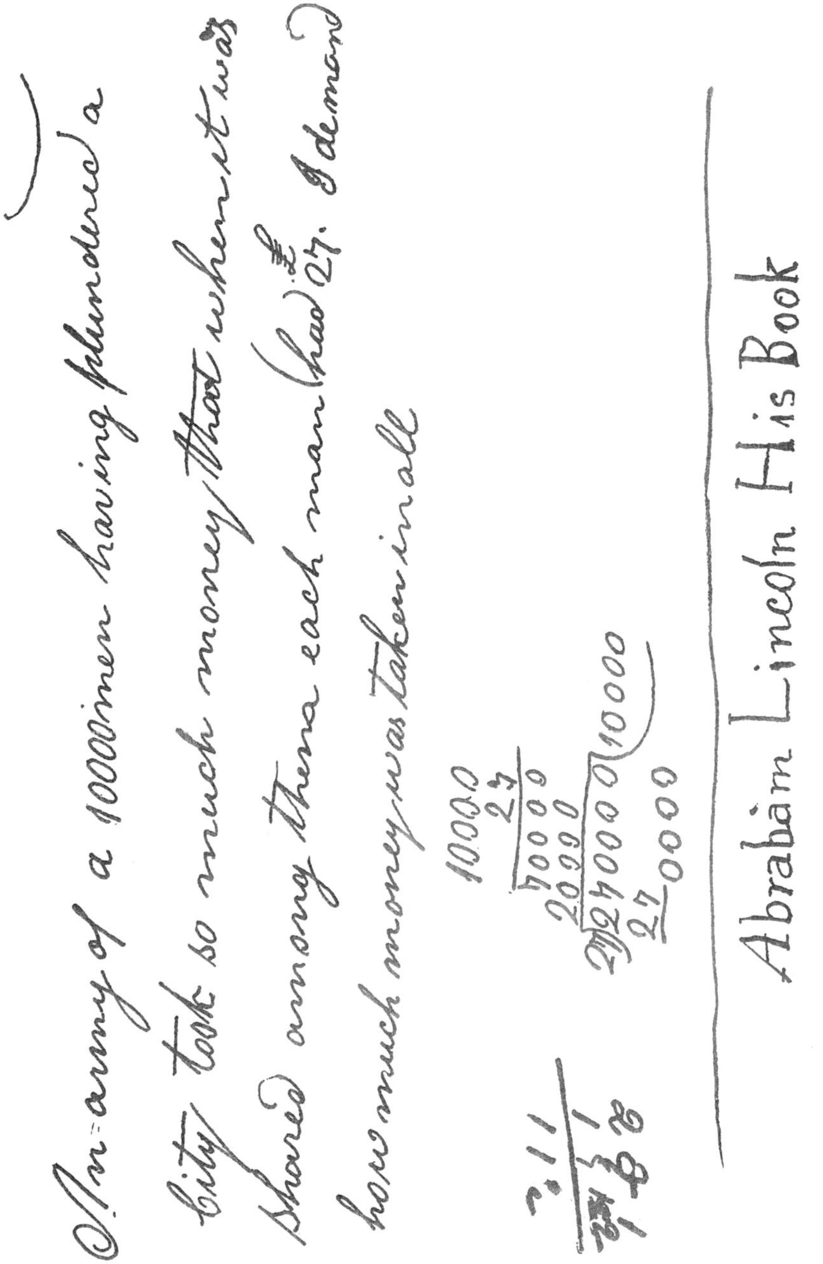

An army of a 10000 men having plundered a

city took so much money/that when it was

shared among them each man (had) £ 27. 8d demand

how much money was taken in all

10000
27
70000
20000
2)0)24000 0(10000
27 0000

FRAGMENT FROM A LEAF OF LINCOLN'S EXERCISE-BOOK.

Abraham Lincoln His Book

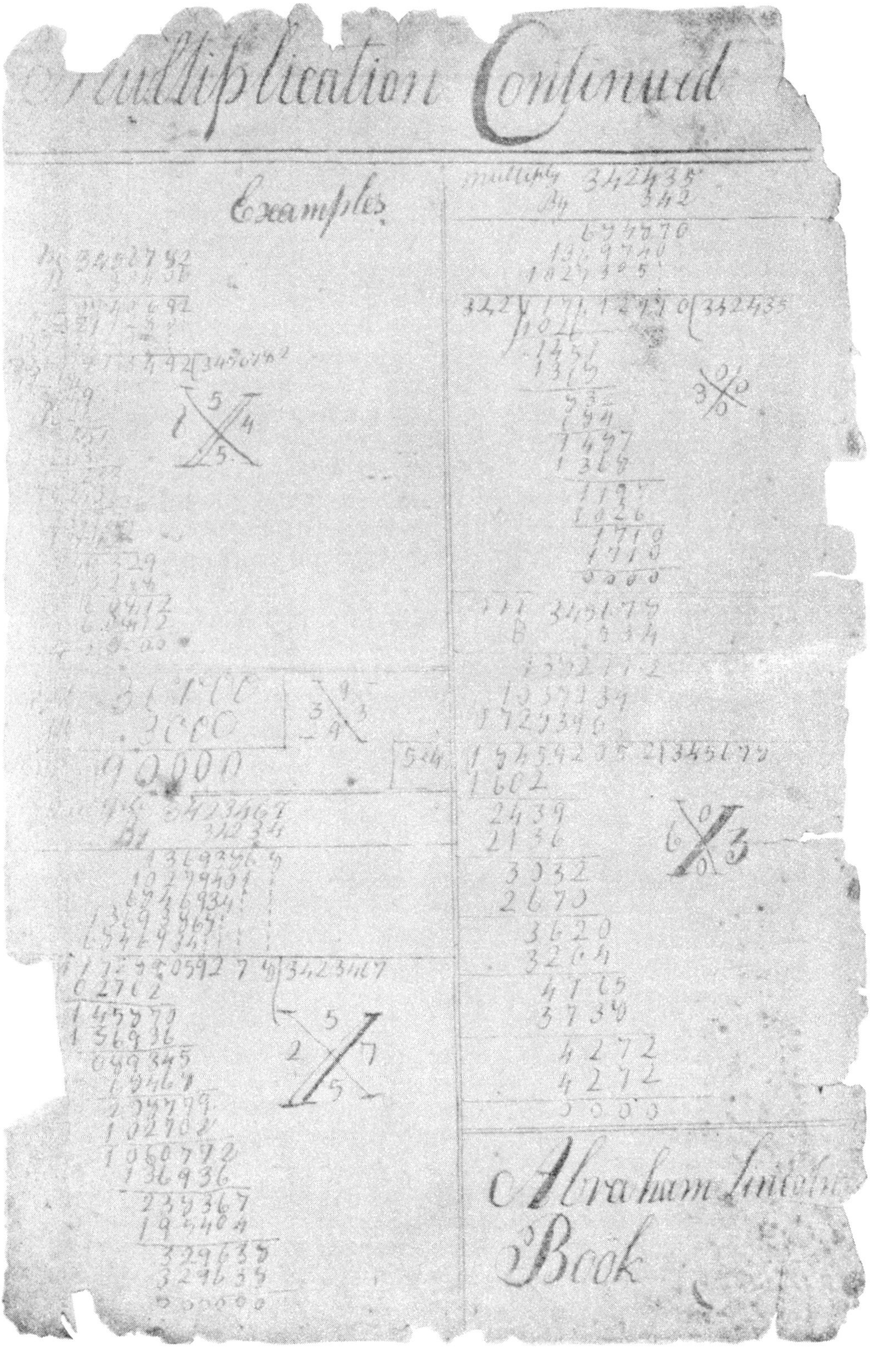

Examples

multiply 342435
By 342

694870
1369740
1027305

342 | 1477 | 0 | 342435

Abraham Lincoln
Book

and "sleds," with tidy cabins w h e r e families lived, and w h e r e one could see the washing stretched, t h e children playing, the mother on pleasant days rocking and sewing ; keel-boats, which dodged in and out and turned inquisitive noses up all the creeks and bayous ; great fleets f r o m the Alleghanies, made up of a score or more of timber rafts, and manned by forty or fifty r o u g h boatmen ; "Orleans boats," loaded with flour, hogs, produce of all kinds ; pirogues, made from great trees; "broad-horns ;" curious nonde-scripts w o r k e d by a wheel; and, after 1812, steamboats.

WILLIAM JONES.

The store in Gentryville in which Lincoln first made his reputation as a debater and story-teller was owned by Mr. Jones. The year before the Lincolns moved to Illinois Abraham clerked in the store, and it is said that when he left Indiana Mr. Jones sold him a pack of goods which he peddled on his journey. Mr. Jones was the representative from Spencer County in the State legislature from 1838 to 1841. He is no longer living. His son, Captain William Jones, is still in Gentryville.

All this traffic w a s leisurely. Men had time to tie up and tell the news and show their wares. Even the steamboats loitered as it pleased them. They knew no schedule. They stopped anywhere to let passengers off. They tied up wherever it was convenient, to wait for fresh wood to be cut and loaded, or for repairs to be made. Waiting for repairs seems, in fact, to have absorbed a great deal of the time of these early steamers. They were continually running on to "sawyers," or "planters," or "wooden islands," and they blew up with a regularity which was monotonous. Even as late as 1842, when Charles Dickens made the trip down the Mississippi, he was often gravely recommended to keep as far aft as possible, "because the steamboats generally blew up forward."

It was this varied river life with which Abraham Lincoln came into contact as a ferryman and boatman. Who can believe that he could see it and be part of it without learning much of the life and the world beyond him? Every time a steamboat or raft tied up near Anderson Creek and he with his companions boarded it and saw its mysteries and talked with its crew, every time he rowed out with passengers to a passing steamer, who can doubt that he came away with new ideas and fresh energy? The trips to New Orleans were, to a thoughtful boy, an education of no mean value. It was the most cosmopolitan and brilliant city of the United States at that date, and there young Lincoln saw life at its intensest.

CHAPTER V.

LINCOLN'S REPUTATION IN INDIANA.—REMINISCENCES OF HIS ASSOCIATES.

IN spite of the crudeness of these early opportunities for learning; in spite of the fact that he had no wise direction, that he was brought up by a father with no settled purpose, and that he lived in a pioneer community, where a young man's life at best is but a series of makeshifts, Lincoln soon developed a determination to make something out of himself, and a desire to know, which led him to neglect no opportunity to learn.

The only unbroken outside influence which directed and stimulated him in his ambitions was that coming first from his mother, then from his step-mother. These two women, both of them of unusual earnestness and sweetness of spirit, were one or the other of them at his side throughout his youth and young manhood. The ideal they held before him was the simple ideal of the early American, that if a boy is upright and industrious he may aspire to any place within the gift of the country. The boy's nature told him they were right. Everything he read confirmed their teachings, and he cultivated, in every way open to him, his passion to know and to be something.

There are many proofs that Lincoln's characteristics were recognized at this period by his associates; that his determination to excel, if not appreciated, yet made its imprint. In 1865, thirty-five years after he left Gentryville, a biographer, anxious to save all that was known of Lincoln in Indiana, went among his old associates, and with a sincerity and thoroughness worthy of

LINCOLN IN 1858.

From a photograph in the possession of Mr. Stuart Brown of Springfield, Illinois. The original of this photograph was bought in 1860, in a Springfield gallery, by Mr. D. McWilliams of Dwight, Illinois. Mr. McWilliams sent the picture to Mr. Milton Hay Jopingfield, an intimate friend of Mr. Lincoln's, and from him received the following letter: " I am greatly pleased with this picture of Lincoln. I think it reproduces the man as he was, in the sober expression most habitual with him, better than any other photograph I have seen of him ; and this is the opinion of all the old familiar acquaintances of his to whom I have shown it."

respect, interviewed them. At that time there were still living numbers of the people with whom Lincoln had been brought up. They all remembered something of him. It is curious to note that all of these people tell of his doing something different from what other boys did, something sufficiently superior to have made a keen impression upon them. In almost every case each person had his own special reason for admiring Lincoln. A facility in making rhymes and writing essays was the admiration of many, who considered it the more remarkable because "essays and poetry were not taught in school," and "Abe took it up on his own account."

Many others were struck by the clever use he made of his gift for writing. The wit he showed in taking revenge for a social slight

GREEN B. TAYLOR, A BOYHOOD FRIEND OF LINCOLN.

Son of James Taylor, for whom Lincoln ran the ferry-boat at the mouth of Anderson Creek. Mr. Taylor, now in his eighty-second year, lives in South Dakota. He remembers Mr. Lincoln perfectly, and says that his father hired Abraham Lincoln for one year, at six dollars a month, and that he was "well pleased with the boy."

by a satire on the Grigsbys, who had failed to invite him to a wedding, made a lasting impression in Gentryville. That he should write so well as to be able to humiliate his enemies more deeply than if he had resorted to the method of taking revenge current in the country, and thrashed them, seemed to his friends a mark of surprising superiority.

Others remembered his quick-wittedness in helping his friends.

"We are indebted to Kate Roby," says Mr. Herndon, "for an incident which illustrates alike his proficiency in orthography and his natural inclination to help another out of the mire. The word 'defied' had been given out by Schoolmaster Crawford, but had been misspelled several times when it came Miss Roby's turn. 'Abe stood on the opposite side of the room,' related Miss Roby to me in 1865, 'and was watching me. I began d-e-f—, and then I stopped, hesitating whether to proceed with an i or a y. Looking up, I beheld Abe, a grin covering his face, and pointing with his index finger to his eye.   I took the hint, spelled the word with an i, and it went through all right.'"

This same Miss Roby it was who said of Lincoln, "He was better read then than the world knows or is likely to know exactly. . . . He often and often commented or talked to me about what he had read—seemed to read it out of the book as he went along—did so to others.   He was the learned boy among us unlearned folks.   He took great pains to explain; could do it so simply.   He was diffident then, too."

One man was impressed by the character of the sentences he had given him for a copy.   "It was considered at that time," said he, "that Abe was the best penman in the neighborhood. One day, w h i l e he was on a visit at my mother's, I asked him to write some copies for me.   He very willingly consented.   He wrote several of them, but one of them I have n e v e r forgotten, although a boy at that time.   It was this:

"'Good boys who to their
        books apply
    Will all be great men
        by and by.'"

All of his comrades remembered his stories and his clearness in argument.   "W h e n he appeared in company,'' says N a t

CABINET MADE BY ABRAHAM LINCOLN.

This cabinet is now in the possession of Captain J. W. Wartman of Evansville, Indiana.   It is of walnut, two feet in height, and very well put together.   Thomas Lincoln is said to have aided his son in making it.

Grigsby, "the boys would gather and cluster around him to hear him talk.   Mr. Lincoln was figurative in his speech, talks, and conversation.   He argued much from analogy, and explained things hard for us to understand by stories, maxims, tales, and figures.   He would almost always point his lesson or idea by

PIGEON CREEK CHURCH, WHICH THE LINCOLNS ATTENDED IN INDIANA.

From a photograph loaned by W. W. Admire of Chicago. This little log church, or "meetin' house," is where the Lincolns attended services in Indiana. The pulpit is said to have been made by Thomas Lincoln. The building was razed about fifteen years ago, after having been used for several years as a tobacco barn.

some story that was plain and near us, that we might instantly see the force and bearing of what he said."

There are many proofs that he was an authority on all subjects, even the country jockeys bringing him their stories and seeking to inspire his enthusiasm. Captain John Lamar of Gentryville, who was a very small boy in the neighborhood when Lincoln was a young man, is still fond of describing a scene he witnessed once, which shows with what care even the "heroes" of the country tried to impress young Lincoln. "Uncle Jimmy Larkins, as everybody called him," says Mr. Lamar, "was a great hero in my childish eyes. Why, I cannot now say, without it was his manners. There had been a big fox-chase, and Uncle Jimmy was telling about it. Of course he was the hero. I was only a little shaver, and I stood in front of Uncle Jimmy, looking up into his eyes; but he never noticed me. He looked at Abraham Lincoln, and said: 'Abe, I've got the best horse in the world; he won the race and never drew a long breath.' But Abe paid no attention to Uncle Jimmy,

THE FIRST LINCOLN MONUMENT.

From a photograph made for this work. When Abraham Lincoln left Indiana, in 1830, his friend James Gentry planted, in remembrance of him, near the Lincoln cabin, a cedar tree. It still stands, sturdy and strong, though it is stripped of twigs as high as one can reach. Those who point out the tree explain the bareness by saying: "The folks who come lookin' around have taken twigs until you can't reach any more very handy."

and I got mad at the big, overgrown fellow, and wanted him to listen to my hero's story. Uncle Jimmy was determined that Abe should hear, and repeated the story. 'I say, Abe, I have the best horse in the world; after all that running he never drew a long breath.' Then Abe, looking down at my little dancing hero, said: 'Well, Larkins, why don't you tell us how many short breaths he drew?' This raised a laugh on Uncle Jimmy, and he got mad, and declared he'd fight Abe if he wasn't so big. He jumped around until Abe quietly said: 'Now, Larkins, if you don't shut up I'll throw you in that water.' I was very uneasy and angry at the way my hero was treated, but I lived to change my views about *heroes*."

There is one other testimony to his character as a boy which should not be omitted. It is that of his stepmother:

"Abe was a good boy, and I can say what scarcely one woman—a mother—can say in a thousand: Abe never gave me a cross word or look, and never refused, in fact or appearance, to do anything I requested him. I never gave him a cross word in all my life. . . . His mind and mine—what little I had—seemed to run together. He was here after he was elected President. He was a dutiful son to me always. I think he loved me truly. I had a son, John, who was raised with Abe. Both were good boys; but I must say, both now being dead, that Abe was the best boy I ever saw, or expect to see."

OLD POST FORD ACROSS THE WABASH RIVER, WHERE THE LINCOLNS CROSSED FROM INDIANA TO ILLINOIS.

From a photograph made for this work. The route by which the Lincolns went into Illinois from Indiana has always been a question in dispute. Some of the acquaintances of the family still living in Indiana claim that they followed the line marked on our map (page 45). Others say that they went from Gentryville to the Old Post Ford across the Wabash. The route on the map was drawn on the supposition that they would have taken the road by which they would have avoided the greatest number of water-courses. Information has come to us since the map was made which shows that they went by Vincennes. Mr. Jesse W. Weik says that Dennis Hanks, who was in the party, told him in 1886 that they went through Vincennes. Colonel Chapman of Charleston, the grandson of Sarah Bush Lincoln, told Mr. Weik that in February, 1861, when Mr. Lincoln visited his mother for the last time, he told him that the settlers passed through Vincennes, where they remained a day. There, Lincoln said, they saw a printing-press for the first time. At Palestine, on the Illinois side of the Wabash, he remembered seeing a large crowd around the United States Land Office, and a travelling juggler performing sleight-of-hand tricks. We also know that they entered Decatur from the south, near the present line of the Illinois Central. This Mr. Lincoln told Mr. H. C. Whitney.

CHAPTER VI.

AMUSEMENTS OF LINCOLN'S LIFE IN INDIANA.—HIS FIRST SORROWS.

F Abraham Lincoln's early struggle for both liveli-
hood and education was rough and hard, his life
was not without amusements. At home the rude
household was overflowing with life.   There were
Abraham and his sister, a stepbrother and two
stepsisters, and a cousin of Nancy Hanks Lincoln, Dennis Hanks, whom misfortune had made
an inmate of the Lincoln home—quite enough to
plan sports and mischief and keep time from
growing dull.   Thomas Lincoln and Dennis Hanks were both
famous story-tellers, and the Lincolns spent many a cozy evening about their cabin fire, repeating the stories they knew.

GRAVE OF LINCOLN'S SISTER.

From a photograph taken for this work. Sarah, or Nancy, Lincoln was born in Elizabethtown,
Kentucky, in 1807. In 1826 she married Aaron Grigsby, and a year later died. She was buried not far
from Gentryville, in what is now called "Old Pigeon Cemetery." Her grave is marked by the rude stone
directly over the star. The marble monument in the centre is that of her husband.

CORN-HUSK BROOMS AND MOPS.

Photographed for this work from the originals, in the United States National Museum at Washington. Corn-husks were used by the pioneers of the West to make brooms, brushes, mats, and horse-collars.

Of course the boys hunted. Not that Abraham ever became a true sportsman; indeed, he seems to have lacked the genuine sporting instinct. In a curious autobiography, written entirely in the third person, which Mr. Lincoln prepared at the request of a friend in 1860,* he says of his exploits as a hunter: "A few days before the completion of his eighth year, in the absence of his father, a flock of wild turkeys approached the new log cabin; and Abraham, with a rifle gun, standing inside, shot through a crack and killed one of them. He has never since pulled the trigger on any larger game." This exploit is confirmed by Dennis

A LINCOLN CHAIR.

This chair was made from rails split by Abraham Lincoln when he was living in Spencer County, Indiana.

Hanks, who says: "No doubt about A. Lincoln's killing the turkey. He done it with his father's rifle, made by William Lutes of Bullitt County, Kentucky. I have killed a hundred deer with her myself; turkeys too numerous to mention."

But there were many other country sports which he enjoyed to the full. He went swimming in the evenings; fished with the other boys in

* Preserved in "Abraham Lincoln. Complete Works." Edited by John G. Nicolay and John Hay. Volume I., page 639. The Century Company.

Pigeon Creek, and caught chubs and suckers enough to delight any boy; he wrestled, jumped, and ran races at the noon rests. He was present at every country horse-race and fox-chase. The sports he preferred were those which brought men together: the spelling-school, the husking-bee, the "raising;" and of all these he was the life by his wit, his stories, his good nature, his doggerel verses, his practical jokes, and by a rough kind of politeness—for even in Indiana in those times there was a notion of politeness, and one of Lincoln's schoolmasters had even given "lessons in manners." Lincoln seems to have profited in a degree by them; for Mrs. Crawford, at whose home he worked some time, declares that he always "lifted his hat and bowed" when he made his appearance.

There was, of course, a rough gallantry among the young people; and Lincoln's old comrades and friends in Indiana have left many tales of how he "went to see the girls," of how he brought in the biggest back-log and made the brightest fire; then of how the young people, sitting around it, watching the way the sparks flew, told their fortunes. He helped pare apples, shell corn, and crack nuts. He took the girls to meeting and to spelling-school, though he was not often allowed to take part in the spelling-match, for the one who "chose first" always chose "Abe Lincoln;" and that was equivalent to winning, as the others knew that "he would stand up the longest."

PIONEER KITCHEN UTENSILS.

Drawn for this work from the original articles, in the United States National Museum, through the courtesy of the director, Mr. G. Brown Goode. The articles in the group are a hominy mortar and pestle, water gourd and gourd dipper, wooden pails and tub, and a wooden piggin.

The nearest

THE HILL NEAR GENTRYVILLE FROM WHICH THE LINCOLNS TOOK THEIR LAST LOOK AT THEIR
INDIANA HOME.

approach to sentiment at this time, of which we know, is recorded in a story Lincoln once told to an acquaintance in Springfield. It was a rainy day, and he was sitting with his feet on the
window-sill, his eyes on the street, watching the rain. Suddenly
he looked up and said:

"Did you ever write out a story in your mind? I did when
I was a little codger. One day a wagon with a lady and two
girls and a man broke down near us, and while they were fixing
up, they cooked in our kitchen. The woman had books and
read us stories, and they were the first I ever had heard. I took
a great fancy to one of the girls; and when they were gone I
thought of her a great deal, and one day when I was sitting out
in the sun by the house I wrote out a story in my mind. I
thought I took my father's horse and followed the wagon, and
finally I found it, and they were surprised to see me. I talked
with the girl and persuaded her to elope with me; and that
night I put her on my horse, and we started off across the prairie.
After several hours we came to a camp; and when we rode up
we found it was the one we had left a few hours before, and we

LINCOLN'S FIRST HOME IN ILLINOIS.

After a photograph owned by H. E. Barker of Springfield, Illinois. A printed description accompanying the photograph says: "The above is an exact reproduction of a photograph taken in 1865 of Abraham Lincoln's cabin on the banks of the Sangamon River. The cabin was located upon Section 28, Harristown Township, Macon County, Illinois." The genuineness of the picture is attested by the Hon. Richard J. Oglesby, at that time Governor of Illinois.

went in. The next night we tried again, and the same thing happened—the horse came back to the same place; and then we concluded that we ought not to elope. I stayed until I had persuaded her father to give her to me. I always meant to write that story out and publish it, and I began once; but I concluded it was not much of a story. But I think that was the beginning of love with me."*

EARLY SORROWS.

His life had its tragedies as well as its touch of romance—tragedies so real and profound that they gave dignity to all the crudeness and poverty which surrounded him, and quickened

* Interview with Mr. T. W. S. Kidd of Springfield, Illinois, editor of "The Morning Monitor."

and intensified the melancholy temperament he had inherited from his mother. Away back in 1816, when Thomas Lincoln had started to find a farm in Indiana, bidding his wife be ready to go into the wilderness on his return, Nancy Lincoln had taken her boy and girl to a tiny grave, that of her youngest child; and the three had there said good-by to a little one whom the c h i l d r e n had scarcely known, but for whom the mother's grief was so keen that the boy never forgot the scene.

LINCOLN'S BROAD-AXE.

This broad-axe is said to have been owned originally by Abram Bales of New Salem; and, according to tradition, it was bought from him by Lincoln. After Lincoln forsook the woods, he sold the axe to one Mr. Irvin. Mr. L. W. Bishop of Petersburg now has the axe, having gotten it directly from Mr. Irvin. There are a number of affidavits attesting its genuineness. The axe has evidently seen hard usage, and is now covered with a thick coat of rust.

Two years later he saw his father make a green pine box and put his dead mother into it, and he saw her buried n o t far f r o m their cabin, almost without prayer. Young as he was, it was his efforts, it is said, which brought a parson from Kentucky, three months later, to preach the sermon and conduct the service which seemed to the child a necessary honor to the dead.* As sad as the death of his mother was that of his only sister, Sarah. Married to Aaron Grigsby in 1826, she had died a year and a half later in child-birth, a death which to her brother must have seemed a horror and a mystery.

Apart from these family sorrows there was all the crime and misery of the community—all of which came to his ears and awakened his nature. He even saw in those days one of his companions go suddenly mad. The young man never recovered his reason, but sank into idiocy. All night he would croon plaintive songs, and Lincoln himself tells how, fascinated by this mysterious malady, he used to rise before daylight to cross the fields and listen to this funeral dirge of the reason. In spite of the poverty and rudeness of his life the depth of his nature was unclouded. He could feel intensely, and his imagination was quick to respond to the touch of mystery.

---

* It still happens frequently in the mountain districts of Tennessee that the funeral services are not held until months after the burial. A gentleman who has lived much in the South tells of a man marrying a second wife at a decent interval after the death of his first, but still *before* the funeral of the first had taken place.

CHAPTER VII.

N the spring of 1830, when Abraham was twenty-one years old, his father, Thomas Lincoln, decided to leave Indiana. The reason Dennis Hanks gives for this removal was a disease called the "milk-sick." Abraham Lincoln's mother, Nancy Hanks Lincoln, and several of their relatives who had followed them from Kentucky had died of it. The cattle had been carried off by it. Neither brute nor human life seemed to be safe. As Dennis Hanks says : "This was reason enough (ain't it?) for leaving." Any one who has travelled through the portions of Spencer County in which the Lincolns settled will respect Thomas Lincoln for his energy in moving. When covered with timber, as the land was when he chose his farm, it no doubt promised well; but fourteen years of hard labor showed him that the soil was niggardly and the future of the country unpromising. To-day, sixty-five years since the Lincolns left Spencer County, the country remains as it was then, dull, commonplace, unfruitful. The towns show no signs of energy or prosperity. There are no leading streets or buildings ; no man's house is better than his neighbor's, and every man's house is ordinary. For a long distance on each side of Gentryville, as one passes by rail, no superior farm is to be seen, no prosperous mine or manufactory. It is a dead, monotonous country, where no possibilities of quick wealth have been discovered, and which only centuries of tilling and fertilizing can make prosperous. Thomas Lincoln did well to leave Indiana.

The place chosen for their new home was the Sangamon country in central Illinois. It was at that day a country of great renown in the West, the name meaning "The land where there is plenty to eat." One of the family—John Hanks, a cousin of Dennis—was already there, and the inviting reports he had sent to Indiana were no doubt what led the Lincolns to decide on Illinois as their future home.

Gentryville saw young Lincoln depart with real regret, and

his friends gave him a score of rude proofs that he would not be forgotten. Even to-day there is not a family living in and around Gentryville, who remembers the Lincolns at all, who has not some legend to repeat of their departure. They tell how in those days "neighbors were like relatives," and everybody offered some kindly service to the movers as a parting sign of good-will. The entire Lincoln family was invited to spend the last n i g h t before starting, with Mr. Gentry. He was so loath to part with Lincoln that he "accompanied the movers along the road a spell." After they were gone, one of his sons, James Gentry, planted a cedar tree in memory of Abraham, which now marks the site of the Lincoln home.

The spot on the hill overlooking Buckthorn valley, where the Lincolns said good-by to their old home and to the

JOHN E. ROLL, WHO HELPED LINCOLN BUILD THE FLATBOAT.

Born in Green Village, New Jersey, June 4, 1814. He went to Illinois in 1830, the year in which Mr. Lincoln went, settling in Sangamon town, where he had relatives. It was here he met Lincoln, and made the "pins" for the flatboat. Later Mr. Roll went to Springfield. A quarter of the city is now known as "Roll's addition." Mr. Roll was well acquainted with Lincoln, and when the President left Springfield he gave Mr. Roll his dog Fido. Mr. Roll knew Stephen A. Douglas well, and carries a watch which once belonged to the "Little Giant."

home of Sarah Lincoln Grigsby, to the grave of the mother and wife, to all their neighbors and friends, is still pointed out. Buckthorn valley held many recollections dear to them all, but to no one of the company was the place dearer than to Abraham. It is certain that he felt the parting keenly, and he certainly never forgot his years in the Hoosier State. One of the most touching experiences he relates in all his published letters is his emotion at visiting his old Indiana home fourteen years after he had left it. So strongly was he moved by the scenes of his first conscious sorrows, efforts, joys, ambitions, that he put into verse the feelings they awakened.*

* Letter to —— Johnston, April 18, 1846. "Abraham Lincoln. Complete Works." Edited by John G. Nicolay and John Hay. Volume I., pages 86, 87. The Century Co.

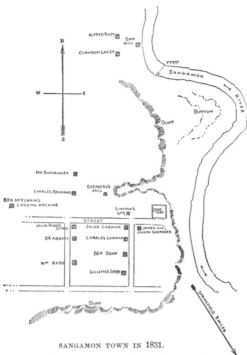

SANGAMON TOWN IN 1831.

Drawn for this work by J. McCan Davis, with
the aid of Mr. John E. Roll, a former resident.

While he never attempted to conceal the poverty and hardship of these days, and would speak humorously of the "pretty pinching times" he saw, he never regarded his life at this time as mean or pitiable. Frequently he talked to his friends in later days of his boyhood, and always with apparent pleasure. "Mr. Lincoln told this story" (of his youth), says Leonard Swett, "as the story of a happy childhood. There was nothing sad or pinched, and nothing of want, and no allusion to want in any part of it. His own description of his youth was that of a joyous, happy boyhood. It was told with mirth and glee, and illustrated by pointed anecdote, often interrupted by his jocund laugh."

And he was right. There was nothing ignoble or mean in this Indiana pioneer life. It was rude, but with only the rudeness which the ambitious are willing to endure in order to push on to a better condition than they otherwise could know. These people did not accept their hardships apathetically. They did not regard them as permanent. They were only the temporary deprivations necessary in order to accomplish what they had home into the country to do. For this reason they endured copefully all that was hard. It is worth notice, too, that there was nothing belittling in their life; there was no pauperism, no shirking. Each family provided for its own simple wants, and had the conscious dignity which comes from being equal to a situation. If their lives lacked culture and refinement, they were rich in independence and self-reliance.

LINCOLN IN 1859.

From a photograph in the collection of H. W. Fay, De Kalb, Illinois. The original was made by S. M. Fassett of Chicago; the negative was destroyed in the Chicago fire. This picture was made at the solicitation of D. B. Cook, who says that Mrs. Lincoln pronounced it the best likeness she had ever seen of her husband. Rajon used the Fassett picture as the original of his etching, and Kruell has made a fine engraving of it.

FROM INDIANA TO ILLINOIS.

The company which emigrated to Illinois included the family of Thomas Lincoln and those of Dennis Hanks and Levi Hall, married to Lincoln's step-sisters—thirteen persons in all. They sold land, cattle, and grain, and much of their household goods, and were ready in March of 1830 for their journey. All the possessions which the three families had to take with them were packed into a big wagon—the first one Thomas Lincoln had ever owned, it is said—to which four oxen were attached, and the caravan was ready. The weather was still cold, the streams were swollen, and the roads were muddy; but the party started out bravely. Inured to hardships, alive to all the new sights on their route, every day brought them amusement and adventures, and especially to young Lincoln the journey must have been of keen interest.

He drove the oxen on this trip, he tells us, and, according to a story current in Gentryville, he succeeded in doing a fair peddler's business on the route. Captain William Jones, in whose father's store Lincoln had spent so many hours in discussion and in story-telling, and for whom he had worked the last winter he was in Indiana, says that before leaving the State Abraham invested all his money, some thirty-odd dollars, in notions. Though the country through which they expected to pass was but sparsely settled, he believed he could dispose of them. " A set of knives and forks was the largest item entered on the bill," says Captain Jones ; " the other items were needles, pins, thread, buttons, and other little domestic necessities. When the Lincolns reached their new home, near Decatur, Illinois, Abraham wrote back to my father, stating that he had doubled his money on his purchases by selling them along the road. Unfortunately we did not keep that letter, not thinking how highly we would have prized it years afterwards."

The pioneers were a fortnight on their journey. All we know of the route they took is from a few chance remarks of Lincoln's to his friends to the effect that they passed through Vincennes, where they saw a printing-press for the first time, and through Palestine, where they saw a juggler performing sleight-of-hand tricks. They reached Macon County, their new home, from the south. Mr. H. C. Whitney says that once in Decatur he and Lincoln passed the court-house together. "Lincoln walked out a few feet in front, and, after shifting his position two or three

MODEL OF ABRAHAM LINCOLN'S DEVICE FOR LIFTING VESSELS OVER SHOALS.

The inscription above this model, which is shown to all visitors to the Model Hall of the Patent Office, reads : " 6469, Abraham Lincoln, Springfield, Illinois. Improvement in method of lifting vessels over shoals. Patented May 22, 1849." The apparatus consists of a bellows placed in each side of the hull of the craft, just below the water-line, and worked by an odd but simple system of ropes and pulleys. When the keel of the vessel grates against the sand or obstruction, the bellows is filled with air ; and, thus buoyed up, the vessel is expected to float over the shoal. The model is about eighteen or twenty inches long, and looks as if it had been whittled with a knife out of a shingle and a cigar box. There is no elaboration in the apparatus beyond that necessary to show the operation of buoying the vessel over the obstructions.

times, said, as he looked up at the building, partly to himself and partly to me : 'Here is the exact spot where I stood by our wagon when we moved from Indiana, twenty-six years ago ; this isn't six feet from the exact spot.' . . . I asked him if he, at that time, had expected to be a lawyer and practise law in that court-house ; to which he replied : 'No ; I didn't know I had sense enough to be a lawyer then.' He then told me he had frequently thereafter tried to locate the route by which they had come, and that he had decided that it was near the main line of the Illinois Central Railroad."

The party settled some ten miles west of Decatur, in Macon

County. Here John Hanks had the logs already cut for their new home, and Lincoln, Dennis Hanks, and Hall soon had a cabin erected. Mr. Lincoln says in his short autobiography of 1860, which he wrote in the third person: "Here they built a log cabin, into which they removed, and made sufficient of rails to fence ten acres of ground, fenced and broke the ground, and raised a crop of sown corn upon it the same year. These are, or are supposed to be, the rails about which so much is being said just now, though these are far from being the first or only rails ever made by Abraham."

If they were far from being his "first and only rails," they certainly were the most famous ones he or anybody else ever split. This was the last work he did for his father, for in the summer of that year (1830) he exercised the right of majority and started out to shift for himself. When he left his home, he went empty-handed. He was already some months over twenty-one years of age, but he had nothing in the world, not even a suit of respectable clothes; and one of the first pieces of work he did was "to split four hundred rails for every yard of brown jeans dyed with white-walnut bark that would be necessary to make him a pair of trousers." He had no trade, no profession, no spot of land, no patron, no influence. Two things recommended him to his neighbors—he was strong, and he was a good fellow.

His strength made him a valuable laborer. Not that he was fond of hard labor. Mrs. Crawford says: "Abe was no hand to pitch into work like killing snakes;" but when he did work, it was with an ease and effectiveness which compensated his employer for the time he spent in practical jokes and extemporaneous speeches. He would lift as much as three ordinary men, and "My, how he would chop!" says Dennis Hanks. "His axe would flash and bite into a sugar-tree or sycamore, and down it would come. If you heard him fellin' trees in a clearin', you would say there was three men at work by the way the trees fell."

Standing six feet four, he could out-lift, out-work, and out-wrestle any man he came in contact with. Friends and employers were proud of his prowess, and boasted of it, never failing to pit him against any hero whose strength they heard vaunted. He himself was proud of it, and throughout his life was fond of comparing himself with tall and strong men. When the committee called on him in Springfield, in 1860, to notify him of his nomination as President, Governor Morgan of New York was of the number, a man of great height and brawn. "Pray, Governor, how tall may you be?" was Mr. Lincoln's first question. There is a story told of a poor man seeking a favor from him once at the White House. He was overpowered by the idea that he was in the presence of the President, and, his errand done, was edging shyly out, when Mr. Lincoln stopped him, insisting that he *measure* with him. The man was the taller, as Mr. Lincoln had thought; and he went away evidently as much abashed that he dared be taller than the President of the United States as that he had dared to venture into his presence.

Governor Hoyt tells an excellent story illustrating this interest of Lincoln's in manly strength, and his involuntary comparison of himself with whoever showed it. It was in 1859, after Lincoln had delivered a speech at the Wisconsin State Agricultural Fair in Milwaukee. Governor Hoyt had asked him to make the rounds of the exhibits, and they went into a tent to see a "strong man" perform. He went through the ordinary exercises with huge iron balls, tossing them in the air and catching them, and rolling them on his arms and back; and Mr. Lincoln, who evidently had never before seen such a combination of agility and strength, watched him with intense interest, ejaculating under his breath now and then, "By George! By George!" When the performance was over, Governor Hoyt, seeing Mr. Lincoln's interest, asked him to go up and be introduced to the athlete. He did so; and, as he stood looking down musingly on the man, who was very short, and evidently wondering that one so much smaller than he could be so much stronger, he suddenly broke out with one of his quaint speeches. "Why," he said, "why, I could lick salt off the top of your hat."

His strength won him popularity, but his good-nature, his wit, his skill in debate, his stories, were still more efficient in gaining him good-will. People liked to have him around, and voted him a good fellow to work with. Yet such were the conditions of his life at this time that, in spite of his popularity, nothing was open to him but hard manual labor. To take the first job which he happened upon—rail-splitting, ploughing, lumbering, boating, store-keeping—and make the most of it, thankful if thereby he earned his bed and board and yearly suit of jeans, was apparently all there was before Abraham Lincoln in 1830, when he started out for himself.

LINCOLN, OFFUTT, AND GREEN ON THE FLATBOAT AT NEW SALEM.

From a painting in the State Capitol, Springfield, Illinois. This picture is crude and inaccurate. The flatboat built by Lincoln, and by him piloted to New Orleans, was larger than the one here portrayed, and the structure over the dam belittles the real mill. There was not only a grist-mill, but also a saw-mill. The mill was built in 1829. March 5, 1830, we find John Overstreet averring before the County Commissioners "that John Cameron and James Rutledge have erected a mill-dam on the Sangamon River which obstructs the navigation of said river ; " and Cameron and Rutledge are ordered to alter the dam so as to restore "safe navigation." James M. Rutledge of Petersburg, a nephew of the mill-owner, helped build the mill, and says : "The mill was a frame structure, and was solidly built. They used to grind corn mostly, though some flour was made. At times they would run day and night. The saw-mill had an old-fashioned upright saw, and stood on the bank." For a time this mill was operated by Denton Offutt, under the supervision of Lincoln. A few stakes, a part of the old dam, still show at low water.

CHAPTER VIII.

FIRST INDEPENDENT WORK.—FIRST APPEARANCE IN SANGAMON COUNTY.—VISIT TO NEW ORLEANS IN 1831.

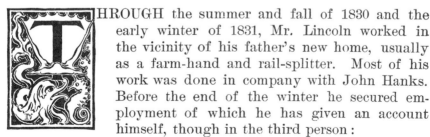

HROUGH the summer and fall of 1830 and the early winter of 1831, Mr. Lincoln worked in the vicinity of his father's new home, usually as a farm-hand and rail-splitter. Most of his work was done in company with John Hanks. Before the end of the winter he secured employment of which he has given an account himself, though in the third person :

"During that winter Abraham, together with his step-mother's son, John D. Johnston, and John Hanks, yet residing in Macon County, hired themselves to Denton Offutt to take a flatboat from Beardstown, Illinois, to New Orleans, and for that purpose were to join him (Offutt) at Springfield, Illinois, so soon as the snow should go off. When it did go off, which was about March 1, 1831, the country was so flooded as to make travelling by land impracticable ; to obviate which difficulty they purchased a large canoe and came down the Sangamon River in it from where they were all living (near Decatur). This is the time and manner of Abraham's first entrance into Sangamon County. They found Offutt at Springfield, but learned from him that he had failed in getting a boat at Beardstown. This led to their hiring themselves to him for twelve dollars per month each, and getting the timber out of the trees, and building a boat at old Sangamon town, on the Sangamon River, seven miles north-west of Springfield, which boat they took to New Orleans, sub-stantially on the old contract."

Sangamon town, where Mr. Lincoln built the flatboat, has, since his day, completely disappeared from the earth ; but then it was one of the flourishing settlements on the river of that name. Lincoln and his friends, on arriving there in March, immediately began work. There is still living in Springfield, Illinois, a man who helped Lincoln at the raft-building—Mr. John Roll, a well-known citizen, and one who has been promi-nent in the material advancement of the city. Mr. Roll remem-bers distinctly Lincoln's first appearance in Sangamon town. "He was a tall, gaunt young man," he says, "dressed in a suit of blue homespun jeans, consisting of a roundabout jacket, waistcoat, and breeches which came to within about four inches of his feet. The latter were encased in rawhide boots, into the tops of which, most of the time, his pantaloons were stuffed. He wore a soft felt hat which had at one time been black, but now, as its owner dryly remarked, 'was sunburned until it was a combine of colors.'"

Mr. Roll's relation to the new-comer soon became something more than that of a critical observer ; he hired out to him, and says with pride, "I made every pin which went into that boat."

LINCOLN'S POPULARITY IN SANGAMON.

It took some four weeks to build the raft, and in that period Lincoln succeeded in captivating the entire village by his story-telling. It was the custom in Sangamon for the "men-folks" to

THOMAS LINCOLN'S HOME IN ILLINOIS.

This cabin was built by Thomas Lincoln in 1831, on Goose Nest Prairie, in Coles County, Illinois, where he had taken up forty acres of land. It was situated nine miles south of Charleston, on what is called Lincoln's Lane. Here Thomas Lincoln died in 1851. The cabin was occupied until 1891, when it was bought by the Lincoln Log Cabin Association to be shown at the World's Fair in 1893.

gather at noon and in the evening, when resting, in a convenient lane near the mill. They had rolled out a long peeled log, on which they lounged while they whittled and talked. Lincoln had not been long in Sangamon before he joined this circle. At once he became a favorite by his jokes and good-humor. As soon as he appeared at the assembly ground the men would start him to story-telling. So irresistibly droll were his "yarns" that, says Mr. Roll, "whenever he'd end up in his unexpected way the boys on the log would whoop and roll off." The result of the rolling off was to polish the log like a mirror. The men, recognizing Lincoln's part in this polishing, christened their seat "Abe's log." Long after Lincoln had disappeared from Sangamon "Abe's log" remained, and until it had rotted away people pointed it out, and repeated the droll stories of the stranger.

AN EXCITING ADVENTURE.

The flatboat was done in about a month, and Lincoln and his friends prepared to leave Sangamon. Before he started, however, he was the hero of an adventure so thrilling that he won new laurels in the community. Mr. Roll, who was a witness to the whole exciting scene, tells the story:

"It was the spring following the winter of the deep snow.* Walter Carman, John Seamon, myself, and at times others of the Carman boys had helped Abe in building the boat, and when he had finished we went to work to make a dug-out, or canoe, to be used as a small boat with the flat. We found a suitable log about an eighth of a mile up the river, and with our axes went to work under Lincoln's direction. The river was very high, fairly 'booming.' After the dug-out was ready to launch we took it to the edge of the water, and made ready to 'let her go,' when Walter Carman and John Seamon jumped in as the boat struck the water, each one anxious to be the first to get a ride. As they shot out from the shore they found they were unable to make any headway against the strong current. Carman had the paddle, and Seamon was in the stern of the boat. Lincoln shouted to them to 'head up-stream,' and 'work back to shore,' but they found themselves powerless against the stream. At last they began to pull for the wreck of an old flatboat, the first ever built on the Sangamon, which had sunk and gone to pieces, leaving one of the stanchions sticking above the water. Just as they reached it Seamon made a grab, and caught hold of the stanchion, when the canoe capsized, leaving Seamon clinging to the old timber, and throwing Carman into the stream. It carried him down with the speed of a mill-race. Lincoln raised his voice above the roar of the flood, and yelled to Carman to swim for an elm tree which stood almost in the channel, which the action of the high water changed.

"Carman, being a good swimmer, succeeded in catching a branch, and pulled himself up out of the water, which was very cold, and had almost chilled him to death; and there he sat shivering and chattering in the tree. Lincoln, seeing Carman

---

* 1830–1831. "The winter of the deep snow" is the date which is the starting point in all calculations of time for the early settlers of Illinois, and the circumstance from which the old settlers of Sangamon County receive the name by which they are generally known, "Snow-birds."

NEW SALEM.

From a painting in the State Capitol, Springfield, Illinois. New Salem was founded by James Rutledge and John Cameron in 1829. In that year they built a dam across the Sanga-mon River, and erected a mill. Under date of October 23, 1829, Reuben Harrison, surveyor, certifies that "at the request of John Cameron, one of the proprietors, I did survey the town of New Salem." The town within two years contained a dozen or fifteen houses, nearly all of them built of logs. New Salem's population probably never exceeded a hundred persons. Its inhabitants, and those of the surrounding country, were mostly Southerners—natives of Kentucky and Tennessee—though there was an occasional Yankee among them. Soon after Lincoln left the place, in the spring of 1837, it began to decline. Petersburg had sprung up two miles down the river, and rapidly absorbed its population and business. By 1840 New Salem was almost deserted. The Rutledge tavern, the first house erected, was the last to succumb. It stood for many years, but at last crumbled away. Salem hill is now only a green cow pasture.

safe, called out to Seamon to let go the stanchion and swim for the tree. With some hesitation he obeyed, and struck out, while Lincoln cheered and directed him from the bank. As Seamon neared the tree he made one grab for a branch, and, missing it, went under the water. Another desperate lunge was successful, and he climbed up beside Carman. Things were pretty exciting now, for there were two men in the tree, and the boat was gone.

"It was a cold, raw April day, and there was great danger of the men becoming benumbed and falling back into the water. Lincoln called out to them to keep their spirits up and he would

save them. The village had been alarmed by this time, and
many people had come down to the bank. Lincoln procured a
rope, and tied it to a log. He called all hands to come and help
roll the log into the water, and after this had been done, he, with
the assistance of several others, towed it some distance up the
stream. A daring young fellow by the name of 'Jim' Dorrell
then took his seat on the end of the log, and it was pushed out
into the current, with the expectation that it would be carried
down stream against the tree where Seamon and Carman were.

"The log was well directed, and went straight to the tree; but
Jim, in his impatience to help his friends, fell a victim to his
good intentions. Making a frantic grab at a branch, he raised
himself off the log, which was swept from under him by the rag-
ing water, and he soon joined· the other two victims upon their
forlorn perch. The excitement on shore increased, and almost
the whole population of the village gathered on the river bank.
Lincoln had the log pulled up the stream, and, securing another
piece of rope, called to the men in the tree to catch it if they
could when he should reach the tree. He then straddled the log
himself, and gave the word to push out into the stream. When
he dashed into the tree, he threw the rope over the stump of a
broken limb, and let it play until he broke the speed of the log,
and gradually drew it back to the tree, holding it there until the
three now nearly frozen men had climbed down and seated themselves astride. He then gave orders to the people on the shore
to hold fast to the end of the rope which was tied to the log, and
leaving his rope in the tree he turned the log adrift. The
force of the current, acting against the taut rope, swung the log
around against the bank, and all 'on board' were saved. The
excited people, who had watched the dangerous experiment with
alternate hope and fear, now broke into cheers for Abe Lincoln
and praises for his brave act. This adventure made quite a hero
of him along the Sangamon, and the people never tired of telling
of the exploit."

A SECOND ADVENTURE.

The flatboat built and loaded, the party started for New
Orleans about the middle of April. They had gone but a few
miles when they met with another adventure. At the village of
New Salem there was a mill-dam. On it the boat stuck, and here
for nearly twenty-four hours it hung, the bow in the air and the

THE NEW SALEM MILL TWENTY-FIVE YEARS AGO.

After a painting by Mrs. Bennett ; reproduced, by permission, from " Menard-Salem-Lincoln Souvenir Album," Petersburg, Illinois, 1893. The Rutledge and Cameron mill, of which Lincoln at one time had charge, stood on the same spot as the mill in the picture, and had the same foundation. From the map on page 116 it will be seen that the mill was below the bluff and east of the town.

stern in the water, the cargo slowly setting backward—shipwreck almost certain. The village of New Salem turned out in a body to see what the strangers would do in their predicament. They shouted, suggested, and advised for a time, but finally discovered that one big fellow in the crew was ignoring them and working out a plan of relief. Having unloaded the cargo into a neighboring boat, Lincoln had succeeded in tilting his craft. Then, by boring a hole in the end extending over the dam, the water was let out. This done, the boat was easily shoved over and reloaded. The ingenuity which he had exercised in saving his boat made a deep impression on the crowd on the bank, and it was talked over for many a day. The proprietor of boat and cargo was even more enthusiastic than the spectators, and vowed he would build a steamboat for the Sangamon and make

A MATRON OF NEW SALEM IN 1832.

This costume, worn by Mrs. Lucy M.
Bennett of Petersburg, Illinois, has been
a familiar attraction at old settlers'
gatherings in Menard County for years.
The dress was made by Mrs. Hill of
New Salem ; and the reticule, or work-
bag, will be readily recognized by those
who have any recollection of the early
days. The bonnet occupied a place in
the store of Samuel Hill at New Salem.
It was taken from the store by Mrs.
Hill, worn for a time by her, and has
been carefully preserved to this day.
It is an imported bonnet—a genuine
Leghorn—and of a kind so costly that
Mr. Hill made only an occasional sale
of one. Its price, in fact, was twenty-
five dollars.

Lincoln the captain. Lincoln himself
was interested in what he had done,
and nearly twenty years later he embodied his reflections on this adventure in a curious invention for getting
boats over shoals.

NEW ORLEANS IN 1831.

The raft over the New Salem dam,
the party went on to New Orleans,
reaching there in May, 1831, and
remaining a month. It must have
been a month of intense intellectual
activity for Lincoln. Since his first
visit, made with young Gentry, New
Orleans had entered upon her "flush
times." Commerce was increasing at
a rate which dazzled speculators, and
drew them from all over the United
States. From 1830 to 1840 no other
American city i n c r e a s e d in such a
ratio ; exports and imports, which in
1831 amounted to $26,000,000, in 1835
had more than
doubled. The
Creole popula-
tion had held
the sway so far
in the city ; but
now it came into
c o m p e t i t i o n,
and often into
conflict, with a
pushing, ambi-
tious, and fre-
q u e n t l y   u n -
s c r u p u l o u s

A NEW SALEM BONNET.

native American party.   To these two pre-
dominating elements were added Germans,
French, Spanish, negroes, and Indians.

THE SITE OF NEW SALEM AS IT APPEARS TO-DAY.

Cosmopolitan in its make-up, the city was even more cosmopolitan in its life. Everything was to be seen in New Orleans in those days, from the idle luxury of the wealthy Creole to the organization of filibustering juntas. The pirates still plied their trade in the Gulf, and the Mississippi River brought down hundreds of river boatmen—one of the wildest, wickedest sets of men that ever existed in any city.

Lincoln and his companions ran their boat up beside thousands of others. It was the custom to tie such craft along the river front where St. Mary's Market now stands, and one could walk a mile, it is said, over the tops of these boats without going ashore.　No doubt Lincoln went, too, to live in the boat-men's rendezvous, called the "swamp," a wild, rough quarter, where roulette, whiskey, and the flint-lock pistol ruled.

All of the picturesque life, the violent contrasts of the city, he would see as he wandered about ; and he would carry away the sharp impressions which are produced when mind and heart are alert, sincere, and healthy.

In this month spent in New Orleans Lincoln must have seen much of slavery.　At that time the city was full of slaves, and the number was constantly increasing ; indeed, one-third of the New Orleans increase in population between 1830 and 1840 was in negroes.　One of the saddest features of the institution was to be seen there in its most aggravated form—the slave market. The better class of slave-holders of the South, who looked on the institution as patriarchal, and who guarded their slaves with conscientious care, knew little, it should be said, of this terrible traffic.　Their transfer of slaves was humane, but in the open markets of the city it was attended by shocking cruelty and degradation.

Lincoln witnessed in New Orleans for the first time the re-volting sight of men and women sold like animals.　Mr. Hern-don says that he often heard Mr. Lincoln refer to this experi-ence.　"In New Orleans for the first time," he writes, "Lincoln beheld the true horrors of human slavery.　He saw 'negroes in chains—whipped and scourged.'　Against this inhumanity his sense of right and justice rebelled, and his mind and conscience were awakened to a realization of what he had often heard and read.　No doubt, as one of his companions has said, 'slavery ran the iron into him then and there.'

"One morning, in their rambles over the city, the trio passed a slave auction.　A vigorous and comely mulatto girl was being sold.　She underwent a thorough examination at the hands of the bidders ; they pinched her flesh, and made her trot up and down the room like a horse, to show how she moved, and in order, as the auctioneer said, that 'bidders might satisfy them-selves' whether the article they were offering to buy was sound or not.　The whole thing was so revolting that Lincoln moved away from the scene with a deep feeling of 'unconquerable hate.' Bidding his companions follow him, he said : 'Boys, let's get away from this.　If ever I get a chance to hit that thing' (mean-ing slavery), 'I'll hit it hard.'"

MR. LINCOLN IN 1857.

The original of this picture is an ambrotype owned by C. F. Gunther of Chicago, who bought it from W. H. Somers of El Cajon, California. Mr. Somers bought the original directly from the artist, a Mr. Alschuler of Urbana, Illinois. In a recent letter he explains why he bought the picture: "At the time I was clerk of the circuit court, and was about as well acquainted with Mr. Lincoln as with most of the forty-odd lawyers who practised law in the circuit. Of course I was then quite a young man, and the fall term of 1857 was my first term as clerk. On the opening day of court, which was always an interesting occasion, largely because we were curious to see what attorneys from a distance were in attendance, while sitting at my desk and watching the lawyers take their places within the bar of the court-room, I observed that Mr. Lincoln was among them; and as I looked in his direction, he arose from his seat, and came forward and gave me a cordial hand-shake, accompanying the action with words of congratulation on my election. I mention this fact because the conduct of Mr. Lincoln was so in contrast with that of the other members of the bar that it touched me deeply, and made me, ever afterwards, his steadfast friend."

Mr. J. O. Cunningham, who was present when the picture was taken, writes us as follows of the circumstances: "One morning I was in the gallery of Mr. Alschuler, when Mr. Lincoln came into the room and said he had been informed that he (Alschuler) wished him to sit for a picture. Alschuler said he had sent such a message to Mr. Lincoln, but he could not take the picture in that coat (referring to a linen duster in which Mr. Lincoln was clad), and asked if he had not a dark coat in which to sit. Mr. Lincoln said he had not; that this was the only coat he had brought with him from his home. Alschuler said he could wear his coat, and gave it to Mr. Lincoln, who pulled off the duster and put on the artist's coat. Alschuler was a very short man, with short arms, but with a body nearly as large as the body of Mr. Lincoln. The arms of the latter extended through the sleeves of the coat of Alschuler a quarter of a yard, making him quite ludicrous, at which he (Lincoln) laughed immoderately, and sat down for the picture to be taken with an effort at being sober enough for the occasion. The lips in the picture show this."

Mr. Herndon gives John Hanks as his authority for this statement. This is plainly an error; for, according to Mr. Lincoln himself, Hanks did not go on to New Orleans, but, having a family, and finding that he was likely to be detained from home longer than he had expected, he turned back at St. Louis. Though there is reason for believing that Lincoln was deeply impressed on this trip by something he saw in a New Orleans slave market, and that he often referred to it, the story told above probably grew to its present proportions by much telling.

CHAPTER IX.

LINCOLN SETTLES IN NEW SALEM.—HE BECOMES A GROCERY CLERK.—HIS POPULARITY IN NEW SALEM.

HE month in New Orleans passed swiftly, and in June, 1831, Lincoln and his companions took passage up the river. He did not return, however, in the usual way of the river boatman "out of a job." According to his own way of putting it, "during this boat-enterprise acquaintance with Offutt, who was previously an entire stranger, he conceived a liking for Abraham, and believing he could turn him to account, he contracted with him to act as a clerk for him on his return from New Orleans, in charge of a store and mill at New Salem." The store and mill were, however, so far only in Offutt's imagination, and Lincoln had to drift about until his employer was ready for him. He made a short visit to his father and mother, now in Coles County, near Charleston (fever and ague had driven the Lincolns from their first home in Macon County), and then, in July, 1831, he went to New Salem, where, as he says, he "stopped indefinitely, and for the first time, as it were, by himself."

The village of New Salem, the scene of Lincoln's mercantile career, was one of the many little towns which, in the pioneer days, sprang up along the Sangamon River, a stream then looked upon as navigable and as destined to be counted among the highways of commerce. Twenty miles northwest of Springfield, strung along the left bank of the Sangamon, parted by hollows and ravines, is a row of high hills. On one of these—a long,

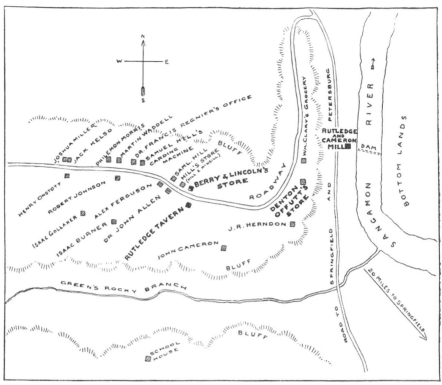

MAP OF NEW SALEM.—MADE ESPECIALLY FOR THIS WORK.

Map drawn by J. McCan Davis, aided by surviving inhabitants of New Salem. Dr. John Allen was the leading physician of New Salem. He was a Yankee, and was at first looked upon with suspicion, but he was soon conducting a Sunday-school and temperance society, though strongly opposed by the conservative church people. Dr. Allen attended Ann Rutledge in her last illness. He was thrifty, and, moving to Petersburg in 1840, became wealthy. He died in 1860. Dr. Francis Regnier was a rival physician and a respected citizen. Samuel Hill and John McNeill (whose real name subsequently proved to be McNamar) operated a general store next to Berry and Lincoln's grocery. Mr. Hill also owned the carding-machine. He moved his store to Petersburg in 1839, and engaged in business there, dying quite wealthy. Jack Kelso followed a variety of callings, being occasionally a school-teacher, now and then a grocery clerk, and always a fisher and hunter. He was a man of some culture, and when warmed by liquor, quoted Shakespeare and Burns profusely, a habit which won for him the close friendship of Lincoln. Joshua Miller was a blacksmith, and lived in the same house with Kelso—a double house. He is said to be still living, somewhere in Nebraska. Miller and Kelso were brothers-in-law. Philemon Morris was a tinner. Henry Onstott was a cooper by trade. He was an elder in the Cumberland Presbyterian Church, and meetings were often held at his house. Rev. John Berry, father of Lincoln's partner, frequently preached there. Robert Johnson was a wheelwright, and his wife took in weaving. Martin Waddell was a hatter. He was the best-natured man in town, Lincoln possibly excepted. The Trent brothers, who succeeded Berry and Lincoln as proprietors of the store, worked in his shop for a time. William Clary, one of the first settlers of New Salem, was one of a numerous family, most of whom lived in the vicinity of "Clary's Grove." Isaac Burner was the father of Daniel Green Burner, Berry and Lincoln's clerk. Alexander Ferguson worked at odd jobs. He had two brothers, John and Elijah. Isaac Gollaher lived in a house belonging to John Ferguson. "Row" Herndon, at whose house Lincoln boarded for a year or more after going to New Salem, moved to the country after selling his store to Berry and Lincoln. John Cameron, one of the founders of the town, was a Presbyterian preacher and a highly esteemed citizen.

narrow ridge, beginning with a sharp and sloping point near the river, running south, and parallel with the stream a little way, and then, reaching its highest point, making a sudden turn to the west, and gradually widening until lost in the prairie—stood this frontier village. The crooked river for a short distance comes from the east, and, seemingly surprised at meeting the bluff, abruptly changes its course, and flows to the north. Across the river the bottom stretches out half a mile back to the highlands. New Salem, founded in 1829 by James Rutledge and John Cameron, and a dozen years later a deserted village, is rescued from oblivion only by the fact that Lincoln was once one of its inhabitants. His first sight of the town had been in April, 1831, when he and his crew had been detained in getting their flatboat over the Rutledge and Cameron mill-dam. When Lincoln walked into New Salem, three months later, he was not altogether a stranger, for the people remembered him as the ingenious flatboatman who had freed his boat

WILLIAM G. GREENE.

William G. Greene was one of the earliest friends of Lincoln at New Salem. He stood on the bank of the Sangamon River on the 19th of April, 1831, and watched Lincoln bore a hole in the bottom of the flatboat which had lodged on the mill-dam, so that the water might run out. A few months later he and Lincoln were both employed by the enterprising Denton Offutt as clerks in the store and managers of the mill which had been leased by Offutt. It was William G. Greene who, returning home from college at Jacksonville on a vacation, brought Richard Yates with him, and introduced him to Lincoln, the latter being found stretched out on the cellar door of Bowling Green's cabin, reading a book. Mr. Greene was born in Tennessee in 1812, and went to Illinois in 1822. After the disappearance of New Salem he removed to Tallula, a few miles away, where in after years he engaged in the banking business. He died in 1894, after amassing a fortune.

from water (and thus enabled it to get over the dam) by resorting to the miraculous expedient of boring a hole in the bottom.

Offutt's goods had not arrived when Mr. Lincoln reached New Salem ; and he "loafed" about, so those who remember his arrival say, good-naturedly taking a hand in whatever he could find to do, and in his droll way making friends of everybody. By chance, a bit of work fell to him almost at once, which introduced him generally and gave him an opportunity to make a

name in the neighborhood.   It was election day.   The village
school-master, Mentor Graham by name, was clerk, but the
assistant was ill.   Looking about for some one to help him, Mr.
Graham saw a tall stranger loitering around the polling-place,
and called to him, "Can you write?" "Yes," said the stranger,
"I can make a few rabbit tracks."   Mr. Graham evidently was
satisfied with the answer, for he promptly initiated him ; and he
filled his place not only to the satisfaction of his employer, but
also to the delectation of the loiterers about the polls, for whenever things dragged he immediately began "to spin out a stock
of Indiana yarns." So droll were they that years afterward
men who listened to Lincoln that day repeated them to their
friends.   He had made a hit in New Salem, to start with, and
here, as in Sangamon town, it was by means of his story-telling.

His next work was to pilot down the Sangamon and Illinois
rivers, as far as Beardstown, a flatboat bearing the family and
goods of a pioneer bound for Texas.   At Beardstown he found
Offutt's goods, waiting to be taken to New Salem.   As he footed
his way home he met two men with a wagon and ox-team going
for the goods.   Offutt had expected Lincoln to wait at Beardstown until the ox-team arrived, and the teamsters, not having
any credentials, asked Lincoln to give them an order for the
goods.   This, sitting down by the roadside, he wrote out ; and
one of the men used to relate that it contained a misspelled word,
which he corrected.

IN CHARGE OF DEN-
   TON OFFUTT'S
   STORE.

The precise date
of the opening of
Denton Offutt's store
is not known.   We
only know that on
J u l y 8, 1831, t h e
County Commission-
ers' Court of Sanga-
mon County granted
Offutt a license to
retail merchandise at

A NEW SALEM SPINNING-WHEEL.

A NEW SALEM INTERIOR, SHOWING GENUINE NEW SALEM COSTUMES AND FURNITURE STILL EXTANT.
Reproduced by permission from "Menard-Salem-Lincoln Souvenir Album," Petersburg, Illinois, 1893.

New Salem, for which he paid five dollars, a fee which supposed him to have one thousand dollars' worth of goods in stock. When the oxen and their drivers returned with the goods, the store was opened in a little log house on the brink of the hill, almost over the river.

The frontier store filled a unique place. Usually it was a "general store," and on its shelves were found most of the articles needed in a community of pioneers. But to be a place for the sale of dry goods and groceries was not its only function; it was a kind of intellectual and social centre. It was the common meeting-place of the farmers, the happy refuge of the village loungers. No subject was unknown there. The *habitués* of the place were equally at home in discussing politics, religion, or sports. Stories were told, jokes were cracked and laughed at, and the news contained in the latest newspaper finding its way into the wilderness was repeated again and again. Such a store was that of Denton Offutt. Lincoln could hardly have chosen surroundings more favorable to the highest development of the art of story-telling, and he had not been there long before his reputation for drollery was established.

THE CLARY'S GROVE BOYS.

But he gained popularity and respect in other ways. There was near the village a settlement called Clary's Grove. The most conspicuous part of the population was an organization known as the "Clary's Grove Boys." They exercised a veritable terror over the neighborhood, and yet they were not a vicious band. Mr. Herndon, who had a cousin living in New Salem at the time, and who knew personally many of the "boys," says :

"They were friendly and good-natured ; they could trench a pond, dig a bog, build a house ; they could pray and fight, make a village or create a State. They would do almost anything for sport or fun, love or necessity. Though rude and rough ; though life's forces ran over the edge of the bowl, foaming and sparkling in pure deviltry for deviltry's sake, yet place before them a poor man who needed their aid, a lame or sick man, a defenceless woman, a widow, or an orphaned child, they melted into sympathy and charity at once. They gave all they had, and willingly toiled or played cards for more. Though there never was under the sun a more generous parcel of rowdies, a stranger's introduction was likely to be the most unpleasant part of his acquaintance with them."

Denton Offutt, Lincoln's employer, was just the man to love to boast before such a crowd. He seemed to feel that Lincoln's physical prowess shed glory on himself, and he declared the country over that his clerk could lift more, throw farther, run faster, jump higher, and wrestle better than any man in Sangamon County. The Clary's Grove Boys, of course, felt in honor bound to prove this false, and they appointed their best man, one Jack Armstrong, to "throw Abe." Jack Armstrong was, according to the testimony of all who remember him, a "powerful twister," "square built and strong as an ox," "the best-made man that ever lived ;" and everybody knew the contest would be close. Lincoln did not like to "tussle and scuffle ;" he objected to "woolling and pulling ;" but Offutt had gone so

VIEW FROM THE TOP OF NEW SALEM HILL.

far that it became necessary to yield. The match was held on the ground near the grocery. Clary's Grove and New Salem turned out generally to witness the bout, and betting on the result ran high, the community as a whole staking their jack-knives, tobacco-plugs, and "treats" on Armstrong. The two men had scarcely taken hold of each other before it was evident that the Clary's Grove champion had met a match. The two men wrestled long and hard, but both kept their feet. Neither could throw the other, and Armstrong, convinced of this, tried a "foul." Lincoln no sooner realized the game of his antagonist than, furious with indignation, he caught him by the throat and, holding him out at arm's length, "shook him like a child."

MENTOR GRAHAM.

Mentor Graham was the New Salem school-master. He it was who assisted Lincoln in mastering Kirkham's Grammar, and later gave him valuable assistance when Lincoln was learning the theory of surveying. He taught in a little log school-house on a hill south of the village, just across Green's Rocky Branch. Among his pupils was Ann Rutledge, and the school was often visited by Lincoln. In 1845 Mentor Graham was defendant in a lawsuit in which Lincoln and Herndon were attorneys for the plaintiff, Nancy Green. It appears from the declaration, written by Lincoln's own hand, that on October 28, 1844, Mentor Graham gave his note to Nancy Green for one hundred dollars, with John Owen and Andrew Beerup as sureties, payable twelve months after date. The note not being paid when due, suit was brought. That Lincoln, even as an attorney, should sue Mentor Graham may seem strange ; but it is no surprise when it is explained that the plaintiff was the widow of Bowling Green—the woman who, with her husband, had comforted Lincoln in an hour of grief. Justice, too, in this case was clearly on her side. The lawsuit seems never to have disturbed the friendly relations between Lincoln and Mentor Graham. The latter's admiration for the former was unbounded to the day of his death. Mentor Graham lived on his farm near the ruins of New Salem until 1860, when he removed to Petersburg. There he lived until 1885, when he removed to Greenview, Illinois. Later he went to South Dakota, where he died about 1892, at the ripe old age of ninety-odd years.

Armstrong's friends rushed to his aid, and for a moment it looked as if Lincoln would be routed by sheer force of numbers. But he held his own so bravely that the "boys," in spite of their sympathies, were filled with admiration. What bade fair to be a general fight ended in a general hand-shake, even Jack Armstrong declaring that Lincoln was the "best fellow who ever broke into the camp." From that day, at the cock-fights and horse-races, which were their common sports, he became the chosen umpire ; and when the entertainment broke up in a row— a not uncommon occurrence —he acted the peacemaker without suffering the peacemaker's usual fate. Such was his reputation with the "Clary's Grove Boys," after three months in New Salem, that when the fall muster came off he was elected captain.

Lincoln showed soon that if he was unwilling to indulge in "woolling and pulling" for amusement, he did not object to it in a case of honor. A man came into the store one day when women were present, and used profane language. Lincoln asked him to stop ; but the man persisted, swearing that nobody should prevent his saying what he wanted to. The women gone, the man began to abuse Lincoln so hotly that the latter finally said, " Well, if you must be whipped, I suppose I might as well whip you as any other man ; " and going outdoors with the fellow, he threw him on the ground, and rubbed smart-weed in his eyes until he bellowed for mercy. New Salem's sense of chivalry was touched, and enthusiasm over Lincoln increased.

His honesty excited no less admiration. Two incidents seem to have particularly im-

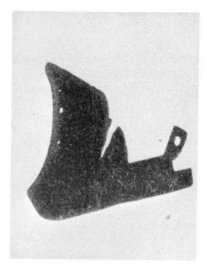

MODEL OF FIRST PLOUGH MADE IN MENARD COUNTY, ILLINOIS.

Reproduced by permission from " Menard-Salem-Lincoln Souvenir Album," Petersburg, Illinois, 1893.

A NEW SALEM CHAIR.

This chair is now in the collection of Mr. Louis Vanuxem of Philadelphia. It was originally owned by Caleb Carmen of New Salem, and was once repaired by Abraham Lincoln.

pressed the community. Having discovered on one occasion that he had taken six and a quarter cents too much from a customer, he walked three miles that evening, after his store was closed, to return the money. Again, he weighed out a half-pound of tea, as he supposed. It was night, and this was the last thing he did before closing up. On entering in the morning he discovered a four-ounce weight on the scales. He saw his mistake, and, closing up shop, hurried off to deliver the remainder of the tea. This unusual regard for the rights of others soon won him the title of "Honest Abe."

LINCOLN STUDIES GRAMMAR.

As soon as the store was fairly under way, Lincoln began to look about for books. Since leaving Indiana, in March, 1830, he had had, in his drifting life, little leisure or opportunity for study, though he had had a great deal for observation. Nevertheless his desire to learn had increased, and his ambition to be somebody had been encouraged. In that time he had found that he really was superior to many of those who were called the "great" men of the country. Soon after entering Macon County, in March, 1830, when he was only twenty-one years old, he had found he could make a better speech than at least one man who was before the public. A candidate had come along where John Hanks and he were at work, and, as John Hanks tells the story, the man made a speech. "It was a bad one, and I said Abe could beat it. I turned down a box, and Abe made his speech. The other man was a candidate, Abe wasn't. Abe beat him to death, his subject being the navigation of the Sangamon River. The man, after Abe's speech was through, took him aside, and asked him where he had learned so much and how he could do so well. Abe replied, stating his manner and method of reading, what he had read. The man encouraged him to persevere."

He had found that people listened to him, that they quoted his opinions, and that his friends were already saying that he was able to fill any position. Offutt even declared the country over that "Abe" knew more than any man in the United States, and that some day he would be President.

Under this stimulus Lincoln's ambition increased. "I have talked with great men," he told his fellow-clerk and friend Greene, "and I do not see how they differ from others." He made up his mind to put himself before the public, and talked of his plans to his friends. In order to keep in practice in speaking he walked seven or eight miles to debating clubs. "Practising polemics" was what he called the exercise. He seems now for the first time to have begun to study subjects. Grammar was what he chose. He sought Mentor Graham, the schoolmaster, and asked his advice. "If you are going before the public," Mr. Graham told him, "you ought to do it." But where could he get a grammar? There was but one, said Mr. Graham, in the neighborhood, and that was six miles away. Without waiting for further information, the young man rose from the breakfast-table, walked immediately to the place, and borrowed this rare copy of Kirkham's Grammar. From that time on for weeks he gave his leisure to mastering its contents. Frequently he asked his friend Greene to hold the book while he recited, and when puzzled he would consult Mr. Graham.

Lincoln's eagerness to learn was such that the whole neighborhood became interested. The Greenes lent him books, the school-master kept him in mind and helped him as he could, and the village cooper let him come into his shop and keep up a fire of shavings sufficiently bright to read by at night. It was not long before the grammar was mastered. "Well," Lincoln said to his fellow-clerk Greene, "if that's what they call a science, I think I'll go at another."

Before the winter was ended he had become the most popular man in New Salem. Although he was but twenty-two years of age in February, 1832 ; had never been at school an entire year ; had never made a speech, except in debating clubs or by the roadside ; had read only the books he could pick up, and known only the men of the poor, out-of-the-way towns in which he had lived, yet, "encouraged by his great popularity among his immediate neighbors," as he says, he announced himself, in March, 1832, as a candidate for the General Assembly of the State.

CHAPTER X.

LINCOLN'S FIRST ANNOUNCEMENT TO THE VOTERS OF SANGAMON COUNTY.—HIS VIEWS ON THE IMPROVEMENT OF THE SANGAMON. —THE MODESTY OF HIS CIRCULAR.

HE only preliminary expected of a candidate for the legislature of Illinois at that date was an announcement stating his "sentiments with regard to local affairs." The circular in which Lincoln complied with this custom was a document of about two thousand words, in which he plunged at once into the subject he believed most interesting to his constituents—"the public utility of internal improvements."

At that time the State of Illinois—as, indeed, the whole United States—was convinced that the future of the country

LINCOLN'S FIRST VOTE.—PHOTOGRAPHED FROM THE ORIGINAL POLL-BOOK, AND NOW FIRST PUBLISHED.
SEE NOTE ON NEXT PAGE.

depended on the opening of canals and railroads, and the clearing out of the rivers. In the Sangamon country the population felt that a quick way of getting to Beardstown on the Illinois River, to which point the steamer came from the Mississippi, was, as Lincoln puts it in his circular, using a phrase of his hero Clay, "indispensably necessary." Of course a railroad was the dream of the settlers; but when it was considered seriously there was always, as Lincoln says, "a heart-appalling shock accompanying the amount of its cost, which forces us to shrink from our pleasing anticipations."

"The probable cost of this contemplated railroad is estimated at two hundred and ninety thousand dollars; the bare statement of which, in my opinion, is sufficient to justify the belief that the improvement of the Sangamon River is an object much better suited to our infant resources.

"Respecting this view, I think I may say, without the fear of being contradicted, that its navigation may be rendered completely practicable as high as the mouth of the South Fork, or probably higher, to vessels of from twenty-five to thirty tons burden, for at least one-half of all common years, and to vessels of much greater burden a part of the time. From my peculiar circumstances, it is probable that for the last twelve months I have given as particular attention to the stage of the water in this river as any other person in the country. In the month of March, 1831, in company with others, I commenced the building of a flatboat on the Sangamon, and finished and took her out in the course of the spring. Since that time I have been concerned in the mill at New Salem. These circumstances are sufficient evidence that I have not been very inattentive to the stages of the water. The time at which we crossed the mill-dam being in the last days of April, the water was lower than it had been since

Note: LINCOLN'S FIRST VOTE.—The original poll-book from which the vote as shown on page 126 is reproduced, is now on file in the County Clerk's office, Springfield, Illinois. Lincoln's first vote was cast at New Salem, " in the Clary's Grove precinct," August 1, 1831. At this election he aided Mr. Graham, who was one of the clerks. In the early days in Illinois, elections were conducted by the *viva voce* method. The people did try voting by ballot, but the experiment was unpopular. It required too much " book larnin," and in 1829 the *viva voce* method of voting was restored. The judges and clerks sat at a table with the poll-book before them. The voter walked up, and announced the candidate of his choice, and it was recorded in his presence. There was no ticket peddling, and ballot-box stuffing was impossible. To this simple system we are indebted for the record of Lincoln's first vote. As will be seen from the fac-simile, Lincoln voted for James Turney for Congressman, Bowling Green and Edmund Greer for Magistrates, and John Armstrong and Henry Sinco for Constables. Of these five men three were elected. Turney was defeated for Congressman by Joseph Duncan. Turney lived in Greene County. He was not then a conspicuous figure in the politics of the State, but was a follower of Henry Clay, and was well thought of in his own district. He and Lincoln, in 1834, served their first terms together in the lower house of the legislature, and later he was a State senator. Joseph Duncan, the successful candidate, was already in Congress. He was a politician of influence. In 1834 he was a strong Jackson man ; but after his election as Governor he created consternation among the followers of " Old Hickory " by becoming a Whig. Sidney Breese, who received only two votes in the Clary's Grove precinct, afterward became the most conspicuous of the five candidates. Eleven years later he defeated Stephen A. Douglas for the United States Senate, and for twenty-five years he was on the bench of the Supreme Court of Illinois, serving under each of the three constitutions. For the office of Magistrate, Bowling Green was elected, but Greer was beaten. Both of Lincoln's candidates for Constable were elected. John Armstrong was the man with whom, a short time afterward, Lincoln had the celebrated wrestling match. Henry Sinco was the keeper of a store at New Salem. Lincoln's first vote for President was not cast until the next year (November 5, 1832), when he voted for Henry Clay.

the breaking of winter, in February, or than it was for several weeks after. The principal difficulties we encountered in descending the river were from the drifted timber, which obstructions all know are not difficult to be removed. Knowing almost precisely the height of water at that time, I believe I am safe in saying that it has as often been higher as lower since.

"From this view of the subject, it appears that my calculations with regard to the navigation of the Sangamon cannot but be founded in reason ; but, whatever may be its natural advantages, certain it is that it never can be practically useful to any great extent without being greatly improved by art. The drifted timber, as I have before mentioned, is the most formidable barrier to this object. Of all parts of this river, none will require as much labor in proportion to make it navigable as the last thirty or thirty-five miles ; and going with the meanderings of the channel, when we are this distance above its mouth, we are only between twelve and eighteen miles from Beardstown in something near a straight direction, and this route is upon such low ground as to retain water in many places during the season, and in all parts such as to draw two-thirds or three-fourths of the river water at all high stages.

"This route is on prairie-land the whole distance, so that it appears to me, by removing the turf a sufficient width, and damming up the old channel, the whole river in a short time would wash its way through, thereby curtailing the distance and increasing the velocity of the current very considerably, while there would be no timber on the banks to obstruct its navigation in future ; and being nearly straight, the timber which might float in at the head would be apt to go clear through. There are also many places above this where the river, in its zigzag course, forms such complete peninsulas as to be easier to cut at the necks than to remove the obstructions from the bends, which, if done, would also lessen the distance.

"What the cost of this work would be, I am unable to say. It is probable, however, that it would not be greater than is common to streams of the same length. Finally, I believe the improvement of the Sangamon River to be vastly important and highly desirable to the people of the country ; and, if elected, any measure in the legislature having this for its object, which may appear judicious, will meet my approbation and receive my support."

Lincoln could not have advocated a measure more popular. At that moment the whole population of Sangamon was in a state of wild expectation. Some six weeks before Lincoln's circular appeared, a citizen of Springfield had advertised that as soon as the ice went off the river he would bring up a steamer, the "Talisman," from Cincinnati, and prove the Sangamon navigable. The announcement had aroused the entire country, speeches were made, and subscriptions taken. The merchants announced goods direct per steamship "Talisman" the country over, and every village from Beardstown to Springfield was laid off in town lots. When the circular appeared the excitement was at its height.

Lincoln's comments in his circular on two other subjects on which all candidates of the day expressed themselves, are amusing in their simplicity. The practice of loaning money at exorbitant rates was then a great evil in the West. Lincoln proposed that the limits of usury be fixed, and he closed his paragraph on the subject with these words, which sound strange enough from a man who in later life showed so profound a reverence for law :

" In cases of extreme necessity, there could always be means found to cheat the law ; while in all other cases it would have its intended effect. I would favor the passage of a law on this subject which might not be very easily evaded. Let it be such that the labor and difficulty of evading it could only be justified in cases of greatest necessity."

A general revision of the laws of the State was the second topic which he felt required a word. "Considering the great probability," he said, " that the framers of those laws were wiser than myself, I should prefer not meddling with them, unless they were attacked by others ; in which case I should feel it both a privilege and a duty to take that stand which, in my view, might tend most to the advancement of justice."

Of course he said a word for education :

" Upon the subject of education, not presuming to dictate any plan or system respecting it, can only say that I view it as the most important subject which we as a people can be engaged in. That every man may receive at least a moderate education, and thereby be enabled to read the histories of his own and other countries, by which he may duly appreciate the value of our free institutions, appears to be an object of vital importance, even on this account alone ; to say nothing of the advantages and satisfaction to be derived from all being able to read the Scriptures and other works, both of a religious and moral nature, for themselves.

" For my part, I desire to see the time when education—and by its means morality, sobriety, enterprise, and industry—shall become much more general than at present, and should be gratified to have it in my power to contribute something to the advancement of any measure which might have a tendency to accelerate that happy period."

The audacity of a young man in his position presenting himself as a candidate for the legislature is fully equalled by the humility of the closing paragraphs of his announcement :

" But, fellow-citizens, I shall conclude. Considering the great degree of modesty which should always attend youth, it is probable I have already been more presuming than becomes me. However, upon the subjects of which I have treated, I have spoken as I have thought. I may be wrong in regard to any or all of them ; but, holding it a sound maxim that it is better only some-

LINCOLN IN 1860.

From an ambrotype in the possession of Mr. Marcus L. Ward of Newark, New Jersey.
This portrait of Mr. Lincoln was made in Springfield, Illinois, on May 20, 1860, for the late
Hon. Marcus L. Ward, Governor of New Jersey. Mr. Ward had gone to Springfield to
see Mr. Lincoln, and while there asked him for his picture. The President-elect replied
that he had no picture which was satisfactory, but would gladly sit for one. The two
gentlemen went out immediately, and in Mr. Ward's presence Mr. Lincoln had the above
picture taken.

ABOVE THE DAM AT NEW SALEM.

Reproduced, by permission, from "Menard-Salem-Lincoln Souvenir Album," Petersburg, Illinois, 1893.

times to be right than at all times to be wrong, so soon as I discover my opinions to be erroneous, I shall be ready to renounce them.

"Every man is said to have his peculiar ambition. Whether it be true or not, I can say, for one, that I have no other so great as that of being truly esteemed of my fellow-men by rendering myself worthy of their esteem. How far I shall succeed in gratifying this ambition is yet to be developed. I am young, and unknown to many of you. I was born, and have ever remained, in the most humble walks of life. I have no wealthy or popular relations or friends to recommend me. My case is thrown exclusively upon the independent voters of the county ; and, if elected, they will have conferred a favor upon me for which I shall be unremitting in my labors to compensate. But, if the good people in their wisdom shall see fit to keep me in the background, I have been too familiar with disappointments to be very much chagrined."

Very soon after Lincoln had distributed his handbills, enthusiasm on the subject of the opening of the Sangamon rose to a fever. The "Talisman" actually came up the river ; scores of men went to Beardstown to meet her, among them Lincoln, of

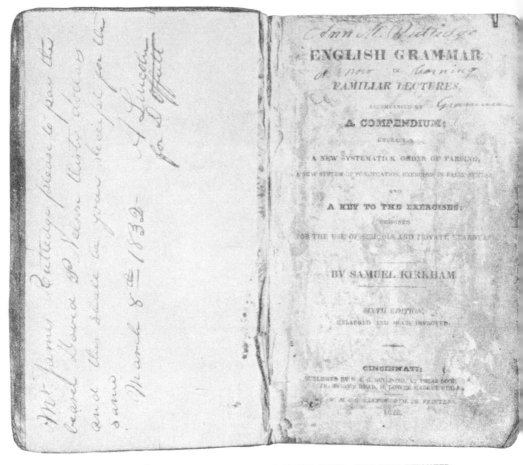

THE KIRKHAM'S GRAMMAR USED BY LINCOLN AT NEW SALEM.—NOW FIRST PUBLISHED.

From a photograph made especially for this work. The copy of Kirkham's Grammar studied by Lincoln belonged to a man named Vaner. Some of the biographers say Lincoln borrowed it; but it appears that he became the owner of the book, either by purchase or through the generosity of Vaner, for it was never returned to the latter. It is said that Lincoln learned this grammar practically by heart. "Sometimes," says Herndon, "he would stretch out at full length on the counter, his head propped up on a stack of calico prints, studying it; or he would steal away to the shade of some inviting tree, and there spend hours at a time in a determined effort to fix in his mind the arbitrary rule that 'adverbs qualify verbs, adjectives, and other adverbs.'" He presented the book to Ann Rutledge, and it has since been one of the treasures of the Rutledge family. After the death of Ann it was studied by her brother Robert, and is now owned by his widow, who resides at Casselton, North Dakota. The title page of the book appears above. The words, "Ann M. Rutledge is now learning grammar," were written by Lincoln. The order on James Rutledge to pay David P. Nelson thirty dollars, and signed "A. Lincoln for D. Offutt," which is shown above, was pasted upon the front cover of the book by Robert Rutledge.

course; and to him was given the honor of piloting her—an honor which made him remembered by many a man who saw him that day for the first time. The trip was made with all the wild demonstrations which always attended the first steamboat. On either bank a long procession of men and boys on foot or horse accompanied the boat. Cannons and volleys of musketry were fired as settlements were passed. At every stop speeches were made, congratulations offered, toasts drunk, flowers presented. It was one long hurrah from Beardstown to Springfield, and foremost in the jubilation was Lincoln the pilot. The "Talisman" went to the point on the river nearest to Springfield, and there tied up for a week. When she went back, Lincoln again had a conspicuous position as pilot. The notoriety this gave him was probably quite as valuable politically as the forty dollars he received for his service was financially.

While the country had been dreaming of wealth through the opening of the Sangamon, and Lincoln had been doing his best to prove that the dream was possible, the store in which he clerked was "petering out"—to use his own expression. The owner, Denton Offutt, had proved more ambitious than wise, and Lincoln saw that an early closing by the sheriff was probable. But before the store was fairly closed, and while the trip of the "Talisman" was yet exciting the country, an event occurred which interrupted all of Lincoln's plans.

A NEW SALEM CENTRE TABLE.

This table is now owned by W. C. Green of Talula, Illinois. Originally it was part of the furniture of the cabin of Bowling Green, near New Salem.

CHAPTER XI.

OUTBREAK OF SACS AND FOXES. — LINCOLN VOLUNTEERS AND IS MADE A CAPTAIN. — INCIDENTS OF HIS SERVICE AS CAPTAIN. — STILLMAN'S DEFEAT.

NE morning in April a messenger from the governor of the State rode into New Salem, scattering circulars. These circulars contained an address from Governor Reynolds to the militia of the northwest section of the State, announcing that the British band of Sacs and other hostile Indians, headed by Black Hawk, had invaded the Rock River country, to the great terror of the frontier inhabitants; and calling upon the citizens who were willing to aid in repelling them, to rendezvous at Beardstown within a week.

The name of Black Hawk was familiar to the people of Illinois. He was an old enemy of the settlers, and had been a tried friend of the British. The land his people had once owned in the northwest of the present State of Illinois had been sold in 1804 to the government of the United States, but with the provision that the Indians should hunt and raise corn there until it was surveyed and sold to settlers. Long before the land was surveyed, however, squatters had invaded the country, and tried to force the Indians west of the Mississippi. Particularly envious were these whites of the lands at the mouth of the Rock River, where the ancient village and burial place of the Sacs

NANCY GREEN.

Nancy Green was the wife of "Squire" Bowling Green. Her maiden name was Nancy Potter. She was born in North Carolina in 1797, and married Bowling Green in 1818. She removed with him to New Salem in 1820, and lived in that vicinity until her death, in 1864. Lincoln was a constant visitor in Nancy Green's home.

stood, and where they came each year to raise corn. Black Hawk had resisted their encroachments, and many violent acts had been committed on both sides.

Finally, however, the squatters, in spite of the fact that the line of settlement was still fifty miles away, succeeded in evading the real meaning of the treaty and in securing a survey of the desired land at the mouth of the river. Black Hawk, exasperated and broken-hearted at seeing his village violated, persuaded himself that the village had never been sold—indeed, that land could not be sold.

"My reason teaches me," he wrote, "that land cannot be sold. The Great Spirit gave it to his children to live upon, and cultivate, as far as is necessary for their subsistence; and so long as they occupy and cultivate it they have the right to the soil, but if they voluntarily leave it, then any other people have a right to settle upon it. Nothing can be sold but such things as can be carried away."

JOHN A. CLARY.

John A. Clary was one of the " Clary's Grove Boys." He was the son of John Clary, the head of the numerous Clary family which settled in the vicinity of New Salem in 1881. He was born in Tennessee in 1815 and died in 1880. He was an intimate associate of Lincoln during the latter's New Salem days.

Supported by this theory, conscious that in some way he did not understand he had been wronged, and urged on by White Cloud, the prophet, who ruled a Winnebago village on the Rock River, Black Hawk crossed the Mississippi in 1831, determined to evict the settlers. A military demonstration drove him back, and he was persuaded to sign a treaty never to return east of the Mississippi. "I touched the goose-quill to the treaty and was determined to live in peace," he wrote afterward; but hardly had he "touched the goose-quill" before his heart smote him. Longing for his home, resentment at the whites, obstinacy, brooding over the bad counsels of White Cloud and his disciple Neapope—an agitating Indian who had recently been East to visit the British and their Indian allies, and who assured Black Hawk that the Winnebagoes, Ottawas, Chippewas, and Pottawottomies would join him in a struggle for his land, and that the British would send him " guns, ammunition, provisions, and clothing early in the spring" —all persuaded the Hawk that he would be successful if he made an effort to drive out the whites. In spite of the advice of many of his friends and of the Indian agent in the country, he crossed the river on April 6, 1832, and with some five hundred braves, his squaws and children, marched to the Prophet's town, thirty-five miles up the Rock River.

As soon as they heard of Black Hawk's invasion, the settlers of the northwestern part of the State fled in a panic to the forts ; and they rained petitions for protection on Governor Reynolds. General Atkinson, who was at Fort Armstrong, wrote to the governor for reënforcements ; and, accordingly, on the 16th of April Governor Reynolds sent out "influential messengers" with a sonorous summons. It was one of these messengers riding into New Salem who put an end to Lincoln's canvassing for the legislature, freed him from Offutt's expiring grocery, and led him to enlist.

There was no time to waste. The volunteers were ordered to be at Beardstown, nearly forty miles from New Salem, on April 22d. Horses, rifles, saddles, blankets were to be secured, a company formed. It was work of which the settlers were not ignorant. Under the laws of the State every able-bodied male inhabitant between eighteen and forty-five was obliged to drill twice a year or pay a fine of one dollar. "As a dollar was hard to raise," says one of the old settlers, "everybody drilled."

LINCOLN A CAPTAIN.

Preparations were quickly made, and by April 22d the men were at Beardstown. The day before, at Richland, Sangamon County, Lincoln had been elected to the captaincy of the company from Sangamon to which he belonged.

His friend Greene gave another reason than ambition to explain his desire for the captaincy. One of the "odd jobs" which Lincoln had taken since coming into Illinois was working in a saw-mill for a man named Kirkpatrick. In hiring Lincoln, Kirkpatrick had promised to buy him a cant-hook with which to move heavy logs. Lincoln had proposed, if Kirkpatrick would give him the two dollars

DUTCH OVEN.

From a photograph made for this work. Owned by Mrs. Ott of Petersburg, Illinois. "A kind of flat-bottomed pot, . . . which stood upon three legs of three inches long, and had an iron lid. Into this bread or meats were put, and baked by placing it on the hearth with a quantity of coals under it and upon the lid, which was made with a rim to keep the coals upon it, and a loop handle to lift it by. It also had a bail like a pot, by which it could be hung over the fire."—*Recollections of Life in Ohio*, by WILLIAM COOPER HOWELLS.

which the cant-hook would cost, to move the logs with a common hand-spike. This the proprietor had agreed to, but when pay-day came he refused to keep his word. When the Sangamon company of volunteers was formed, Kirkpatrick aspired to the captaincy, and Lincoln, knowing it, said to Greene : " Bill, I believe I can now make Kirkpatrick pay that two dollars he owes me on the cant-hook. I'll run against him for captain ; " and he became a candidate. The vote was taken in a field, by directing the men at the command " march " to assemble around the one they wanted for captain. When the order was given, three-fourths of the men gathered around Lincoln.* In Lincoln's curious third-person autobiography he says he was elected, " to his own surprise ; " and adds, " He says he has not since had any success in life which gave him so much satisfaction."

The company was a motley crowd of men. Each had secured for his outfit what he could get, and no two were equipped alike. Buckskin breeches prevailed, and there was a sprinkling of coon-skin caps. Each man had a blanket of the coarsest texture. Flint-lock rifles were the usual arms, though here and there a man had a Cramer. Over the shoulder of each was slung a powder-horn. The men had, as a rule, as little regard for discipline as for ap-pearances, and when the new captain gave an order were as likely to jeer at it as to obey it. To drive the Indians out was their mission, and any orders which did not bear directly on that point were little respected. Lincoln himself was not familiar with military tactics, and made many blunders, of which he used to tell afterwards with relish. One of his early experiences in handling his company is particularly amusing. He was march-ing with a front of over twenty men across a field, when he desired to pass through a gateway into the next inclosure.

" I could not for the life of me," said he, " remember the proper word of command for getting my company *endwise,* so that it could get through the gate ; so, as we came near the gate, I shouted, ' This company is dismissed for two minutes, when it will fall in again on the other side of the gate ! ' "

Nor was it only his ignorance of the manual which caused him trouble. He was so unfamiliar with camp discipline that he once had his sword taken from him for shooting within limits.

---

* This story of Kirkpatrick's unfair treatment of Lincoln we owe to the courtesy of Colonel Clark E. Carr of Galesburg, Illinois, to whom it was told several times by Greene himself.

VIEW OF THE SANGAMON RIVER NEAR NEW SALEM.
The town lay along the ridge marked by the star.

Another disgrace he suffered was on account of his disorderly company. The men, unknown to him, stole a quantity of liquor one night, and the next morning were too drunk to fall in when the order was given to march. For their lawlessness Lincoln wore a wooden sword two days.

But none of these small difficulties injured his standing with the company. Lincoln was tactful, and he joined his men in sports as well as duties. They soon grew so proud of his quick wit and great strength that they obeyed him because they ad-

SITE OF DENTON OFFUTT'S STORE.

From a photograph taken for this work. The building in which Lincoln clerked for Denton Offutt was standing as late as 1836, and presumably stood until it rotted down. A slight depression in the earth, evidently once a cellar, is all that remains of Offutt's store. Out of this hole in the ground have grown three trees, a locust, an elm, and a sycamore, seeming to spring from the same roots, and curiously twined together. High up on the sycamore some genius has chiselled the face of Lincoln.

mired him. No amount of military tactics could have secured from the volunteers the cheerful following he won by his personal qualities.

The men soon learned, too, that he meant what he said, and would permit no dishonorable actions. A helpless I n d i a n took refuge in the camp o n e day ; and the men, who were inspired by what G o v e r n o r R e y n o l d s calls *Indian ill-will—* that wanton mixture of selfishness, u n r e a s o n, and c r u e l t y w h i c h seems to seize a frontiersman as soon as he scents a red man—were determined to kill the refuge. He had a safe conduct from General Cass; but the men, having come out to kill Indians and not h a v i n g succeeded, threatened

JOHN POTTER, NEIGHBOR OF LINCOLN'S AT NEW SALEM.

From a recent photograph. John Potter, born November 10, 1808, was a few months older than Lincoln. He is now living at Petersburg, Illinois. He settled in the country one and one-half miles from New Salem in 1820. Mr. Potter remembers Lincoln's first appearance in New Salem, in July, 1831. He corroborates the stories told of his store, of his popularity in the community, and of the general impression that he was an unusually promising young man.

to take revenge on the helpless savage. Lincoln boldly took the man's part, and, though he risked his life in doing it, he cowed the company and saved the Indian.

It was on the 27th of April that the force of sixteen hundred men organized at Beardstown started out. The spring was cold, the roads heavy, the streams turbulent. The army marched first to Yellow Banks on the Mississippi ; then to Dixon on the Rock River, which they reached on May 12th. At Dixon they camped, and near here occurred the first bloodshed of the war.

A body of about three hundred and forty rangers under

Major Stillman, but not of the regular army, asked to go ahead as scouts, to look for a body of Indians under Black Hawk, rumored to be about twelve miles away. The permission was given, and on the night of the 14th of May, Stillman and his men went into camp. Black Hawk heard of their presence. By this time the poor old chief had discovered that the promises of aid from the Indian tribes and the British were false, and, dismayed, he had resolved to recross the Mississippi. When he heard of the whites near, he sent three braves with a white flag to ask for a parley and permission to descend the river. Behind them he sent five men to watch proceedings. Stillman's rangers were in camp when the bearers of the flag of truce appeared. The men were many of them half drunk, and when they saw the Indian truce-bearers, they rushed out in a wild mob, and ran them into camp. Then catching sight of the five spies, they started after them, killing two. The three who reached Black Hawk reported that the truce-bearers had been killed, as well as their two companions. Furious at this violation of faith, Black Hawk raised a yell, and sallied forth with forty braves to meet Stillman's band, who by this time were out in search of the Indians. Black Hawk, too maddened to think of the difference of numbers, attacked the whites. To his surprise the enemy turned, and fled in a wild riot. Nor did they stop at their camp, which from its position was almost impregnable ; they fled in complete panic, *sauve qui peut*, through their camp, across prairie and rivers and swamps, to Dixon, twelve miles away. The first arrival reported that two thousand savages had swept down on Stillman's camp and slaughtered all but himself. Before the next night all but eleven of the band had arrived.

Stillman's defeat, as this disgraceful affair is called, put all notion of peace out of Black Hawk's mind, and he started out in earnest on the warpath. By the morning of the 15th, Governor Reynolds and his army were in pursuit of Black Hawk. But it was like pursuing a shadow. The Indians purposely confused their trail. Sometimes it was a broad path, then it suddenly radiated to all points. The whites broke their bands, and pursued the savages here and there, never overtaking them, though now and then coming suddenly on some terrible evidences of their presence—a frontier home deserted and burned, slaughtered cattle, scalps suspended where the army could not fail to see them.

BOWLING GREEN'S HOUSE.

From a photograph made for this work. Bowling Green's log cabin, half a mile north of New Salem, just under the bluff, still stands, but long since ceased to be a dwelling-house, and is now a tumble-down old stable. Here Lincoln was a frequent boarder, especially during the period of his closest application to the study of the law. Stretched out on the cellar door of this cabin, reading a book, he met for the first time " Dick " Yates, then a college student at Jacksonville, and destined to become the great " War Governor " of the State. Yates had come home with William G. Greene to spend his vacation, and Greene took him around to Bowling Green's house to introduce him to " his friend, Abe Lincoln." Unhappily there is nowhere in existence a picture of the original occupant of this humble cabin. Bowling Green was one of the leading citizens of the county. He was County Commissioner from 1826 to 1828 ; he was for many years a justice of the peace ; he was a prominent member of the Masonic fraternity, and a very active and uncompromising Whig. The friendship between him and Lincoln, beginning at a very early day, continued until his death, in 1842.

This fruitless warfare exasperated the volunteers ; they threatened to leave, and their officers had great difficulty in making them obey orders. On reaching a point on the Rock River, beyond which lay the Indian country, the men under Colonel Zachary Taylor refused to cross, urging that they had volunteered only to defend the State, and had the right to refuse to go out of its borders. Taylor heard them to the end, and then said : " I feel that all gentlemen here are my equals ; in reality, I am persuaded that many of them will, in a few years, be my superiors, and perhaps, in the capacity of members of Congress, arbiters of the fortunes and reputation of humble servants of the Republic, like myself. I expect then to obey them as interpreters of the will of the people ; and the best proof that I will obey them is now to observe the orders of those whom the people have already put in the place of authority to which many gentlemen around me justly aspire. In plain English, gentlemen and fellow-citizens, the word has been passed on to me from

Washington to follow Black Hawk and to take you with me as soldiers. I mean to do both. There are the flatboats drawn up on the shore, and here are Uncle Sam's men drawn up behind you on the prairie." The volunteers knew true grit when they met it. They dissolved their meeting and crossed the river without Uncle Sam's men being called into action.

CHAPTER XII.

LINCOLN AN INDEPENDENT RANGER.—MAJOR ILES'S REMINISCENCES OF THE CAMPAIGN.—END OF THE BLACK HAWK WAR.

HE march in pursuit of the Indians led the army to Ottawa, where the volunteers became so dissatisfied that on May 27th and 28th Governor Reynolds mustered them out. But a force in the field was essential until a new levy was raised, and a few of the men were patriotic enough to offer their services, among them Lincoln, who, on May 29th, was mustered in, at the mouth of the Fox River, by a man in whom, thirty years later, he was to have a keen interest—General Robert Anderson, commander at Fort Sumter in 1861. Lincoln became a private in Captain Elijah Iles's company of Independent Rangers, not brigaded—a company made up, says Captain Iles in his "Footsteps and Wanderings," of "generals, colonels, captains, and distinguished men from the disbanded army." General Anderson says that at this muster Lincoln's arms were valued at forty dollars, his horse and equipment at one hundred and twenty dollars. The Independent Rangers were a favored body, used to carry messages and to spy on the enemy. They had no camp duties, and "drew rations as often as they pleased;" so that as a private Lincoln was really better off than as a captain.*

---

* William Cullen Bryant, who was in Illinois in 1832, at the time of the Black Hawk War, used to tell of meeting in his travels in the State a company of Illinois volunteers, commanded by a "raw youth" of "quaint and pleasant" speech, who, he learned afterwards, was Abraham Lincoln. As Lincoln's captaincy ended on May 27th, and Mr. Bryant did not reach Illinois until June 12th, and as he never came nearer than fifty miles to the Rapids of the Illinois, where the body of rangers to which Lincoln belonged was encamped, it is evident that the "raw youth" could not have been Lincoln, much as one would like to believe that it was.

ABRAHAM LINCOLN.—HITHERTO UNPUBLISHED.

From a photograph in the collection of T. H. Bartlett, the sculptor, of Boston, Massachusetts. Mr. Bartlett regards this as his earliest portrait of Mr. Lincoln, but does not know when or where it was taken. This portrait is also in the Oldroyd collection at Washington, D. C., where it is dated 1856. The collection of Lincoln portraits owned by Mr. Bartlett is the most complete and the most intelligently arranged which we have examined. Mr. Bartlett began collecting fully twenty years ago, his aim being to secure data for a study of Mr. Lincoln from a physiognomical point of view. He has probably the earliest portrait which exists, the one here given, excepting the early daguerreotype owned by Mr. Robert Lincoln. He has a large number of the Illinois pictures made from 1858 to 1860, such as the Gilmer picture (page 209); a large collection of Brady photographs, the masks, Volk's bust, and other interesting portraits. These he has studied from a sculptor's point of view, comparing them carefully with the portraiture of other men, as Webster and Emerson. Mr. Bartlett has embodied his study of Mr. Lincoln in an illustrated lecture, which is a model of what such a lecture should be, suggestive, human, delightful. All his fine collection of Lincoln portraits Mr. Bartlett has put freely at our disposal, an act of courtesy and generosity for which the readers of this work, as well as the authors, cannot fail to be deeply grateful.

The achievements and tribulations of the body of rangers to which he belonged are told with interesting detail by Major Iles.

"While the other companies were ordered to scout the country," says Major Iles, "mine was held by General Atkinson in camp as a reserve. One company was ordered to go to Rock River (now Dixon) and report to Colonel Taylor (afterwards President), who had been left there with a few United States soldiers to guard the army supplies. The place was also made a point of rendezvous. Just as the company got to Dixon, a man came in, and reported that he and six others were on the road to Galena, and, in passing through a point of timber about twenty miles north of Dixon, they were fired on and six killed, he being the only one to make his escape. . . . Colonel Taylor ordered the company to proceed to the place, bury the dead, go on to Galena, and get all the information they could about the Indians. But the company took fright, and came back to the Illinois River, helter-skelter.

"General Atkinson then called on me, and wanted to know how I felt about taking the trip ; that he was exceedingly anxious to open communication with Galena, and to find out, if possible, the whereabouts of the Indians before the new troops arrived. I answered the general that myself and men were getting rusty, and were anxious to have something to do, and that nothing would please us better than to be ordered out on an expedition ; that I would find out how many of my men had good horses and were otherwise well equipped, and what time we wanted to prepare for the trip. I called on him again at sunset, and reported that I had about fifty men well equipped and eager, and that we wanted one day to make preparations. He said go ahead, and he would prepare our orders.

"The next day was a busy one, running bullets and getting our flint-locks in order—we had no percussion locks then. General Henry, one of my privates, who had been promoted to the position of major of one of the companies, volunteered to go with us. I considered him a host, as he had served as lieutenant in the war of 1812, under General Scott, and was in the battle of Lundy's Lane, and several other battles. He was a good drill officer, and could aid me much. . . . After General Atkinson handed me my orders, and my men were mounted and ready for the trip, I felt proud of them, and was confident of our success, although numbering only forty-eight. Several good men failed to go, as they had gone down to the foot of the Illinois Rapids, to aid in bringing up the boats of army supplies. We wanted to be as little encumbered as possible, and took nothing that could be dispensed with, other than blankets, tin cups, coffee-pots, canteens, a wallet of bread, and some fat side meat, which we ate raw or broiled.

" When we arrived at Rock River, we found Colonel Taylor on the opposite side, in a little fort built of prairie sod. He sent an officer in a canoe to bring me over. I said to the officer that I would come over as soon as I got my men in camp. I knew of a good spring half a mile above, and I determined to camp at it. After the men were in camp I called on General Henry, and he accompanied me. On meeting Colonel Taylor (he looked like a man born to command) he seemed a little piqued that I did not come over and camp with him. I told him we felt just as safe as if quartered in his one-horse fort ; besides, I knew what his orders would be, and wanted to try the mettle of my men before starting on the perilous trip I knew he would order. He said the trip was perilous, and that since the murder of the six men all communication with Galena had been cut off, and it might be besieged ; that he wanted me to proceed to Galena, and that he would have my orders for me in the morning, and asked what outfit I wanted. I answered, 'Nothing but coffee, side meat, and bread.'

" In the morning my orders were to collect and bury the remains of the six men murdered, proceed to Galena, make a careful search for the signs of Indians, and find out whether they were aiming to escape by crossing the river below Galena, and get all information at Galena of their possible whereabouts before the new troops were ready to follow them.

" John Dixon, who kept a house of entertainment here, and had sent his family to Galena for safety, joined us, and hauled our wallets of corn and grub in his wagon, which was a great help. Lieutenant Harris, U.S.A., also joined us. I now had fifty men to go with me on the march. I detailed two to march on the right, two on the left, and two in advance, to act as lookouts to prevent a surprise. They were to keep in full view of us, and to remain out until we camped for the night. Just at sundown of the first day, while we were at lunch, our advance scouts came in under whip and reported Indians. We bounced

THE BLACK HAWK.

From a photograph made for this work. After a portrait by George Catlin, in the National Museum at Washington, D. C., and here reproduced by the courtesy of the director, Mr. G. Brown Goode. Makataimeshekiakiak, the Black Hawk Sparrow, was born in 1767, on the Rock River. He was not a chief by birth, but through the valor of his deeds became the leader of his village. He was imaginative and discontented, and bred endless trouble in the Northwest by his complaints and his visionary schemes. He was completely under the influence of the British agents, and in 1812 joined Tecumseh in the war against the United States. After the close of that war the Hawk was peaceable until driven to resistance by the encroachments of the squatters. After the battle of Bad Axe he escaped, and was not captured until betrayed by two Winnebagoes. He was taken to Fort Armstrong, where he signed a treaty of peace, and then was transferred as a prisoner of war to Jefferson Barracks, now St. Louis, where Catlin painted him. Catlin, in his "Eight Years," says : "When I painted this chief he was dressed in a plain suit of buckskin, with a string of wampum in his ears and on his neck, and held in his hand his medicine-bag, which was the skin of a black hawk, from which he had taken his name, and the tail of which made him a fan, which he was almost constantly using." In April, 1833, Black Hawk and the other prisoners of war were transferred to Fortress Monroe. They were released in June, and made a trip through the Atlantic cities before returning West. Black Hawk settled in Iowa, where he and his followers were given a small reservation in Davis County. He died in 1838.

to our feet, and, having a full view of the road for a long distance, could see a large body coming toward us. All eyes were turned to John Dixon, who, as the last one dropped out of sight coming over a ridge, pronounced them Indians. I stationed my men in a ravine crossing the road, where any one approaching could not see us until within thirty yards; the horses I had driven back out of sight in a valley. I asked General Henry to take command. He said, 'No; stand at your post,' and walked along the line, talking to the men in a low, calm voice. Lieutenant Harris, U.S.A., seemed much agitated; he ran up and down the line, and exclaimed, 'Captain, we will c a t c h hell!' He h a d horsepistols, belt-pistols, and a doublebarrelled gun. He would pick the flints, reprime, and lay the horsepistols at his feet. When he got all ready he passed along the line slowly, and seeing the nerves of the men all quiet—after General Henry's talk to them—said, 'Captain, we are safe; we can whip five hundred Indians.' Instead of Indians, they proved to be the command of General Dodge, from Galena, of one hundred and fifty men, *en route* to find out what had become of General Atkinson's army, as, since the murder of the six men, communi-

WHITE CLOUD, THE PROPHET.

From a photograph made for this work. After a painting in the collection of the State Historical Society of Wisconsin, and here reproduced through the courtesy of the secretary, Mr. Reuben G. Thwaites. The chief of an Indian village on the Rock River. White Cloud was half Winnebago, half Sac. He was false and crafty, and it was largely his counsels which induced Black Hawk to recross the Mississippi in 1832. He was captured with Black Hawk, was a prisoner at both Jefferson Barracks and Fortress Monroe, and made the tour of the Atlantic cities with his friends. The above portrait was made at Fortress Monroe by R. M. Sully. Catlin also painted White Cloud at Jefferson Barracks in 1832. He describes him as about forty years old at that time, "nearly six feet high, stout and athletic." He said he let his hair grow out to please the whites. Catlin's picture shows him with a very heavy head of hair. The prophet, after his return from the East, remained among his people until his death in 1840 or 1841.

cation had been stopped for more than ten days. My look-out at the top of the hill did not notify us, and we were not undeceived until they got within thirty steps of us. My men then raised a yell and ran to finish their lunch. . . .

" When we got within fifteen miles of Galena, on Apple Creek, we found a stockade filled with women and children and a few men, all terribly frightened. The Indians had shot at and chased two men that afternoon, who made their escape to the stockade. They insisted on our quartering in the fort, but instead we camped one hundred yards outside, and slept — what little sleep we did get — with our

BLACK HAWK.

From a photograph made for this work. After an improved replica of the original portrait painted by R. M. Sully at Fortress Monroe in 1833, and now in the Museum of the State Historical Society of Wisconsin, at Madison. It is reproduced through the courtesy of the secretary of the society, Mr. Rueben G. Thwaites.

WHIRLING THUNDEK.

From a photograph made for this work. After a painting by R. M. Sully in the collection of the State Historical Society of Wisconsin, and here reproduced through the courtesy of the secretary, Mr. Reuben G. Thwaites. Black Hawk had two sons: the elder was the Whirling Thunder, the younger the Roaring Thunder; both were in the war, and both were taken prisoners with their father, and were with him at Jefferson Barracks and at Fortress Monroe and on the trip through the Atlantic cities. At Jefferson Barracks Catlin painted them, and the pictures are in the National Museum. While at Fortress Monroe the above picture of Whirling Thunder was painted. A pretty anecdote is told of the Whirling Thunder. While on their tour through the East the Indians were invited to various gatherings, and much was done for their entertainment. On one of these occasions a young lady sang a ballad. Whirling Thunder listened intently, and when she ended he plucked an eagle's feather from his head-dress and, giving it to a white friend, said: "Take that to your mocking-bird squaw." Black Hawk's sons remained with him until his death in 1838, and then removed with the Sacs and Foxes to Kansas.

guns on our arms. General Henry did not sleep, but drilled my men all night; so the moment they were called they would bounce to their feet and stand in two lines, the front ready to fire, and fall back to reload, while the others stepped forward to take their places. They were called up a number of times, and we got but little sleep. We arrived at Galena the next day, and found the citizens prepared to defend the place. They were glad to see us, as it had been so long since they had heard from General Atkinson and his army. The few Indians prowling about Galena and murdering were simply there as a ruse.

"On our return from Galena, near the forks of the Apple River and Gratiot roads, we could see General Dodge on the Gratiot road, on his return from Rock River. His six scouts had discovered my two men that I had allowed to drop in the rear—

ZACHARY TAYLOR.

At the breaking out of the Black Hawk War, Zachary Taylor, afterwards general in the Mexican War, and finally President of the United States, was colonel of the First Infantry. He joined Atkinson at the beginning of the war, and was in active service until the end of the campaign.

two men who had been in Stillman's defeat, and, having weak horses, were allowed to fall behind. Having weak horses they had fallen in the rear about two miles, and each took the other to be Indians, and such an exciting race I never saw, until they got sight of my company; then they came to a sudden halt, and after looking at us a few moments, wheeled their horses and gave up the chase. My two men did not know but that they were Indians until they came up with us and shouted 'Indians!' They had thrown away their wallets and guns, and used their ramrods as whips.

"The few houses on the road that usually accommodated the travel were all standing, but vacant, as we went. On our return we found them burned by the Indians. On my return to the Illinois River I reported to General Atkinson, saying that, from all we could learn, the Indians were aiming to escape by going north, with the intention of crossing the Mississippi River above Galena. The new troops had just arrived and were being mustered into service. My company had only been organized for twenty days, and as the time had now expired, the men were mustered out. All but myself again volunteered for the third time."

LINCOLN AND HIS COMPANY ENTER MICHIGAN TERRITORY.

On June 20th Lincoln was mustered in again, by Major Anderson, as a member of an independent company under Captain Jacob M. Early. His arms were valued this time at only fifteen dollars, his horse and equipment at eighty-five dollars.*

* See "Wisconsin Historical Collections," Volume X., for Major Anderson's reminiscences of the Black Hawk War.

Tomahawk. Indian Pipe. Powder-horn.
Flint-lock Rifle. Indian Flute.
Indian Knife.

BLACK HAWK WAR RELICS.

From a photograph made for this work. This group of relics of the Black Hawk War was selected for us from the collection in the museum of the Wisconsin Historical Society by the secretary, Mr. Reuben G. Thwaites. The coat and chapeau belonged to General Dodge, an important leader in the war. The Indian relics are a tomahawk, a Winnebago pipe, a Winnebago flute, and a knife. The powder-horn and the flint-lock rifle are the only volunteer articles. One of the survivors of the war, Mr. Elijah Herring of Stockton, Illinois, says of the flintlock rifles used by the Illinois volunteers : "They were constructed like the old-fashioned rifle, only in place of a nipple for a cap they had a pan in which was fixed an oil flint which the hammer struck when it came down, instead of the modern cap. The pan was filled with powder grains, enough to catch the spark and communicate it to the load in the gun. These guns were all right, and rarely missed fire on a dry, clear day; but unless they were covered well, the dews of evening would dampen the powder, and very often we were compelled to withdraw the charge and load them over again. We had a gunsmith with us, whose business it was to look after the guns for the whole regiment ; and when a gun was found to be damp, it was his duty to get his tools and 'draw' the load. At that time the Cramer lock and triggers had just been put on the market, and my rifle was equipped with these improvements, a fact of which I was very proud. Instead of one trigger my rifle had two, one set behind the other—the hind one to cock the gun, and the front one to shoot it. The man Cramer sold his lock and triggers in St. Louis, and I was one of the first to use them."

The army moved up Rock River soon after the middle of June. Black Hawk was overrunning the country, and scattering death wherever he went. The settlers were wild with fear, and most of the settlements were abandoned. At a sudden sound, at the merest rumor, men, women, and children fled. "I well remember those troublesome times," says one old Illinois woman. "We often left our bread-dough unbaked, to rush to the Indian fort near by." When Mr. John Bryant, a brother of William Cullen Bryant, visited the colony in Princeton, in 1832, he found it nearly broken up on account of the war. Everywhere the crops were neglected, for the able-bodied men were volunteering. William Cullen Bryant, who, in June, 1834, travelled on horseback from Petersburg to near Pekin, and back, wrote home: "Every few miles on our way we fell in with bodies of Illinois militia proceeding to the American camp, or saw where they had encamped for the night. They generally stationed themselves near a stream or a spring in the edge of a wood, and turned their horses to graze on the prairie. Their way was barked or girdled, and the roads through the uninhabited country were as much beaten and as dusty as the highways on New York Island. Some of the settlers complained that they made war upon the pigs and chickens. They were a hard-looking set of men, unkempt and unshaved, wearing shirts of dark calico, and sometimes calico capotes."

Soon after the army moved up the Rock River, the independent spy company, of which Lincoln was a member, was sent with a brigade to the northwest, near Galena, in pursuit of the Hawk. The nearest Lincoln came to an actual engagement in the war was here. The skirmish of Kellogg's Grove took place on June 25th ; Lincoln's company came up soon after it was over, and helped bury the five men killed. It was probably to this experience that he referred when he told a friend once of coming on a camp of white scouts one morning just as the sun was rising. The Indians had surprised the camp, and had killed and scalped every man.

" I remember just how those men looked," said Lincoln, "as we rode up the little hill where their camp was. The red light of the morning sun was streaming upon them as they lay heads towards us on the ground. And every man had a round red spot on the top of his head, about as big as a dollar, where the redskins had taken his scalp. It was frightful, but it was grotesque ; and the red sunlight seemed to paint everything all over." Lincoln paused, as if recalling the vivid picture, and added, somewhat irrelevantly, " I remember that one man had buckskin breeches on."

By the end of the month the troops crossed into Michigan Territory—as Wisconsin was then called—and July was passed floundering in swamps and stumbling through forests, in pursuit of the now nearly exhausted Black Hawk. On July 10th, three weeks before the last battle of the war, that of Bad Axe, in which the whites finally massacred most of the Indian band, Lincoln's company was disbanded at Whitewater, Wisconsin, and he and his friends started for home. The volunteers in returning suffered much from hunger. Mr. Durley of Hennepin, Illinois, who walked home from Rock Island, Illinois, says all he had to eat on the journey was meal and water baked in rolls of bark laid by the fire. Lincoln was little better off. The night before his company started from Whitewater he and one of his messmates had their horses stolen ; and, excepting when their more fortunate companions gave them a lift, they walked as far as Peoria, Illinois, where they bought a canoe, and paddled down the Illinois River to Havana. Here they sold the canoe, and walked across the country to New Salem.

CHAPTER XIII.

ELECTIONEERING IN 1832 IN ILLINOIS.—LINCOLN DEFEATED OF
ELECTION TO THE ASSEMBLY.—BUYS A STORE.

N returning to New Salem, Lincoln at once plunged into electioneering. He ran as "an avowed Clay man," and the county was stiffly Democratic. However, in those days political contests were almost purely personal. If the candidate was liked he was voted for irrespective of principles. "The Democrats of New Salem worked for Lincoln out of their personal regard for him," said Stephen T. Logan, a young lawyer of Springfield, who made Lincoln's acquaintance in the campaign. "He was as stiff as a man could be in his Whig doctrines. They did this for him simply because he was popular ; because he was Lincoln."

It was the custom for the candidates to appear at every gathering which brought the people out, and, if they had a chance, to make speeches. Then, as now, the farmers gathered at the county-seat, or at the largest town within their reach, on Saturday afternoons, to dispose of produce, buy supplies, see their neighbors, and get the news. During election times candidates were always present, and a regular feature of the day

was listening to their speeches. Public sales, also, were gatherings which they never missed, it being expected that after the
"vandoo" the candidates would take the auctioneer's place.

Lincoln let none of these chances to be heard slip. Accompanied by his friends, generally including a few Clary's Grove
Boys, he always was present. The first speech he made was
after a sale at Pappsville. What he said there is not remembered; but an illustration of the kind of man he was, interpo-
lated into his discourse, made a lasting impression. A fight broke
out in his audience while he was on the stand, and observing
that one of his friends was being worsted, he bounded into
the group of contestants, seized the fellow who had his supporter
down, threw him "ten or twelve feet," remounted the platform,
and finished the speech. Sangamon County could appreciate
such a performance, and the crowd that day at Pappsville never
forgot Lincoln.

His appearance at Springfield at this time was of great importance to him. Springfield was not then a very attractive
place. Bryant, visiting it in June, 1832, said that the houses

SCENE OF STILLMAN'S DEFEAT.
From a photograph loaned by S. J. Dodds of Lena, Illinois.

were not as good as at Jacksonville, "a considerable proportion of them being log cabins,
and the whole town having an
appearance of dirt and discom-
fort." Nevertheless it was the
largest town in the county, and
among its inhabitants were many
young men of education, birth,
and energy. One of these men
Lincoln had b e c o m e well acquainted with in the Black Hawk
War, Major John Stuart,* at
that time a lawyer, and, like
Lincoln, a candidate for the
General A s s e m b l y. He met
others at this time who were to
be associated with him more or
less closely in the future in both
law and politics, such as Judge
Logan and W i l l i a m Butler.
With these men the manners
which had won him the day at
Pappsville were of no value;
what impressed them was his
"very sensible speech," and his
decided individuality and origin-
ality.

The e l e c t i o n came off on
August 6th. Lincoln was de-

From a photograph in the war collection of Mr. Robert
Coster.

MAJOR ROBERT ANDERSON.

Born in Kentucky in 1805. In 1825 graduated
at West Point. Anderson was on duty at the St.
Louis Arsenal when the Black Hawk War broke
out. He asked permission to join General Atkinson, who commanded the expedition against the
Indians; was placed on his staff as Assistant In-
spector-General, and was with him until the end
of the war. Anderson twice mustered Lincoln
into the service and once out. When General
Scott was sent to take Atkinson's place, Anderson was ordered to report to the former for duty,
and was sent by him to take charge of the Indians captured at Bad Axe. It was Anderson who
conducted Black Hawk to Jefferson Barracks.
His adjutant in this task was Lieutenant Jefferson Davis. From 1835–37 Anderson was an in-
structor at West Point. He served in the Florida
War in 1837–38, and was wounded at Molino del
Rey in the Mexican War. In 1857 he was appointed Major of the First Artillery. On November 20, 1860, Anderson assumed command of the
troops in Charleston Harbor. On April 14th he
surrendered Fort Sumter, marching out with the
honors of war. He was made brigadier-general
by Lincoln for his service. On account of failing
health he was relieved from duty in October, 1861.
In 1865 he was brevetted major-general. He died
in France in 1871.

* There were many prominent Americans
in the Black Hawk War, with some of whom
Lincoln became acquainted. Among the
best known were General Robert Anderson;
Colonel Zachary Taylor; General Scott,
afterwards candidate for President, and
Lieutenant-General; Henry Dodge, Gover-
nor of the Territory of Wisconsin, and United
States Senator; Hon. William L. D. Ewing and Hon. Sidney Breese, both United States
Senators from Illinois; William S. Hamilton, a son of Alexander Hamilton; Colonel
Nathan Boone, son of Daniel Boone; Lieutenant Albert Sydney Johnston, afterwards a
Confederate general. Jefferson Davis was not in the war, according to the muster-rolls
of his company, which report him absent on furlough from March 26 to August 18, 1832.

feated. "This was the only time Abraham was ever defeated on a direct vote of the people," say his autobiographical notes. He had a consolation in his defeat, however, for in spite of the pronounced Democratic sentiments of his precinct, he received two hundred and seventy-seven votes out of three hundred cast. The facts upon this point are here stated for the first time. The biographers, as a rule, have agreed that Lincoln received all of the votes cast in the New Salem precinct, except three. Mr. Herndon places the total vote at 208 ; Nicolay and Hay, at 277 ; and Mr. Lincoln himself, in his autobiography, has said that he received all but seven of a total of 277 votes, basing his statement, no doubt, upon memory. An examination of the official poll-book in the county clerk's office at Springfield shows that all of these figures are erroneous ; exactly three hundred votes were cast. Of these Lincoln received 277. The fact remains, however—and it is a fact which has been commented upon by several of the biographers as showing his phenomenal popularity—that the vote for Lincoln was far in excess of that given any other candidate. The twelve candidates, with the number of votes of each, were : Abraham Lincoln, 277 ; John T. Stewart, 182 ; William Carpenter, 136 ; John Dawson, 105 ; E. D. Taylor, 88 ; Archer G. Herndon, 84 ; Peter Cartwright, 62 ; Achilles Morris, 27; Thomas M. Neal, 21 ; Edward Robeson, 15 ; Zachariah Peters, 4 ; Richard Dunston, 4.

Of the twenty-three who did not vote for Lincoln, ten refrained from voting for representative at all, thus leaving only thirteen votes actually cast against Lincoln. Lincoln is not recorded as voting. This defeat did not take him out of politics. The first civil office Lincoln ever held was that of clerk of the next election, in September. The report in his hand still exists ; as far as we know, it is his first official document.

LOOKING FOR WORK.

It was in August, 1832, that Lincoln made his unsuccessful canvass for the Illinois Assembly. The election over, he began to look for work. One of his friends, an admirer of his physical strength, advised him to become a blacksmith, but it was a trade which afforded little leisure for study, and for meeting and talking with men ; and he had already resolved, it is evident, that books and men were essential to him. The only employment in New Salem which offered both support and the opportunities

BAD AXE BATTLE-GROUND.

From a copy of a painting by Samuel M. Brookes, in the Museum of the Wisconsin Historical Society. The remnant of Black Hawk's force was slaughtered here on August 1st and 2d, while attempting to cross the Mississippi. Only about one hundred and fifty of his original band of one thousand escaped.

he sought, was clerking in a store. But the stores of New Salem were in more need of customers than of clerks. The business had been greatly overdone. In the fall of 1832 there were at least four stores in New Salem. The most pretentious was that of Hill and McNeill, which carried a large line of dry goods. The three others, owned respectively by the Herndon brothers, Reuben Radford, and James Rutledge, were groceries.

DECIDES TO BUY A STORE.

Failing to secure employment at any of these establishments, Lincoln resolved to *buy* a store. He was not long in finding an opportunity to purchase. James Herndon had already sold out his half interest in Herndon Brothers' store to William F. Berry; and Rowan Herndon, not getting along well with Berry, was only too glad to find a purchaser of his half in the person of "Abe" Lincoln. Berry was as poor as Lincoln; but that was not a serious obstacle, for their notes were accepted for the Herndon stock of goods. They had barely hung out their sign when something happened which threw another store into their hands. Reuben Radford had made himself obnoxious to the Clary's Grove Boys, and one night they broke in his doors and windows, and overturned his counters and sugar barrels. It was too much for Radford, and he sold out next day to William G. Green for a four-hundred-dollar note signed by Green. At the latter's request, Lincoln made an inventory of the stock, and then offered him six hundred and fifty dollars for it —a proposition which was cheerfully accepted. Berry and Lincoln, being unable to pay cash, assumed the four-hundred-dollar note payable to Radford, and gave Green their joint note for two hundred and fifty dollars. The little grocery owned by James Rutledge was the next to succumb. Berry and Lincoln bought it at a bargain, their joint note taking the place of cash. The three stocks were consolidated. Their aggregate cost must have been not less than fifteen hundred dollars. Berry and Lincoln had secured a monopoly of the grocery business in New Salem. Within a few weeks two penniless men had become the proprietors of three stores, and had stopped buying only because there were no more to purchase.

William F. Berry, the partner of Lincoln, was the son of a Presbyterian minister, the Rev. John Berry, who lived on Rock Creek, five miles from New Salem. The son had strayed from the footsteps of the father, for he was a hard drinker, a gambler, a fighter, and "a very wicked young man." Lincoln cannot in truth be said to have chosen such a partner, but rather to have accepted him from the force of circumstances. It required only a little time to make plain that the partnership was wholly uncongenial. Lincoln displayed little business capacity. He trusted largely to Berry, and Berry rapidly squandered the profits of the business in riotous living. Lincoln loved books as Berry loved liquor, and hour after hour he was stretched out on the counter of the store, or under a shade tree, reading Shakespeare or Burns.

His acquaintance with the works of these two writers dates from this period. In New Salem there was one of those curious individuals sometimes found in frontier settlements, half poet, half loafer, incapable of earning a living in any steady employment, yet familiar with good literature and capable of enjoying it—Jack Kelso. He repeated passages from Shakespeare and Burns incessantly over the odd jobs he under-

LINCOLN IN 1860.—HITHERTO UNPUBLISHED.

From a photograph loaned by H. W. Fay of DeKalb, Illinois. After Lincoln's nomination for the presidency, Alexander Hesler of Chicago published a portrait he had made of Lincoln in 1857 (see page 49). At the same time he put out a portrait of Douglas. The contrast was so great between the two, and in the opinion of the politicians so much in Douglas's favor, that they told Hesler he must suppress Lincoln's picture; accordingly the photographer wrote to Springfield, requesting Lincoln to call and sit again. Lincoln replied that his friends had decided that he remain in Springfield during the canvass, but that if Hesler would come to Springfield he would be "dressed up" and give him all the time he wanted. Hesler went to Springfield, and made at least four negatives, three of which are supposed to have been destroyed in the Chicago fire. The fourth is owned by Mr. George Ayers of Philadelphia. The photograph reproduced above is a print from one of the lost negatives.

took, or as he idled by the streams—for he was a famous fisherman—and Lincoln soon became one of his constant companions. The taste he formed in company with Kelso he retained through life.

William D. Kelley records an incident which shows that Lincoln had a really intimate knowledge of Shakespeare. Mr. Kelley had taken McDonough, an actor, to call at the White House, and Lincoln began the conversation by saying:

" 'I am very glad to meet you, Mr. McDonough, and am grateful to Kelley for bringing you in so early, for I want you to tell me something about Shakespeare's plays as they are constructed for the stage. You can imagine that I do not get much time to study such matters, but I recently had a couple of talks with Hackett—Baron Hackett, as they call him—who is famous as Jack Falstaff, from whom I elicited few satisfactory replies, though I probed him with a good many questions.'

"Mr. McDonough," continues Mr. Kelley, "avowed his willingness to give the President any information in his possession, but protested that he feared he would not succeed where his friend Hackett had failed. 'Well, I don't know,' said the President, 'for Hackett's lack of information impressed me with a doubt as to whether he had ever studied Shakespeare's text, or had not been content with the acting edition of his plays.' He arose, went to a shelf not far from his table, and having taken down a well-thumbed volume of the 'Plays' of Shakespeare, resumed his seat, arranged his glasses, and having turned to 'Henry VI.' and read with fine discrimination an extended passage, said: 'Mr. McDonough, can you tell me why those lines are omitted from the acting play? There is nothing I have read in Shakespeare, certainly nothing in "Henry VI." or the "Merry Wives of Windsor," that surpasses its wit and humor.' The actor suggested the breadth of its humor as the only reason he could assign for its omission, but thoughtfully added that it was possible that if the lines were spoken they would require the rendition of another or other passages which might be objectionable.

" 'Your last suggestion,' said Mr. Lincoln, 'carries with it greater weight than anything Mr. Hackett suggested, but the first is no reason at all;' and after reading another passage, he said, 'This is not withheld, and where it passes current there can be no reason for withholding the other.' . . . And, as if

MONUMENT AT KELLOGG'S GROVE.

On June 24, 1832, Black Hawk attacked Apple River Fort, fourteen miles east of Galena, Illinois, but was unable to drive out the inmates. The next day he attacked a spy battalion of one hundred and fifty men at Kellogg's Grove, sixteen miles farther east. A detachment of volunteers relieved the battalion, and drove off the savages, about fifteen of whom were killed. The whites lost five men, who were buried at various points in the grove. During the summer of 1886 the remains of these men were collected and, with those of five or six other victims of the war, were placed together under the monument here represented.—See "The Black Hawk War," by Reuben G. Thwaites, Vol. XII. in Wisconsin Historical Collections. This account of the Black Hawk War is the most trustworthy, complete, and interesting that has been made.

feeling the impropriety of preferring the player to the parson [there was a clergyman in the room], he turned to the chaplain and said: 'From your calling it is probable that you do not know that the acting plays which people crowd to hear are not always those planned by their reputed authors. Thus, take the stage edition of "Richard III." It opens with a passage from "Henry VI.," after which come portions of "Richard III.," then another scene from "Henry VI.;" and the finest soliloquy in the play, if we may judge from the many quotations it furnishes, and the frequency with which it is heard in amateur exhibitions, was never seen by Shakespeare, but was written—was it not, Mr. McDonough?—after his death, by Colley Cibber.'

"Having disposed, for the present, of questions relating to the stage editions of the plays, he recurred to his standard copy, and . . . read, or repeated from memory, extracts from several of the plays, some of which embraced a number of lines. . . . He interspersed his remarks with extracts striking from their similarity to, or contrast with, something of Shakespeare's, from Byron, Rogers, Campbell, Moore, and other English poets."*

* "Reminiscences of Abraham Lincoln." Edited by Allen Thorndike Rice, 1886.

JOHN REYNOLDS, GOVERNOR OF ILLINOIS 1831–1834.

After a steel engraving in the Governor's office, Springfield, Illinois. John Reynolds, Governor of Illinois from 1831 to 1834, was born in Montgomery County, Pennsylvania, February 26, 1788. He was of Irish parentage. When he was six months old his parents moved to Tennessee. In 1800 they removed to Illinois. When twenty years old, John Reynolds went to Knoxville, Tennessee. to college, where he spent two years. He was admitted to the bar at Kaskaskia in 1812. In the war of 1812 he rendered distinguished service, earning the title of "the Old Ranger." He began the practice of law in the spring of 1814. In 1818 he was made an associate justice of the Supreme Court ; in 1826 he was elected a member of the legislature ; and in 1830, after a stirring campaign, he was chosen Governor of Illinois. The most important event of his administration was the Black Hawk War. He was prompt in calling out the militia to subdue the Black Hawk, and went upon the field in person. In November, 1834, just before the close of his term as Governor, he resigned to become a member of Congress. In 1837, aided by others, he built the first railroad in the State—a short line of six miles from his coal mine in the Mississippi bluff to the bank of the river opposite St. Louis. It was operated by horse-power. He again became a member of the legislature in 1846 and 1852, during the latter term being Speaker of the House. In 1860, in his seventy-third year, he was an anti-Douglas delegate to the Charleston convention, and received the most distinguished attentions from the Southern delegates. After the October elections, when it became apparent that Lincoln would be elected, he issued an address advising the support of Douglas. His sympathies were with the South, though in 1832 he strongly supported President Jackson in the suppression of the South Carolina nullifiers. He died in Belleville in May, 1865. Governor Reynolds was a quaint and forceful character. He was a man of some learning ; but in conversation (and he talked much) he rarely rose above the odd Western vernacular of which he was so complete a master. He was the author of two books ; one an autobiography, and the other "The Pioneer History of Illinois."

CHAPTER XIV.

I T was not only Burns and Shakespeare that inter-
fered with the grocery-keeping; Lincoln had
begun seriously to read law.   His first acquaintance with the subject had been made when he
was a mere lad in Indiana and a copy of the
"Revised Statutes of Indiana" had fallen into
his hands.   The very copy he used is still in
existence, and, fortunately, in hands where it is
safe.   The book was owned by Mr. David Turn-
ham of Gentryville, and was given in 1865 by him to Mr. Herndon,
who placed it in the Lincoln Memorial collection of Chicago.   In
December, 1894, this collection was sold in Philadelphia, and the
"Statutes of Indiana" was bought by Mr. William Hoffman
Winters, Librarian of the New York Law Institute, and through
his courtesy I have been allowed to examine it.   The book is
worn, the title page is gone, and a few leaves from the end are
missing.   The title page of a duplicate volume which Mr. Winters kindly showed me reads: "The Revised Laws of Indiana,
adopted and enacted by the General Assembly at their eighth
session.   To which are prefixed the Declaration of Independence, the Constitution of the United States, the Constitution of
the State of Indiana, and sundry other documents connected
with the Political History of the Territory and State of Indiana.
Arranged and published by authority of the General Assembly.
Corydon: Printed by Carpenter and Douglass, 1824."

We know from Dennis Hanks, from Mr. Turnham, to whom
the book belonged, and from other associates of Lincoln's at the
time, that he read the book intently and discussed its contents
intelligently.   It was a remarkable volume for a thoughtful lad
whose mind had been fired already by the history of Washington ; for it opened with that wonderful document, the Declaration
of Independence, a document which became, as Mr. John G.
Nicolay says, "his political chart and inspiration."   Following
the Declaration of Independence was the Constitution of the

United States, the Act of Virginia passed in 1783 by which the "Territory North Westward of the river Ohio" was conveyed to the United States, and the Ordinance of 1787 for governing this territory, containing that clause on which Lincoln in the future based many an argument on the slavery question. This article, No. 6 of the Ordinance, reads: "There shall be neither slavery nor involuntary servitude in the said territory, otherwise than in the punishment of crimes, whereof the party shall have been duly convicted: provided always, that any person escaping into the same, from whom labor or service is lawfully claimed in any one of the original States, such fugitive may be lawfully reclaimed, and conveyed to the person claiming his or her labour or service, as aforesaid."

Following this was the Constitution and the Revised Laws of Indiana, three hundred and seventy-five pages, of five hundred words each, of statutes—enough law, if thoroughly digested, to make a respectable lawyer. When Lincoln finished this book, as he had, probably, before he was eighteen, we have reason to believe that he understood the principles on which the nation was founded, how the State of Indiana came into being, and how it was governed. His understanding of the subject was clear and practical, and he applied it in his reading, thinking, and discussion.

It was after he had read the Laws of Indiana that Lincoln had free access to the library of his admirer, Judge John Pitcher of Rockport, Indiana, where, undoubtedly, he examined many law-books. But from the time he left Indiana in 1830 he had no legal reading until one day soon after the grocery was started, when there happened one of those trivial incidents which so often turn the current of a life. It is best told in Lincoln's own words.* "One day a man who was migrating to the West drove up in front of my store with a wagon which contained his family and household plunder. He asked me if I would buy an old barrel for which he had no room in his wagon, and which he said contained nothing of special value. I did not want it, but

---

* This incident was told by Lincoln to Mr. A. J. Conant the artist, who in 1860 painted his portrait in Springfield. Mr. Conant, in order to catch Mr. Lincoln's animated expression, had engaged him in conversation, and had questioned him about his early life ; and it was in the course of their conversation that this incident came out. It is to be found in a delightful and suggestive article entitled, "My Acquaintance with Abraham Lincoln," contributed by Mr. Conant to the "Liber Scriptorum," and by his permission quoted here.

From a photograph made for this biography.

ELIJAH ILES, CAPTAIN OF ONE OF THE
COMPANIES IN WHICH LINCOLN SERVED
AS PRIVATE IN THE BLACK HAWK WAR.

After a painting by the late Mrs. Obed
Lewis, niece of Major Iles, and owned
by Mr. Obed Lewis, Springfield, Illinois.
Elijah Iles was born in Kentucky, March
28, 1796, and when young went to Missouri. There he heard marvellous stories
about the Sangamon Valley, and he resolved to go thither. Springfield had just
been staked out in the wilderness, and he
reached the place in time to erect the first
building—a rude hut in which he kept a
store. This was in 1821. "In the early
days in Illinois," he wrote in 1883, "it was
hard to find good material for law-makers.
I was elected a State Senator in 1826, and
again for a second term. The Senate then
comprised thirteen members, and the House
twenty-five." In 1827 he was elected major
in the command of Colonel T. NcNeal, intending to fight the Winnebagoes, but no
fighting occurred. In the Black Hawk
War of 1832, after his term as a private in
Captain Dawson's company had expired,
he was elected captain of a new company
of independent rangers. In this company
Lincoln reënlisted as a private. Major Iles
lived at Springfield to the end of his life.
He died September 4, 1883.

to oblige him I bought it, and paid
him, I think, half a dollar for it.
Without further examination, I put
it away in the store, and forgot all
about it. Some time after, in over-
hauling things, I came upon the
barrel, and emptying it upon the
floor to see what it contained, I
found at the bottom of the rubbish
a complete edition of Blackstone's
Commentaries. I began to read
those famous works, and I had
plenty of time ; for during the long
summer days, when the farmers
were busy with their crops, my customers were few and far between.
The more I read " — this he said
with unusual emphasis—" the more
intensely interested I became.
Never in my whole life was my
mind so thoroughly absorbed. I
read until I devoured them."

BERRY AND LINCOLN GET A TAVERN LICENSE.

But all this was fatal to business, and by spring it was evident
that something must be done to
stimulate the grocery sales.

On the 6th of March, 1833, the
County Commissioner's Court of
Sangamon County granted the firm
of Berry and Lincoln a license to
keep a tavern at New Salem.

It is probable that the license was
procured to enable the firm to retail
the liquors which they had in stock,
and not for keeping a tavern. In a community in which liquor-
drinking was practically universal, at a time when whiskey was
as legitimate an article of merchandise as coffee or calico, when

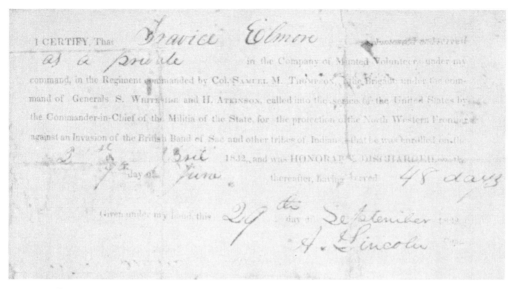

A DISCHARGE FROM SERVICE IN THE BLACK HAWK WAR SIGNED BY ABRAHAM LINCOLN AS CAPTAIN.—
NOW FIRST PUBLISHED.

no family was without a jug, when the minister of the gospel
could take his "dram" without any breach of propriety, it is not
surprising that a reputable young man should have been found
selling whiskey. Liquor was sold at all groceries, but it could
not be lawfully sold in a smaller quantity than one quart. The
law, however, was not always rigidly observed, and it was the
custom of storekeepers to treat their patrons. Each of the three
groceries which Berry and Lincoln acquired had the usual supply of liquors, and it was only good business that they should
seek a way to dispose of the surplus quickly and profitably—
an end which could be best accomplished by selling it over the
counter by the glass. To do this lawfully required a tavern
license ; and it is a warrantable conclusion that such was the
chief aim of Berry and Lincoln in procuring a franchise of this
character. We are fortified in this conclusion by the coincidence
that three other grocers of New Salem—William Clary, Henry
Sincoe, and George Warberton—were among those who took out
tavern licenses. To secure the lawful privilege of selling whiskey by the "dram" was no doubt their purpose ; for their
"taverns" were as mythical as the inn of Berry and Lincoln.
Lincoln may, of course, have desired to go into the tavern business and so have taken out a license, but it is certain that he

never realized his ambition and that it was only in the grocery that he sold liquor.

The license issued to Berry and Lincoln read as follows:

Ordered that William F. Berry, in the name of Berry and Lincoln, have a license to keep a tavern in New Salem to continue 12 months from this date, and that they pay one dollar in addition to the six dollars heretofore paid as per Treasurer's receipt, and that they be allowed the following rates (viz.) :

French Brandy per ¼ pt			25
Peach " " "			18¼
Apple " " "			12
Holland Gin " "			18¼
Domestic " "			12¼
Wine " "			25
Rum " "			18¼
Whiskey " "			12¼
Breakfast, dinner or supper			25
Lodging per night			12¼
Horse per night			25
Single feed			12¼
Breakfast, dinner or supper for Stage Passengers			37¼

who gave bond as required by law.

At the granting of a tavern license, the applicants therefor were required by law to file a bond. The bond given in the case of Berry and Lincoln was as follows:

Know all men by these presents, we, William F. Berry, Abraham Lincoln and John Bowling Green, are held and firmly bound unto the County Commissioners of Sangamon County in the full sum of three hundred dollars to which payment well and truly to be made we bind ourselves, our heirs, executors and administrators firmly by these presents, sealed with our seal and dated this 6th day of March A.D. 1833. Now the condition of this obligation is such that Whereas the said Berry & Lincoln has obtained a license from the County Commissioners Court to keep a tavern in the Town of New Salem to continue one year. Now if the said Berry & Lincoln shall be of good behavior and observe all the laws of this State relative to tavern keepers—then this obligation to be void or otherwise remain in full force.

ABRAHAM LINCOLN [Seal]
WM. F. BERRY   [Seal]
BOWLING GREEN   [Seal]

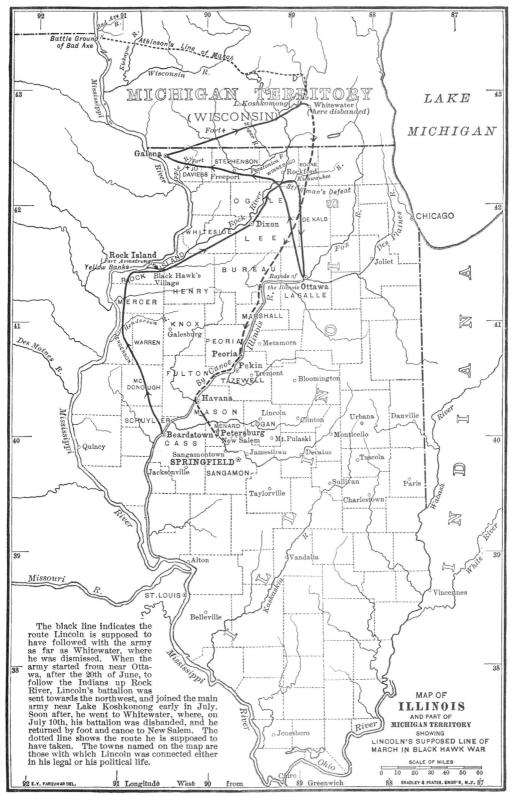

The black line indicates the route Lincoln is supposed to have followed with the army as far as Whitewater, where he was dismissed. When the army started from near Ottawa, after the 20th of June, to follow the Indians up Rock River, Lincoln's battalion was sent towards the northwest, and joined the main army near Lake Koshkonong early in July. Soon after, he went to Whitewater, where, on July 10th, his battalion was disbanded, and he returned by foot and canoe to New Salem. The dotted line shows the route he is supposed to have taken. The towns named on the map are those with which Lincoln was connected either in his legal or his political life.

MAP OF
ILLINOIS
AND PART OF
MICHIGAN TERRITORY
SHOWING
LINCOLN'S SUPPOSED LINE OF
MARCH IN BLACK HAWK WAR

SCALE OF MILES
0   10   20   30   40   50   60

E. V. FARQUHAR DEL.   Longitude   West   from   Greenwich   BRADLEY & POATES, ENGR'S, N.Y.

MAP OF ILLINOIS IN 1832.—PREPARED SPECIALLY FOR THIS WORK.

This bond appears to have been written by the clerk of the Commissioners' Court ; and Lincoln's name was signed by some one other than himself, very likely by his partner Berry.

THE FIRM HIRES A CLERK.

The license seems to have stimulated the business, for the firm concluded to hire a clerk. The young man who secured this position was Daniel Green Burner, son of Isaac Burner, at whose house Lincoln for a time boarded. He is still living on a farm near Galesburg, Illinois, and is in the eighty-second year of his age. " The store building of Berry and Lincoln," says Mr. Burner, "was a frame building, not very large, one story in height, and contained two rooms. In the little back room Lincoln had a fireplace and a bed. There is where we slept. I clerked in the store through the winter of 1833–34, up to the 1st of March. While I was there they had nothing for sale but liquors. They may have had some groceries before that, but I am certain they had none then. I used to sell whiskey over their counter at six cents a glass—and charged it, too. N. A. Garland started a store, and Lincoln wanted Berry to ask his father for a loan, so they could buy out Garland ; but Berry refused, saying this was one of the last things he would think of doing."

Among the other persons yet living who were residents with Lincoln of New Salem or its near neighborhood, are Mrs. Parthenia W. Hill, aged seventy-nine years, widow of Samuel Hill, the New Salem merchant ; James McGrady Rutledge, aged eighty-one years ; John Potter, aged eighty-seven years ; and Thomas Watkins, aged seventy-one years—all now living at Petersburg, Illinois. Mrs. Hill, a woman of more than ordinary intelligence, did not become a resident of New Salem until 1835, the year in which she was married. Lincoln had then gone out of business, but she knew much of his store. " Berry and Lincoln," she says, "did not keep any dry goods. They had a grocery, and I have always understood they sold whiskey." Mr. Rutledge, a nephew of James Rutledge the tavern-keeper, has a vivid recollection of the store. He says: " I have been in Berry and Lincoln's store many a time. The building was a frame—one of the few frame buildings in New Salem. There were two rooms, and in the small back room they kept their whiskey. They had pretty much everything, except dry goods—sugar, coffee, some

At an election held at the house of John McNeil in the New Salem precinct in the County of Sangamon and State of Illinois on the 20th day of September in the year of our Lord one thousand eight hundred and thirtytwo the following named persons received the number of votes annexed to their respective names— for Constable—

John Clary had Fortyone Votes for Constable
John R. Herndon had Twentytwo votes for Constable
William McNeely had Thirteen Votes for Constable
Baxter B. Berry had Nine— votes for Constable
Edmund Greer had Four— votes for Constable

James Rutledge
Hugh Armstrong   } *Judges of the election*
James White

Attest
A. Lincoln
William Green   } *Clerks of the election*

I certify that the above Judges and clerks were qualified according to law
September 20 - 1832
Bowling Green

From the original now on file in the county clerk's office, Springfield, Illinois. The first civil office Lincoln ever held was that of election clerk, and the return made by him, of which a facsimile is here presented, was his first official document. All the men whose names appear on this election return are now dead, except William McNeely, now residing at Petersburg. John Clary lived at Clary's Grove; John R. Herndon was "Row" Herndon, whose store Berry and Lincoln purchased, and at whose house Lincoln for a time boarded; Baxter Berry was a relative of Lincoln's partner in the grocery business, and Edmund Greer was a school-teacher, and afterwards a justice of the peace and a surveyor; James Rutledge was the keeper of the Rutledge tavern and the father of Ann Rutledge; Hugh Armstrong was one of the numerous Armstrong family; "Uncle Jimmy" White lived on a farm five miles from New Salem, and died about thirty years ago, in the eightieth year of his age; William Green was father of William G. Greene, Lincoln's associate in Offutt's store; and as to Bowling Green, more is said elsewhere. In the following three or four years, very few elections were held in New Salem at which Lincoln was not a clerk. It is a somewhat singular fact that Lincoln, though clerk of this election, is not recorded as voting.

To the Travelling Public.
FOUR HORSE COACH.
FROM SPRINGFIELD TO THE YELLOW BANKS.

VIA Sangamotown, New Salem, Petersburgh, Huron, Havana, Lewistown, Canton, Knoxville, Monmouth, to the Yellow Banks.

Leave Springfield every Wednesday morning at 6 o'clock, arrive at Monmouth on Friday evenings at 6 o'clock, and at the Yellow Banks on the Mississippi, next day at 12 M. Return the same days to Monmouth, and arrive at Springfield on Tuesday evenings at 6 o'clock. Fare through to the Yellow Banks, nine dollars; way passengers six and a fourth cents per mile. Baggage at the risk of the owners. The proprietors have procured good carriages and horses, and careful drivers, and every attention will be paid to the comfort and convenience of passengers.

The country through which this coach passes is well worthy the attention of emigrants. The patronage of the public is solicited for this new enterprize.

April 30.—34   TRACY & RENY.

A STAGE-COACH ADVERTISEMENT, 1834.

This advertisement appeared in the "Sangamo Journal" in April, 1834, and held a place in the paper through the next three years. As the "Four Horse Coach" ran through Sangamontown and New Salem, it doubtless had Lincoln as a passenger now and then; but not often, probably, for the fare from New Salem to Springfield was one dollar and twenty-five cents, and walking, or riding upon a borrowed horse, must generally have been preferred by Lincoln to so costly a mode of travelling.

crockery, a few pairs of shoes (not many), some farming implements, and the like. Whiskey, of course, was a necessary part of their stock. I remember one transaction in particular which I had with them. I sold the firm a load of wheat, which they turned over to the mill." Mr. Potter, who remembers the morning when Lincoln, then a stranger on his way to New Salem, stopped at his father's house and ate breakfast, knows less about the store, but says: "It was a grocery, and they sold whiskey, of course." Thomas Watkins says that the store contained "a little candy, tobacco, sugar, and coffee, and the like;" though Mr. Watkins, being then a young boy, and living a mile in the country, was not a frequent visitor at the store.

CHAPTER XV.

VEN after the license was granted, however, business was not so brisk in Berry and Lincoln's store that the junior partner did not welcome an appointment as postmaster which he received in May, 1833. The appointment of a Whig by a Democratic administration seems to have been made without comment. "The office was too insignificant to make his politics an objection," say the autobiographical notes. The duties of the new office were not arduous, for letters were few, and their comings far between. At that date the mails were carried by four-horse post-coaches from city to city, and on horseback from central points into the country towns. The rates of postage were high. A single-sheet letter carried thirty miles or under cost six cents; thirty to eighty miles, ten cents; eighty to one hundred and fifty miles, twelve and one-half cents; one hundred and fifty to four hundred miles, eighteen and one-half cents; over four hundred miles, twenty-five cents. A copy of this magazine sent from New York to New Salem would have cost fully twenty-five cents. The mail was irregular in coming as well as light in its contents. Though supposed to arrive twice a week, it sometimes happened that a fortnight or more passed without any mail. Under these conditions the New Salem post-office was not a serious care.

A large number of the patrons of the office lived in the country—many of them miles away—but generally Lincoln delivered the letters at their doors. These letters he would carefully place in the crown of his hat, and distribute them from house to house. Thus it was in a measure true that he kept the New Salem post-office in his hat. The habit of carrying papers in his hat clung to Lincoln; for, many years later, when he was a practising lawyer in Springfield, he apologized for failing to

BERRY AND LINCOLN'S STORE IN 1895.—NOW FIRST PUBLISHED.

From a recent photograph by C. S. McCullough, Petersburg, Illinois. The little frame store building occupied by Berry and Lincoln at New Salem is now standing at Petersburg, Illinois, in the rear of L. W. Bishop's gun-shop. Its history after 1834 is somewhat obscure, but there is no reason for doubting its identity. According to tradition it was bought by Robert Bishop, the father of the present owner, about 1835, from Mr. Lincoln himself ; but it is difficult to reconcile this legend with the sale of the store to the Trent brothers, unless, upon the flight of the latter from the country and the closing of the store, the building, through the leniency of creditors, was allowed to revert to Mr. Lincoln, in which event he no doubt sold it at the first opportunity, and applied the proceeds to the payment of the debts of the firm. When Mr. Bishop bought the store building, he removed it to Petersburg. It is said that the removal was made in part by Lincoln himself ; that the job was first undertaken by one of the Bales, but that, encountering some difficulty, he called upon Lincoln to assist him, which Lincoln did. The structure was first set up adjacent to Mr. Bishop's house, and converted into a gun-shop. Later it was removed to a place on the public square ; and soon after the breaking out of the late war, Mr. Bishop, erecting a new building, pushed Lincoln's store into the back yard, and there it still stands. Soon after the assassination of Mr. Lincoln, the front door was presented to some one in Springfield, and has long since been lost sight of. It is remembered by Mr. Bishop that in this door there was an opening for the reception of letters—a circumstance of importance as tending to establish the genuineness of the building, when it is remembered that Lincoln was postmaster while he kept the store. The structure, as it stands to-day, is about eighteen feet long, twelve feet in width, and ten feet in height. The back room, however, has disappeared, so that the building as it stood when occupied by Berry and Lincoln was somewhat longer. Of the original building there only remain the frame-work, the black walnut weather-boarding on the front end, and the ceiling of sycamore boards. One entire side has been torn away by relic-hunters. In recent years the building has been used as a sort of store-room. Just after a big fire in Petersburg some time ago, the city council condemned the Lincoln store building and ordered it demolished. Under this order a portion of one side was torn down, when Mr. Bishop persuaded the city authorities to desist, upon giving a guarantee that if Lincoln's store ever caught fire, he would be responsible for any loss which might ensue.

LINCOLN EARLY IN 1861.—PROBABLY THE EARLIEST PORTRAIT SHOWING HIM WITH A BEARD.

From a photograph in the collection of H. W. Fay of De Kalb, Illinois, taken probably in Springfield early in 1861. It is supposed to have been the first, or at least one of the first, portraits made of Mr. Lincoln after he began to wear a beard. As is well known, his face was smooth until about the end of 1860; and when he first allowed his beard to grow, it became a topic of newspaper comment, and even of caricature. A pretty story relating to Lincoln's adoption of a beard is more or less familiar. A letter written to the authors of this Life, under date of December 6, 1895, by Mrs. Grace Bedell Billings, tells this story, of which she herself as a little girl was the heroine, in a most charming way:

DELPHOS, KANSAS, *December 6, 1895.*

In reply to your letter of recent date inquiring about the incident of my childhood and connected with Mr. Lincoln, I would say that at the time of his first nomination to the Presidency I was a child of eleven years, living with my parents in Chautauqua County, New York.

My father was an ardent Republican, and possessed of a profound admiration for the character of

answer a letter promptly, by explaining: "When I received your letter I put it in my old hat, and buying a new one the next day, the old one was set aside, and so the letter was lost sight of for a time."

But whether the mail was delivered by the postmaster him-

the grand man who was the choice of his party. We younger children accepted his opinions with unquestioning faith, and listened with great delight to the anecdotes of his life current at that time, and were particularly interested in reading of the difficulties he encountered in getting an education. So much did it appeal to our childish imaginations that *we* were firmly persuaded that if we could only study our lessons prone before the glow and cheer of an open fire in a great fireplace, *we* too might rise to heights which now we could never attain. My father brought to us, one day, a large poster, and my mind still holds a recollection of its crude, coarse work and glaring colors. About the edges were grouped in unadorned and exaggerated ugliness the pictures of our former Presidents, and in the midst of them were the faces of "Lincoln and Hamlin," surrounded by way of a frame with a rail fence. We are all familiar with the strong and rugged face of Mr. Lincoln; the deep lines about the mouth, and the eyes have much the same sorrowful expression in all the pictures I have seen of him. I think I must have felt a certain disappointment, for I said to my mother that he would look much nicer if he wore whiskers; and straightway gave him the benefit of my opinion in a letter, describing the poster, and hinting, rather broadly, that his appearance might be improved if he would let his whiskers grow. Not wishing to wound his feelings, I added that the rail fence around his picture looked real pretty! I also asked him if he had any little girl, and if so, and he was too busy to write and tell me what he thought about it, if he would not let her do so; and ended by assuring him I meant to try my best to induce two erring brothers of the Democratic faith to cast their votes for him. I think the circumstance would have speedily passed from my mind but for the fact that I confided to an elder sister that I had written to Mr. Lincoln, and had she not expressed a doubt as to whether I had addressed him properly. To prove that I had, and was not as ignorant as she thought me, I rewrote the address for her inspection: "*Hon. Abraham Lincoln Esquire.*"

My mortification at the laughter and ridicule excited was somewhat relieved by my mother's remarking that "there would be no mistake as to whom the letter belonged." The reply to my poor little letter came in due time, and the following is a copy of the original, which is *still in my possession.*

"*Private.*
"SPRINGFIELD, ILLINOIS, *October* 19, 1860.
"MISS GRACE BEDELL.

"*My Dear little Miss:*—Your very agreeable letter of the 15th inst. is received. I regret the necessity of saying I have no daughter. I have three sons; one seventeen, one nine, and one seven years of age. They, with their mother, constitute my whole family. As to the whiskers, having never worn any, do you not think people would call it a piece of silly affectation if I were to begin wearing them now? Your very sincere well-wisher,

"A. LINCOLN."

Probably the frankness of the child appealed to the humorous side of his nature, for the suggestion was acted upon. After the election, and on his journey from Springfield to Washington, he inquired of Hon. G. W. Patterson, who was one of the party who accompanied him on that memorable trip, and who was a resident of our town, if he knew of a family bearing the name of Bedell. Mr. Patterson replying in the affirmative, Mr. Lincoln said he had "received a letter from a little girl called Grace Bedell, advising me to wear whiskers, as she thought it would improve my looks." He said the character of the "letter was so unique, and so different from the many self-seeking and threatening ones he was daily receiving, that it came to him as a relief and a pleasure." When the train reached Westfield, Mr. Lincoln made a short speech from the platform of the car, and in conclusion said he had a correspondent there, relating the circumstance and giving my name, and if she were present would like to see her. I was present, but in the crowd had neither seen nor heard the speaker; but a gentleman helped me forward, and Mr. Lincoln stepped down to the platform where I stood, shook my hand, kissed me, and said: "You see I let these whiskers grow for you, Grace." The crowd cheered, Mr. Lincoln reëntered the car, and I ran quickly home, looking at and speaking to no one, with a much dilapidated bunch of roses in my hand, which I had hoped might be passed up to Mr. Lincoln with some other flowers which were to be presented, but which in my confusion I had forgotten. Gentle and genial, simple and warm-hearted, how full of anxiety must have been his life in the days which followed! These words seem to fitly describe him: "A man of sorrows and acquainted with grief."   Very sincerely,

GRACE BEDELL BILLINGS.

FACSIMILE OF A TAVERN LICENSE ISSUED TO BERRY AND LINCOLN MARCH 6, 1833, BY THE COUNTY COM-
MISSIONERS' COURT OF SANGAMON COUNTY.

The only tavern in New Salem in 1833 was that kept by James Rutledge—a two-story log structure of
five rooms, standing just across the street from Berry and Lincoln's store. Here Lincoln boarded. It
seems entirely probable that he may have had an ambition to get into the tavern business, and that he and
Berry obtained a license with that end in view, possibly hoping to make satisfactory terms for the purchase of the Rutledge hostelry. The tavern of sixty years ago, besides answering the purposes of the
modern hotel, was the dramshop of the frontier. The business was one which, in Illinois, the law strictly
regulated. Tavern-keepers were required to pay a license fee, and to give bonds to insure their good
behavior. Minors were not to be harbored, nor did the law permit liquor to be sold to them ; and the sale
to slaves of any liquors " or strong drink, mixed or unmixed, either within or without doors," was likewise
forbidden. Nor could the poor Indian get any "fire-water" at the tavern or the grocery. If a tavern-
keeper violated the law, two-thirds of the fine assessed against him went to the poor people of the county. The
Rutledge tavern was the only one at New Salem of which we have any authentic account. There were
other landlords besides Mr. Rutledge ; but nothing can be more certain than that Lincoln was not one of
them. The few surviving inhabitants of the vanished village, and of the country round about, have a clear
recollection of Berry and Lincoln's store ; but not one has been found with the faintest remembrance of a
tavern kept by Lincoln, or by Berry, or by both. Stage passengers jolting into New Salem sixty-two years
ago must, if Lincoln was inn-keeper, have partaken of his hospitality by the score ; but if they did, they
all died many, many years ago, or have all maintained an unaccountable and most perplexing silence.

self, or the recipient came to the store to inquire, " Anything
for me ? " it was the habit " to stop and visit awhile." He who
received a letter read it and told the contents ; if he had a newspaper, usually the postmaster could tell him in advance what it
contained, for one of the perquisites of the early postmaster was
the privilege of reading all printed matter before delivering it.
Every day, then, Lincoln's acquaintance in New Salem, through
his position as postmaster, became more intimate.

A NEW OPENING.

As the summer of 1833 went on, the condition of the store became more and more unsatisfactory. As the position of post-master brought in only a small revenue, Lincoln was forced to take any odd work he could get. He helped in other stores in the town, split rails, and looked after the mill; but all this yielded only a scant and uncertain support, and when in the fall he had an opportunity to learn surveying, he accepted it eagerly.

The condition of affairs in Illinois in the thirties made a de-mand for the services of surveyors. The immigration had been phenomenal. There were thousands of farms to be surveyed and thousands of corners to be located. Speculators bought up large tracts, and mapped out cities on paper. It was years before the first railroad was built in Illinois, and, as all inland travelling was on horseback or in the stage-coach, each year hundreds of miles of wagon road were opened through woods and swamps and prairies. As the county of Sangamon was large, and eagerly sought by immigrants, the county surveyor in 1833, one John Calhoun, needed deputies ; but in a country so new it was no easy matter to find men with the requisite capacity.

With Lincoln, Calhoun had little, if any, personal acquaint-ance, for they lived twenty miles apart. Lincoln, however, had made himself known by his meteoric race for the legislature in 1832, and Calhoun had heard of him as an honest, intelligent, and trustworthy young man. One day he sent word to Lincoln by Pollard Simmons, who lived in the New Salem neighborhood, that he had decided to appoint him a deputy surveyor if he would accept the position.

Going into the woods, Simmons found Lincoln engaged in his old occupation of making rails. The two sat down together on a log, and Simmons told Lincoln what Calhoun had said. It was a surprise to Lincoln. Calhoun was a "Jackson man ;" he was for Clay. What did he know about surveying, and why should a Democratic official offer him a position of any kind ? He im-mediately went to Springfield, and had a talk with Calhoun. He would not accept the appointment, he said, unless he had the assurance that it involved no political obligation, and that he might continue to express his political opinions as freely and frequently as he chose. This assurance was given. The only difficulty then in the way was the fact that he knew absolutely nothing of surveying. But Calhoun, of course, understood this, and agreed that he should have time to learn.

With the promptness of action with which he always undertook anything he had to do, he procured Flint and Gibson's treatise on surveying, and sought Mentor Graham for help. At a sacrifice of some time, the schoolmaster aided him to a partial mastery of the intricate subject. Lincoln worked literally day and night, sitting up night after night until the crowing of the cock warned him of the approaching dawn. So hard did he study that his friends were greatly concerned at his haggard face. But in six weeks he had mastered all the books within reach relating to the subject—a task which, under ordinary circumstances, would hardly have been achieved in as many months. Reporting to Calhoun for duty (greatly to the amazement of that gentleman), he was at once assigned to the territory in the northwest part of the county, and the first work he did of which there is any authentic record was in January, 1834. In that month he surveyed a piece of land for Russell Godby, dating the certificate January 14, 1834, and signing it "J. Calhoun, S. S. C., by A. Lincoln."

Lincoln was frequently employed in laying out public roads, being selected for that purpose by the County Commissioners' Court. So far as can be learned from the official records, the first road he surveyed was "from Musick's Ferry, on Salt Creek, via New Salem, to the county line in the direction of Jacksonville." For this he was allowed fifteen dollars for five days' service, and two dollars and fifty cents for a plat of the new road. The next road he surveyed, according to the records, was that leading from Athens to Sangamon town. This was reported to the County Commissioners' Court, November 4, 1834. But road surveying was only a small portion of his work. He was more frequently employed by private individuals.

SURVEYING WITH A GRAPEVINE.

According to tradition, when he first took up the business he was too poor to buy a chain, and, instead, used a long, straight grapevine. Probably this is a myth, though surveyors who had experience in the early days say it may be true. The chains commonly used at that time were made of iron. Constant use wore away and weakened the links, and it was no unusual thing

THE STATE-HOUSE AT VANDALIA, ILLINOIS.—NOW USED AS A COURT-HOUSE.

Vandalia was the State capital of Illinois for twenty years, and three different State-houses were built and occupied there. The first, a two-story frame structure, was burned down December 9, 1823. The second was a brick building, and was erected at a cost of twelve thousand, three hundred and eighty-one dollars and fifty cents, of which the citizens of Vandalia contributed three thousand dollars. The agitation for the removal of the capital to Springfield began in 1833, and in the summer of 1836 the people of Vandalia, becoming alarmed at the prospect of their little city's losing its prestige as the seat of the State government, tore down the old capitol (much complaint being made about its condition), and put up a new one at a cost of sixteen thousand dollars. The tide was too great to be checked ; but after the "Long Nine" had secured the passage of the bill taking the capital to Springfield, the money which the Vandalia people had expended was refunded. The State-house shown in this picture was the third and last one. In it Lincoln served as a legislator. Ceasing to be a capitol July 4, 1839, it was converted into a court-house for Fayette County, and is still so used.

for a chain to lengthen six inches after a year's use. "And a good grapevine," to use the words of a veteran surveyor, "would give quite as satisfactory results as one of those old-fashioned chains."

Lincoln's surveys had the extraordinary merit of being correct. Much of the government work had been rather indifferently done, or the government corners had been imperfectly preserved, and there were frequent disputes between adjacent landowners about boundary lines. Frequently Lincoln was called upon in such cases to find the corner in controversy. His verdict was

DANIEL GREEN BURNER, BERRY AND LINCOLN'S CLERK.

From a recent photograph. Mr. Burner lived at New Salem from 1829 to 1834. Lincoln for many months lodged with his father, Isaac Burner. He now lives on a farm near Galesburg, Illinois. Mr. Burner is over eighty years of age.

THE REV. JOHN M. CAMERON, A NEW SALEM FRIEND OF LINCOLN.

From a photograph in the possession of the Hon. W. J. Orendorff of Canton, Illinois. John M. Cameron, a Cumberland Presbyterian minister, and a devout, sincere, and courageous man, was held in the highest esteem by his neighbors. Yet, according to Daniel Green Burner, Berry and Lincoln's clerk—and the fact is mentioned merely as illustrating a universal custom among the pioneers

—" John Cameron always kept a barrel of whiskey in the house." He was a powerful man physically, and a typical frontiersman. He was born in Kentucky in 1791, and, with his wife, moved to Illinois in 1815. He settled in Sangamon County in 1818, and in 1829 took up his abode in a cabin on a hill overlooking the Sangamon River, and, with James Rutledge, founded the town of New Salem. According to tradition, Lincoln for a time lived with the Camerons. In the early thirties they moved to Fulton County, Illinois ; then, in 1841 or 1842, to Iowa ; and finally, in 1849, to California. In California they lived to a ripe old age—Mrs. Cameron dying in 1875, and her husband following her three years later. They had twelve children, eleven of whom were girls. Mr. Cameron is said to have officiated at the funeral of Ann Rutledge in 1835.

JAMES SHORT, WHO SAVED LINCOLN'S HORSE AND SURVEYING INSTRUMENTS FROM A CREDITOR.

From a photograph taken at Jacksonville, Illinois, about thirty years ago. James Short lived on Sand Ridge, a few miles north of New Salem. When Lincoln's horse and surveying instruments were levied upon by a creditor and sold, Mr. Short bought them in, and made Lincoln a present of them. Lincoln, when President, made his old friend an Indian agent in California. Mr. Short died in Iowa many years ago. His acquaintance with Lincoln began in rather an interesting way. His sister, who lived in New Salem, had made Lincoln a pair of jeans trousers. The material supplied by Lincoln was scant, and the trousers came out conspicuously short in the legs. One day when James Short was visiting with his sister, he pointed to a man walking down the street, and asked, " Who is that man in the short breeches ? " " That is Lincoln." And Mr. Short went out and introduced himself.

A GROUP OF LINCOLN'S OLD NEIGHBORS.

SAMUEL HILL, AT WHOSE STORE LINCOLN KEPT
THE POST-OFFICE.

SQUIRE COLEMAN SMOOT, ONE OF LINCOLN'S FIRST
POLITICAL SUPPORTERS.

Coleman Smoot was born in Virginia, February 13, 1794 ; removed to Kentucky when a child ; married Rebecca Wright, March 17, 1817 ; came to Illinois in 1831, and lived on a farm across the Sangamon River from New Salem until his death, March 21, 1876. Lincoln met him for the first time in Offutt's store in 1831. "Smoot," said Lincoln, "I am disappointed in you ; I expected to see a man as ugly as old Probst," referring to a man reputed to be the homeliest in the county. "And I am disappointed," replied Smoot ; "I had expected to see a good-looking man when I saw you." After Lincoln's election to the legislature in 1834, he called on Smoot and said: "I want to buy some clothes and fix up a little, and I want you to loan me two hundred dollars." The loan was cheerfully made, and, of course, was subsequently repaid.

From an old daguerreotype. Samuel Hill was among the earliest inhabitants of New Salem. He opened a general store there in partnership with John McNeill—the John McNeill who became betrothed to Ann Rutledge, and whose real name was afterwards discovered to be John McNamar. When McNeill left New Salem and went East, Mr. Hill became sole proprietor of the store. He also owned the carding machine at New Salem. Lincoln, after going out of the grocery business, made his headquarters at Samuel Hill's store. There he kept the post-office, entertained the loungers, and on busy days helped Mr. Hill wait on customers. Mr. Hill is said to have once courted Ann Rutledge himself, but he did not receive the encouragement which was bestowed upon his partner, McNeill. In 1835 he married Miss Parthenia W. Nance, who still lives at Petersburg. In 1839 he moved his store to Petersburg, and died there in 1857.

MARY ANN RUTLEDGE, MOTHER OF ANN MAYES RUTLEDGE.

From an old tintype. Mary Ann Rutledge was the wife of James Rutledge and the mother of Ann She was born October 21, 1787, and reared in Kentucky. She lived to be ninety-one years of age, dying in Iowa, December 26, 1878. The Rutledges left New Salem in 1833 or 1834, moving to a farm a few miles northward. On this farm Ann Rutledge died, August 25, 1835 ; and here also, three months later (December 3, 1835), died her father, broken-hearted, no doubt, by the bereavement. In the following year the family moved to Fulton County, Illinois, and some three years later to Birmingham, Iowa. Of James Rutledge there is no portrait in existence. He was born in South Carolina, May 11, 1781. He and his sons, John and David, served in the Black Hawk War.

A GROUP OF LINCOLN'S OLD NEIGHBORS.

invariably the end of the dispute, so general was the confidence in his honesty and skill. Some of these old corners located by him are still in existence. The people of Petersburg proudly remember that they live in a town which was laid out by Lincoln. This he did in 1836, and it was the work of several weeks.

Lincoln's pay as a surveyor was three dollars a day, more than he had ever before earned. Compared with the compensation for like services nowadays, it seems small enough ; but at that time it was really princely. The governor of the State received a salary of only one thousand dollars a year, the Secretary of State six hundred dollars, and good board and lodging could be obtained for one dollar a week. But even three dollars a day did not enable him to meet all his financial obligations. The heavy debts of the store hung over him. He was obliged to help his father's family in Coles County. The long distances he had to travel in his new employment had made it necessary to buy a horse, and for it he had gone into debt.

"My father," says Thomas Watkins of Petersburg, "sold Lincoln the horse, and my recollection is that Lincoln agreed to pay him fifty dollars for it. Lincoln was a little slow in making the payments, and after he had paid all but ten dollars, my father, who was a high-strung man, became impatient, and sued him for the balance. Lincoln, of course, did not deny the debt, and raised the money and paid it. I do not often tell this," Mr. Watkins adds, "because I have always thought there never was such a man as Lincoln, and I have always been sorry father sued him."

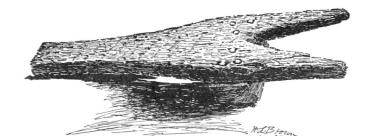

BOOT-JACK MADE AND USED BY LINCOLN WHEN A YOUNG MAN.

From Libby Prison Museum, Chicago, Illinois. By permission of C. F. Gunther.

FACSIMILE OF A LETTER AND RECEIPT WRITTEN BY LINCOLN WHILE POSTMASTER AT NEW SALEM.

Reproduced by permission from "Menard-Salem-Lincoln Souvenir Album," Petersburg, 1893.

CHAPTER XVI.

BUSINESS REVERSES.—LINCOLN FOR THE SECOND TIME A
CANDIDATE FOR THE LEGISLATURE.—IS ELECTED.

BETWEEN his duties as deputy surveyor and postmaster, Lincoln had little leisure for the store, and its management passed into the hands of Berry. The stock of groceries was on the wane. The numerous obligations of the firm were maturing, with no money to meet them. Both members of the firm, in the face of such obstacles, lost courage ; and when, early in 1834,

Alexander and William Trent asked if the store was for sale, an affirmative answer was eagerly given. A price was agreed upon, and the sale was made. Now, neither Alexander Trent nor his brother had any money ; but as Berry and Lincoln had bought without money, it seemed only fair that they should be willing to sell on the same terms. Accordingly the notes of the Trent brothers were accepted for the purchase price, and the store was turned over to the new owners. But about the time their notes fell due the Trent brothers disappeared. The few groceries in the store were seized by creditors, and the doors were closed, never to be opened again.

Misfortunes now crowded upon Lincoln. His late partner, Berry, soon reached the end of his wild career, and one morning a farmer from the Rock Creek neighborhood drove into New Salem with the news that he was dead.

The appalling debt which had accumulated was thrown upon Lincoln's shoulders. It was then too common a fashion among men who became deluged in debt to "clear out," in the expressive language of the pioneer, as the Trents had done ; but this was not Lincoln's way. He quietly settled down among the men he owed, and promised to pay them. For fifteen years he carried this burden—a load which he cheerfully and manfully bore, but one so heavy that he habitually spoke of it as the "national debt." Talking once of it to a friend, Lincoln said: "That debt was the greatest obstacle I have ever met in life. I had no way of speculating, and could not earn money except by labor ; and to earn by labor eleven hundred dollars, besides my living, seemed the work of a lifetime. There was, however, but one way. I went to the creditors, and told them that if they would let me alone, I would give them all I could earn over my living, as fast as I could earn it." As late as 1848, so we are informed by Mr. Herndon, Mr. Lincoln, then a member of Congress, sent home money, saved from his salary, to be applied on these obligations. All the notes, with interest at the high rates then prevailing, were at last paid.

With a single exception, Lincoln's creditors seem to have been lenient. One of the notes given by him came into the hands of a Mr. Van Bergen, who, when it fell due, brought suit. The amount of the judgment was more than Lincoln could pay, and his personal effects were levied upon. These consisted of his horse, saddle and bridle, and surveying instruments. James

New Salem, Ills
Nov 3 1835.

Messrs
Your subscriber at this place
John C. Vance, is dead; and no
person takes the paper from the
office

Respectfully,
A. Lincoln P.M.

Blair & Rives.

FACSIMILE OF A LETTER WRITTEN BY LINCOLN WHILE POSTMASTER AT NEW SALEM.—HITHERTO UNPUBLISHED.

From the collection of Mr. C. F. Gunther of Chicago.

JOHN CALHOUN, UNDER WHOM LINCOLN LEARNED SUR-
VEYING.

From a steel engraving in the possession of R. W. Diller,
Springfield, Illinois. John Calhoun was born in Boston,
Massachusetts, October 14, 1806. In 1830 he removed to
Springfield, Illinois, and after serving in the Black Hawk
War was appointed surveyor of Sangamon County. He was
a Democratic Representative in 1838 ; Democratic presidential
elector in 1844 ; candidate for Governor before the Democratic
State Convention in 1846 ; Mayor of Springfield in 1849, 1850,
and 1851. In 1854, President Pierce appointed him Surveyor-
General of Kansas, and he became conspicuous in Kansas
politics. He was president of the Lecompton Convention.
He died at St. Joseph, Missouri, October 25, 1859. Mr. Frederick Hawn, who was his boyhood friend, and afterward
married a sister of Calhoun's wife, is now living at Leaven-
worth, Kansas, at the age of eighty-five years. In an interesting letter to the writer he says : " It has been related that
Calhoun induced Lincoln to study surveying in order to become his deputy. Presuming that he was ready to graduate
and receive his commission, he called on Calhoun, then living with his father-in-law, Seth R. Cutter, on Upper Lick
Creek. After the interview was concluded, Mr. Lincoln,
about to depart, remarked : 'Calhoun, I am entirely unable
to repay you for your generosity at present. All that I have
you see on me, except a quarter of a dollar in my pocket.'
This is a family tradition. However, my wife, then a miss of
sixteen, says, while I am writing this sketch, that she distinctly remembers this interview. After Lincoln was gone
she says she and her sister, Mrs. Calhoun, commenced making jocular remarks about his uncanny appearance, in the
presence of Calhoun, to which in substance he made this
rejoinder: 'For all that, he is no common man.' My wife
believes these were the exact words."

Short, a well-to-do farmer living on Sand Ridge, a few miles north of New Salem, heard of the trouble w h i c h had befallen his young friend. Without advising Lincoln of his plans, he attended the sale, bought in the horse and surveying instruments for one hundred and twenty dollars, and turned them over to their former owner. By this kind act of "Uncle Jimmy," the young surveyor was enabled to continue his business.

Lincoln never forgot a benefactor. He not only repaid the money with interest, but nearly thirty years later remembered the kindness in a most substantial way. After Lincoln left New Salem, financial reverses came to James Short, and he removed to the far West to seek his fortune anew. Early in Lincoln's presidential term he heard that "Uncle J i m m y" was living in California. One day Mr. Short received a letter from Washington. Tearing it open, he read the gratifying announcement that he had been commissioned an Indian agent.

LINCOLN'S SURVEYING INSTRUMENTS.

Photographed for this work. After Lincoln gave up surveying, he sold his instruments to John B. Gum, afterward county surveyor of Menard County. Mr. Gum kept them until a few years ago, when he presented the instruments to the Lincoln Monument Association, and they are now on exhibition at the monument in Springfield, Illinois.

THE KINDNESS SHOWN LINCOLN IN NEW SALEM.

The kindness of Mr. Short was not exceptional in Lincoln's New Salem career. When the store had "winked out," as he put it, and the post-office had been left without headquarters, one of his neighbors, Samuel Hill, invited the homeless post-master into his store. There was hardly a man or woman in the community who would not have been glad to do as much. It was a simple recognition of Lincoln's friendliness to them. He was what they called "obliging"—a man who instinctively did the thing which he saw would help another, no matter how trivial or homely it was. In the home of Rowan Herndon, where he had boarded when he first came to the town, he had made himself loved by his care of the children. "He nearly always had one of them around with him," says Mr. Herndon. In the Rutledge tavern, where he afterwards lived, the land-lord told with appreciation how, when his house was full, Lincoln gave up his bed, went to the store, and slept on the counter, his pillow a web of calico. If a traveller "stuck in the mud" in New Salem's one street, Lincoln was always the first to help pull out the wheel. The widows praised him because he "chopped their wood;" the overworked, because he was always ready to give them a lift. It was the spontaneous, unobtrusive helpful-ness of the man's nature which endeared him to everybody, and which inspired a general desire to do all possible in return.

There are many tales told of homely service rendered him, even
by the hard-working farmers' wives around New Salem.　There
was not one of them who did not gladly "put on a plate" for
Abe Lincoln when he appeared, or did not darn or mend for
him when she knew he needed it.　Hannah Armstrong, the wife of
the hero of Clary's Grove, made him one of her family.　"Abe
would come out to our house," she said, "drink milk, eat mush,
cornbread and butter, bring the children candy, and rock the
cradle while I got him something to eat. 　. 　. 　. 　Has stayed at
our house two or three weeks at a time."　Lincoln's pay for his
first piece of surveying came in the shape of two buckskins, and
it was Hannah who "foxed" them on his trousers.

His relations were equally friendly in the better homes of the
community ; even at the minister, the Rev. John Cameron's, he
was perfectly at home, and Mrs. Cameron was by him affection-
ately called "Aunt Polly."　It was not only his kindly service
which made Lincoln loved ; it was his sympathetic comprehen-
sion of the duties and joys and sorrows and interests of the people.
Whether it was Jack Armstrong and his wrestling, Hannah and
her babies, Kelso and his fishing and poetry, the schoolmaster
and his books—with one and all he was at home.　He possessed
in an extraordinary degree the power of entering into the interests
of others, a power found only in reflective, unselfish natures endowed with a humorous sense of human foibles, and with great
tenderness of heart.　Men and women amused Lincoln, but so
long as they were sincere he loved them and sympathized with
them.　He was human in the best sense of that fine word.

LINCOLN'S ACQUAINTANCE IN SANGAMON COUNTY IS EXTENDED.

Now that the store was closed and his surveying increased,
Lincoln had an excellent opportunity to extend his acquaintance,
for he was travelling about the country.　Everywhere he won
friends.　The surveyor, naturally, was respected for his calling's
sake ; but the new deputy surveyor was admired for his friendly
ways, his willingness to lend a hand indoors as well as out, his
learning, his ambition, his independence.　Throughout the
county he began to be regarded as "a right smart young man."
Some of his associates appear even to have comprehended his
peculiarly great character, and dimly to have foreseen a splendid

LINCOLN IN THE SUMMER OF 1860.—HITHERTO UNPUBLISHED.

From a copy (made by E. A. Bromley of the Minneapolis "Journal" staff) of a photograph owned by Mrs. Cyrus Aldrich, whose husband, now dead, was a Congressman from Minnesota. We owe the photograph to the courtesy of Mr. Daniel Fish of Minneapolis. In the summer of 1860 Mr. M. C. Tuttle, a photographer of St. Paul, wrote to Mr. Lincoln, requesting that he have a negative taken and sent to him for local use in the campaign. The request was granted, but the negative was broken in transit. On learning of the accident, Mr. Lincoln sat again, and with the second negative he sent a jocular note wherein he referred to the fact, disclosed by the picture, that in the interval he had "got a new coat." A few copies of the picture were made by Mr. Tuttle, and distributed among the Republican editors of the State. It has never before been reproduced. Mrs. Aldrich's copy was presented to her by William H. Seward when he was entertained at the Aldrich homestead (now the Minneapolis City Hospital) in September, 1860. A fine copy of this same photograph is owned by Mr. Ward Monroe of Jersey City, New Jersey.

future. "Often," says Daniel Green Burner, Berry and Lincoln's clerk in the grocery, "I have heard my brother-in-law, Dr. Duncan, say he would not be surprised if some day Abe Lincoln got to be Governor of Illinois. Lincoln," Mr. Burner adds, "was thought to know a little more than anybody else among the young people. He was a good debater, and liked it. He read much, and seemed never to forget anything."

Lincoln was fully conscious of his popularity, and it seemed to him in 1834 that he could safely venture to try again for the legislature. Accordingly he announced himself as a candidate, spending much of the summer of 1834 in electioneering. It was a repetition of what he had done in 1832, though on the larger scale made possible by wider acquaintance. In company with the other candidates, he rode up and down the county, making speeches at the public sales, in shady groves, now and then in a log schoolhouse. In his speeches he soon distinguished himself by the amazing candor with which he dealt with all questions, and by his curious blending of audacity and humility. Wherever he saw a crowd of men he joined them, and he never failed to adapt himself to their point of view in asking for votes. If the degree of physical strength was their test for a candidate, he was ready to lift a weight, or wrestle with the countryside champion; if the amount of grain a man could cradle would recommend him, he seized the cradle and showed the swath he could cut. The campaign was well conducted, for in August he was elected one of the four assemblymen from Sangamon. The

LINCOLN'S SADDLE-BAGS.—PHOTOGRAPHED FOR THIS BIOGRAPHY.

These saddle-bags, now in the Lincoln Monument at Springfield, are said to have been used by Lincoln while he was a surveyor.

vote at this election stood : Dawson, 1390 ; Lincoln, 1376 ; Carpenter, 1170 ; Stuart, 1164.

With one exception, the biographers of Lincoln have given
him the first place on the ticket in 1834.   He really stood second
in order.   Herndon gives the correct vote, although he is in error
in saying that the chief authority he quotes, a document owned
by Dr. A. W. French of Springfield, Illinois, is an "official
return."   It is a statement, made out in Lincoln's writing, and
certified to by the county clerk, of the total number of votes
cast in the whole county for each of the several candidates for
the legislature.   The official returns are on file in the Springfield
court-house.

VIEW OF THE SANGAMON RIVER NEAR NEW SALEM.

Reproduced, by permission, from " Menard-Salem-Lincoln Souvenir Album," Petersburg, Illinois, 1893.

CHAPTER XVII.

HE best thing which Lincoln did in the canvass of 1834 was not winning votes; it was coming to a determination to read law, not for pleasure, but as a business. In his autobiographical notes he says: "During the canvass, in a private conversation, Major John T. Stuart (one of his fellow-candidates) encouraged Abraham to study law. After the election he borrowed books of Stuart, took them home with him, and went at it in good earnest. He never studied with anybody." He seems to have thrown himself into the work with an almost impatient ardor. As he tramped back and forth from Springfield, twenty miles away, to get his law-books, he read sometimes forty pages or more on the

STEPHEN A. DOUGLAS.

Born at Brandon, Vermont, April 23, 1813 ; died in Chicago, June 3, 1861. Douglas learned a trade when a boy, but abandoned it to study law. Obliged to support himself, he went to Illinois in 1833, where he taught school until admitted to the bar. In 1835 he was elected State Attorney-General, but resigned at the end of the year, having been elected to the General Assembly. In 1837 he was appointed register of the land-office at Springfield ; in 1838 was defeated in a contest for Congress ; in 1840 was appointed Secretary of State ; in 1841 was elected judge of the Supreme Court of Illinois. From 1843 to 1846 he was in Congress, and for fourteen years after was a United States Senator. The Lincoln and Douglas debates took place in his last senatorial canvass. In 1860 Mr. Douglas was the Democratic candidate for President, and was defeated by Lincoln. He died in 1861.

REPORT OF A ROAD SURVEY BY LINCOLN.—HITHERTO UNPUBLISHED.

Photographed for this biography from the original, now on file in the County Clerk's office, Springfield, Illinois. The survey here reported was made in pursuance of an order of the County Commissioners' Court, September 1, 1834, in which Lincoln was designated as the surveyor.

way. Often he was seen wandering at random across the fields, repeating aloud the points in his last reading. The subject seemed never to be out of his mind. It was the great absorbing interest of his life. The rule he gave twenty years later to a young man who wanted to know how to become a lawyer, was the one he practised:

"Get books, and read and study them carefully. Begin with Blackstone's 'Commentaries,' and after reading carefully through, say twice, take up Chitty's 'Pleadings,' Greenleaf's 'Evidence,' and Story's 'Equity,' in succession. Work, work, work, is the main thing."

Having secured a book of legal forms, he was soon able to write deeds, contracts, and all sorts of legal instruments; and he was frequently called upon by his neighbors to perform services of this kind. " In 1834," says Daniel Green Burner, Berry and Lincoln's clerk, " 'my father, Isaac Burner, sold out to Henry Onstott, and he wanted a deed written. I knew how handy Lincoln was that way,

A MAP MADE BY LINCOLN OF A PIECE OF ROAD IN MENARD COUNTY, ILLINOIS.—HITHERTO UNPUBLISHED.

Photographed from the original for this biography. This map, which, as here reproduced, is about one-half the size of the original, accompanied Lincoln's report of the survey of a part of the road between Athens and Sangamon town. For making this map, Lincoln received fifty cents. He received three dollars for the day he spent in relocating the road. (See report, page 198.) The road evidently was located " on good ground," and was " necessary and proper," as the report says, for it is still the main travelled highway leading into the country south of Athens, Menard County.

and suggested that we get him. We found him sitting on a stump. 'All right,' said he, when informed what we wanted. 'If you will bring me a pen and ink and a piece of paper I will write it here.' I brought him these articles, and, picking up a shingle and putting it on his knee for a desk, he wrote out the deed.''

As there was no practising lawyer nearer than Springfield, Lincoln was often employed to act the part of advocate before the village squire, at that time Bowling Green. He realized that this experience was valuable, and never, so far as known, demanded or accepted a fee for his services in these petty cases.

Justice was sometimes administered in a summary way in Squire Green's court. Precedents and the venerable rules of law had little weight. The "Squire" took judicial notice of a great many facts, often going so far as to fill, simultaneously, the two functions of witness and court. But his decisions were generally just.

James McGrady Rutledge tells a story in which several of Lincoln's old friends figure, and which illustrates the legal practices of New Salem. "Jack Kelso," says Mr. Rutledge, "owned, or claimed to own, a white hog. It was also claimed by John Ferguson. The hog had often wandered around Bowling Green's place, and he was somewhat acquainted with it. Ferguson sued Kelso, and the case was tried before 'Squire' Green. The plaintiff produced two witnesses who testified positively that the hog belonged to him. Kelso had nothing to offer, save his own unsupported claim.

" ' Are there any more witnesses ? ' inquired the court.

"He was informed that there were no more.

" ' Well,' said 'Squire' Green, 'the two witnesses we have heard have sworn to a —— lie. I know this shoat, and I know it belongs to Jack Kelso. I therefore decide this case in his favor.' "

An extract from the record of the County Commissioners' Court illustrates the nature of the cases that came before the justice of the peace in Lincoln's day. It also shows the price put upon the privilege of working on Sunday, in 1832 :

" JANUARY 29, 1832.—Alexander Gibson found guilty of Sabbath-breaking, and fined 12½ cents. Fine paid into court.

" (Signed) EDWARD ROBINSON, J. P."

THE ILLINOIS ASSEMBLY OF 1834.

The session of the ninth Assembly began December 1, 1834, and Lincoln went to the capital, then Vandalia, seventy-five miles southeast of New Salem, on the Kaskaskia River, in time for the opening. Vandalia was a town which had been called into existence in 1820 especially to give the State government an abiding-place. Its very name had been chosen, it is said, because it "sounded well" for a State capital. As the tradition goes, while the commissioners were debating what they should call the town they were making, a wag suggested that it be named Vandalia, in honor of the Vandals, a tribe of Indians which, said he, had once lived on the borders of the Kaskaskia ; this, he argued, would conserve a local tradition while giving a euphonious title. The commissioners, pleased with so good a suggestion, adopted the name. When Lincoln first went to Vandalia it was a town of about eight hundred inhabitants ; its noteworthy features, according to Peck's "Gazetteer" of Illinois for 1834, being a brick court-house, a two-story brick edifice "used by State officers," "a neat framed house of worship for the Presbyterian Society, with a cupola and bell," "a framed meeting-house for the Methodist Society," three taverns, several stores, five lawyers, four physicians, a land-office, and two newspapers. It was a much larger town than Lincoln had ever lived in before, though he was familiar with Springfield, then twice as large as Vandalia, and he had seen the cities of the Mississippi.

The Assembly which he entered was composed of eighty-one members—twenty-six senators and fifty-five representatives. As a rule, these men were of Kentucky, Tennessee, or Virginia origin, with here and there a Frenchman. There were but few Eastern men, for there was still a strong prejudice in the State against Yankees. The close bargains and superior airs of the emigrants from New England contrasted so unpleasantly with the open-handed hospitality and the easy ways of the Southerners and French, that a pioneer's prospects were blasted at the start if he acted like a Yankee. A history of Illinois in 1837, published, evidently, to "boom" the State, cautioned the emigrant that if he began his life in Illinois by "affecting superior intelligence and virtue, and catechizing the people for their habits of plainness and simplicity, and their apparent want of

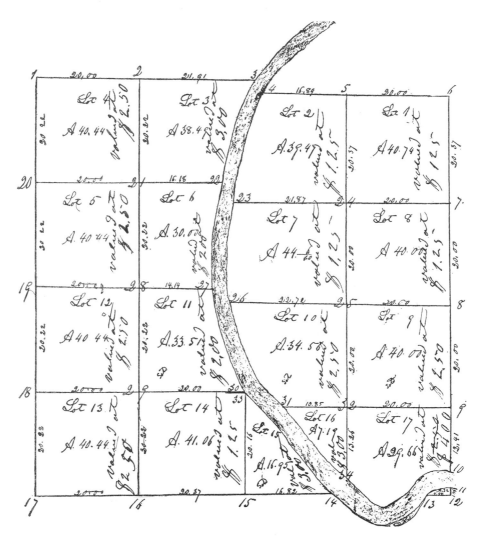

I certify that the foregoing are an accurate Plat and Field Notes for Section 16 in Township 17 North of Range 6 West of the 3rd Principal Meridian; as surveyed by me.

A. Lincoln
for J. M. Neale. S.S.C.

May 10th - 1836

SURVEY OF A SECTION OF LAND BY LINCOLN.—NOW

From the original, in the possession of Z. A. Enos, Springfield, Illinois. "The Sangamon River runs through this section," says Mr. Enos, himself a veteran surveyor, " and the section lines in the government survey were not extended across, but closed on the river, without any connection being made between the opposite marginal corners or lines ; and though shown on the government plats as being continuous straight east or west lines across the river, they were, in fact, surveyed by the government surveyor as represented by Mr. Lin-

Corners	Bearing trees	Diam	Course	Link Dist
1	W.Oak	18	N57W	132
2	W.Oak	24	S5W	66
3	W.Oak	12	S74W	19
4	Ash	14	N51S	55
5	Post & mound			
6	Elm	16	N86E	410
7	Post & mound			
8	Elm	16	S24W	41
9	Hick	6	S84W	25
10	S.Oak	36	N73E	16
11	Maple	7	S60W	21
12	Lucan	30	N26W	47
13	Lian	24	S0W	15
14	Cotton	10	S6W	30
15	W.Oak	10	N10W	37
16	W.Oak	3	N73E	8
17	Hick	12	S24W	58
18	Hick	3	N6E	9
19	B.Oak	32	S9E	79
20	Post & mound			
21	W.Oak	22	N84W	3
22	Elm	14	N44E	29
23	B.Oak	22	corner	
24	Post & mound			
25	Ash	24	N80W	4
26	Hick	12	corner	
27	Elm	15	corner	
28	B.Oak	12	S57E	23
29	Post & mound			
30	Lynn	11	N50E	20
31	Hick	14	N50W	17
32	Hick	8	N32W	8
33	W.Oak	22	corner	
34	Cotton	17	S25E	7

FIRST PUBLISHED.

coln's plat." This plat is also interesting as "showing," as Mr. Enos says, "how Illinois lands were valued at that date, as indicated by the value of the several lots in the school section, as determined by the trustees, and marked by them on each tract, and at those estimated values the lots were then subject to purchase."

those things which he imagines indispensable to comfort," he must expect to be forever marked as "a Yankee," and to have his prospects correspondingly defeated. A "hard-shell" Baptist preacher of this date showed the feeling of the people when he said, in preaching of the richness of the grace of the Lord : "It tuks in the isles of the sea and the uttermust part of the yeth. It embraces the Esquimaux and the Hottentots, and some, my dear brethering, go so far as to suppose that it tuks in the poor benighted Yankees; but *I don't go that fur.*" When it came to an election of legislators, many of the people "didn't go that fur" either.

There was a preponderance of jean suits like Lincoln's in the Assembly, and there were occasional coonskin caps and buckskin trousers. Nevertheless, more than one member showed a studied garb and a courtly manner. Some of the best blood of the South went into the making of Illinois, and it showed itself from the first in the Assembly. The surroundings of the legislators were quite as simple as the attire of the plainest of them. The court-house, in good old Colonial style, with square pillars and belfry, was finished with wooden desks and benches. The State furnished her law-makers few perquisites beyond their three dollars a day. A cork inkstand, a certain number of quills, and a limited amount of stationery were all the extras an Illinois legislator in 1834 got from his position. Scarcely more could be expected from a State whose revenues from December 1, 1834, to December 1, 1836, were only about one hundred and twenty-five thousand dollars, with expenditures during the same period amounting to less than one hundred and sixty-five thousand dollars.

Lincoln thought little of these things, no doubt. To him the absorbing interest was the men he met. To get acquainted with them, measure them, compare himself with them, and discover wherein they were his superiors and what he could do to make good his deficiency—this was his chief occupation. The men he met were good subjects for such study. Among them were William L. D. Ewing, Jesse K. Dubois, Stephen T. Logan, Thomas Ford, and Governor Duncan—men destined to play large parts in the history of the State. One whom he met that winter in Vandalia was destined to play a great part in the history of the nation—the Democratic candidate for the office of State attorney for the first judicial district of Illinois—a man four years younger than Lincoln (he was only twenty-one at the time) ; a new-comer, too, in the State, having arrived about a year before, under no very promising auspices either, for he had only thirty-seven cents in his pockets, and no position in view ; but a man of metal, it was easy to see, for already he had risen so high in the district where he had settled, that he dared contest the office of State attorney with John J. Hardin, one of the most successful lawyers of the State. This young man was Stephen A. Douglas. He had come to Vandalia from Morgan County to conduct his campaign, and Lincoln met him first in the halls of the old court-house, where he and his friends carried on with success their contest against Hardin.

The ninth Assembly gathered in a more hopeful and ambitious mood than any of its predecessors. Illinois was feeling well. The State was free from debt. The Black Hawk War had stimulated the people greatly, for it had brought a large amount of

LINCOLN IN 1861. NOW FIRST PUBLISHED.

From a photograph loaned by Mr. Frank A. Brown of Minneapolis, Minnesota. This beautiful photograph was taken, probably early in 1861, by Alexander Hesler of Chicago. It was used by Leonard W. Volk, the sculptor, in his studies of Lincoln.

money into circulation. In fact, the greater portion of the eight to ten million dollars the war had cost, had been circulated among the Illinois volunteers. Immigration, too, was increasing at a bewildering rate. In 1835 the census showed a population of 269,974. Between 1830 and 1835 two-fifths of this number had come in. In the northeast, Chicago had begun to rise. "Even for Western towns" its growth had been unusually rapid, declared Peck's "Gazetteer" of 1834 ; the harbor building there, the proposed Michigan and Illinois canal, the rise in town lots—all promised to the State a great metropolis. To meet the rising tide of prosperity, the legislators of 1834 felt that they must devise some worthy scheme, so they chartered a new State bank, with a capital of one million five hundred thousand dollars, and revived a bank which had broken twelve years before, granting it a charter of three hundred thousand dollars. There was no surplus money in the State to supply the capital ; there were no trained bankers to guide the concern ; there was no clear notion of how it was all to be done ; but a banking capital of one million eight hundred thousand dollars would be a good thing in the State, they were sure ; and if the East could be made to believe in Illinois as much as her legislators believed in her, the stocks would go ; and so the banks were chartered.

But even more important to the State than banks was a highway. For thirteen years plans of the Illinois and Michigan canal had been constantly before the Assembly. Surveys had been ordered, estimates reported, the advantages extolled, but nothing had been done. Now, however, the Assembly, flushed by the first thrill of the coming "boom," decided to authorize a loan of a half-million on the credit of the State. Lincoln favored both these measures. He did not, however, do anything especially noteworthy for either of the bills, nor was the record he made in other directions at all remarkable. He was placed on the committee of public accounts and expenditures, and attended meetings with great fidelity. His first act as a member was to give notice that he would ask leave to introduce a bill limiting the jurisdiction of justices of the peace—a measure which he succeeded in carrying through. He followed this by a motion to change the rules, so that it should not be in order to offer amendments to any bill after the third reading, which was not agreed to ; though the same rule, in effect, was adopted some years later, and is to this day in force in both branches of the Illinois

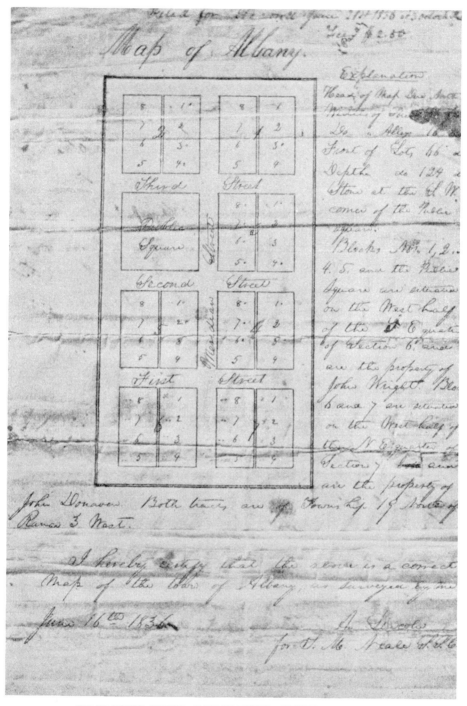

MAP OF ALBANY, ILLINOIS. MADE BY LINCOLN.—HITHERTO UNPUBLISHED.

The original of this plat is owned by Mr. J. Davidson Burns of Kalamazoo, Michigan, to whose courtesy we owe the right of reproduction.

Assembly. He next made a motion to take from the table a report which had been submitted by his committee, which met a like fate. His first resolution, relating to a State revenue to be derived from the sales of the public lands, was denied a reference, and laid upon the table. Neither as a speaker nor as an organizer did he make any especial impression on the body.

CHAPTER XVIII.

LINCOLN'S FIRST ACQUAINTANCE WITH ANN RUTLEDGE.—THE STORY OF THEIR LOVE.

N the spring of 1835 the young representative from Sangamon returned to New Salem to take up his duties as postmaster and deputy surveyor, and to resume his law studies. He exchanged his rather exalted position for the humbler one, with a light heart. New Salem held all that was dearest in the world to him at that moment, and he went back to the poor little town with a hope, which he had once supposed honor forbade his acknowledging even to himself, glowing warmly in his heart. He loved a young girl of the village, and now for the first time, though he had known her since he first came to New Salem, was he free to tell his love.

One of the most prominent families of the settlement in 1831, when Lincoln first appeared there, was that of James Rutledge. The head of the house was one of the founders of New Salem, and at that time the keeper of the village tavern. He was a high-minded man, of a warm and generous nature, and had the universal respect of the community. He was a South Carolinian by birth, but had lived many years in Kentucky before coming to Illinois. Rutledge came of a distinguished family : one of his ancestors signed the Declaration of Independence ; another was Chief Justice of the Supreme Court of the United States by appointment of Washington, and another was a conspicuous leader in the American Congress.

The third of the nine children in the Rutledge household was a daughter, Ann Mayes, born in Kentucky, January 7, 1813.

ABRAHAM LINCOLN IN 1858.

From an ambrotype owned by Miss Hattie Gilmer of Pittsfield, Illinois. The Gilmer ambrotype was taken by C. Jackson, in Pittsfield, October 1, 1858, during the Lincoln and Douglas campaign, immediately after Lincoln had made a speech in the public square. Lincoln was the guest of his friend D. H. Gilmer, a lawyer. He sat for two pictures, one of which was finished for Mr. Gilmer. The other picture is supposed to have been destroyed.

When Lincoln first met her she was nineteen years old, and as fresh as a flower. Many of those who knew her at that time have left tributes to her beauty and gentleness, and even to-day there are those living who talk of her with moistened eyes and softened tones. "She was a beautiful girl," says her cousin, James McGrady Rutledge, "and as bright as she was pretty. She was well educated for that early day, a good conversationalist, and always gentle and cheerful; a girl whose company people liked." So fair a maid was not, of course, without suitors. The most determined of those who sought her hand was one John McNeill, a young man who had arrived in New Salem from New York soon after the founding of the town. Nothing was known of his antecedents, and no questions were asked. He was understood to be merely one of the thousands who had come West in search of fortune. That he was intelligent, industrious, and frugal, with a good head for business, was at once apparent; for he and S a m u e l H i l l opened a general store, and they soon d o u b l e d their capital, and their business continued to grow remarkably. In four years from his first appearance in the settlement, besides having a half-interest in the store, McNeill owned a large farm a few miles north of New Salem. His neighbors believed him to be worth about twelve thousand dollars.

TWO NEW SALEM CHAIRS.

Now owned by Mrs. Samuel Hill, Petersburg, Illinois.

ANN RUTLEDGE'S ENGAGEMENT TO JOHN McNEILL.

John McNeill was an unmarried man—at least so he represented himself to be—and very soon after becoming a resident of New Salem he formed the acquaintance of Ann Rutledge, then a girl of seventeen. It was a case of love at first sight, and the two soon became engaged, in spite of the rivalry of Samuel Hill,

McNeill's partner. But Ann was as yet only a young girl ; and it was thought very sensible in her, and very gracious and considerate in her lover, that both acquiesced in the wishes of Ann's parents that, for some time, at least, the marriage be postponed.

Such was the situation when Lincoln appeared in New Salem. He naturally soon became acquainted with the girl. She was a pupil in Mentor Graham's school, w h e r e he fre-q u e n t l y visited, a n d rumor says that he first met her there. However that may be, it is certain that in the latter part of 1832 he went to board at the Rutledge tavern, and there was thrown daily into her company.

During the next year, 1833, John McNeill, in spite of his fair prospects, became restless and discontented. He wanted to see his people, he said, and before the end of the year he had decided to go East for a visit. To secure perfect f r e e d o m from his business while gone, he sold out his interest in the store. To Ann he said that he hoped to bring

MAJOR JOHN T. STUART, THE MAN WHO INDUCED LIN-
COLN TO STUDY LAW.

After a photograph owned by his widow, Mary Nash Stuart, Springfield, Illinois. John T. Stuart was born in Fayette County, Kentucky, seven miles east of Lexington, November 10, 1807. He was a son of Robert Stuart, a Presbyterian minister, and professor of languages in Transylvania University. His mother's maiden name was Hannah Todd. She was a daughter of General Levi Todd, and a sister of Robert S. Todd, the father of Mrs. Abraham Lincoln. John T. Stuart graduated at Center College, Danville, Kentucky, in 1826, and after studying law in Richmond, Kentucky, he went to Springfield, Illinois. This was in 1828. Here he at once began the practice of the law. In the Black Hawk War he was major of the battalion in which Lincoln commanded a company, and here his acquaintance with Lincoln seems to have been formed. In 1832 he was elected a representative in the State legislature, and was reëlected in 1834. In 1836 he was an unsuccessful Whig candidate for Congress. Two years later he was again a candidate, and this time was elécted, defeating Stephen A. Douglas. He was reëlected in 1840. Lincoln, upon his removal to Springfield in the spring of 1837, became Major Stuart's law partner. The partnership continued until April 14, 1841, when Lincoln became the partner of Judge Stephen T. Logan. For many years Major Stuart was the senior member of the law firm of Stuart, Edwards and Brown, the two other members being Benjamin S. Edwards and Christopher C. Brown. In 1837, at Jacksonville, Illinois, he was married to Mary V. Nash, who is still living. Major Stuart died in 1885.

back his father and mother, and to place them on his farm. "This duty done," was his farewell word, "you and I will be married." In the spring of 1834 McNeill started East. The journey overland by foot and horse was in those days a trying one, and on the way McNeill fell ill with chills and fever. It was late in the summer before he reached his home and wrote back to Ann, explaining his silence. The long wait had been a severe strain on the girl, and Lincoln had watched her anxiety with softened heart. It was to him, the New Salem postmaster, that she came to inquire for letters. It was to him she entrusted those she sent. In a way the postmaster must have become the girl's confidant ; and his tender heart, which never could resist suffering, must have been deeply touched. After the long silence was broken, and McNiell's first letter of explanation came, the cause of anxiety seemed removed ; but, strangely enough, other letters followed only at long intervals, and finally they ceased altogether. Then it was that the young girl told her friends a secret which McNiell had confided to her before leaving New Salem.

He had told her what she had never even suspected before, that John McNeill was not his real name, but that it was John Mc-Namar. Shortly before he came to New Salem, he explained, his father had suffered a disastrous failure in business. He was the oldest son ; and in the hope of retrieving the lost fortune, he resolved to go West, expecting to return in a few years and share his riches with the rest of the family. Anticipating parental opposition, he ran away from home ; and, being sure that he could never accumulate anything with so numer-

A WAYSIDE WELL NEAR NEW SALEM, KNOWN AS "ANN RUTLEDGE'S WELL."

ous a family to support, he endeavored to lose himself by a change of name. All this Ann had believed and not repeated ; but now, worn out by waiting, she took her secret to her friends.

With few exceptions, they pronounced the story a fabrication and McNamar an impostor. Why had he worn this mask ? His excuse seemed flimsy. At best, they declared, he was a mere adventurer ; and was it not more probable that he was a fugitive from justice—a thief, a swindler, or a murderer? And who knew how many wives he might have ? With all New Salem declaring John McNamar false, Ann Rutledge could hardly be blamed for imagining that he either was dead or that he had ceased to love her.

ANN'S ENGAGEMENT TO LINCOLN.

It was not until McNeill, or McNamar, had been gone many months, and gossip had become offensive, that Lincoln ventured to show his love for Ann, and then it was a long time before the girl would listen to his suit. Convinced at last, however, that her former lover had deserted her, she yielded to Lincoln's wishes, and promised, in the spring of 1835, soon after Lincoln's return from Vandalia, to become his wife. But Lincoln had nothing on which to support a family—indeed, he found it no trifling task to support himself. As for Ann, she was anxious to go to school another year. It was decided that in the autumn she should go with her brother to Jacksonville and spend the winter there in an academy. Lincoln was to devote himself to his law studies ; and the next spring, when she returned from school and he was a member of the bar, they were to be married.

A happy spring and summer followed. New Salem took a cordial interest in the two lovers, and presaged a happy life for them ; and all would undoubtedly have gone well if the young girl could have dismissed the haunting memory of her old lover. The possibility that she had wronged him ; that he might reappear ; that he loved her still, though she now loved another ; that perhaps she had done wrong—a torturing conflict of memory, love, conscience, doubt, and morbidness lay like a shadow across her happiness, and wore upon her until she fell ill. Gradually her condition became hopeless ; and Lincoln, who had been shut from her, was sent for. The lovers passed an hour alone in an anguished parting, and soon after, on August 25, 1835, Ann died.

LINCOLN IN 1858.

After a photograph owned by Mrs. Harriet Chapman of Charleston, Illinois. Mrs. Chapman is a grand-daughter of Sarah Bush Lincoln, Lincoln's step-mother. Her son, Mr. R. N. Chapman of Charleston, Illinois, writes us : " In 1858 Lincoln and Douglas had a series of joint debates in this State, and this city was one place of meeting. Mr. Lincoln's step-mother was making her home with my father and mother at that time. Mr. Lincoln stopped at our house, and as he was going away my mother said to him : 'Uncle Abe, I want a picture of you.' He replied, 'Well, Harriet, when I get home I will have one taken for you and send it to you.' Soon after, mother received the photograph, which she still has, already framed, from Springfield, Illinois, with a letter from Mr. Lincoln, in which he said, 'This is not a very good-looking picture, but it's the best that could be produced from the poor subject.' He also said that he had it taken solely for my mother. The photograph is still in its original frame, and I am sure is the most perfect and best picture of Lincoln in existence. We suppose it must have been taken in Springfield, Illinois."

The 11th Section of the act of Congress, approved Feb. 11, 1805, prescribing rules for the subdivision of Sections of lands within the United States system of Surveys, standing unrepealed, in my opinion, is binding on the respective purchasers of different parts of the same Section, and furnishes the true rule for Surveyors in establishing lines between them — That law, being in force at the time each became a purchaser, becomes a condition of the purchase —

And, by that law, I think the true rule for dividing into quarters, any interior Section, or Section which is not fractional, is to run straight lines through the Section from the opposite quarter section corners, fixing the point where such straight lines cross, or intersect each other, as the middle, or center of the Section —

Nearly, perhaps quite, all the original surveys are to some extent, erroneous, and in some of the Sections, greatly so — In each of the latter, it is obvious that a more equitable mode of division than the above, might be adopted; but as error is infinitely various, perhaps no better single rule can be prescribed. At all events I think the above has been prescribed by the competent authority —

Springfield, Jany. 6. 1859.   A. Lincoln.

FACSIMILE OF A LEGAL OPINION BY LINCOLN.—NOW FIRST PUBLISHED.

From the original, in the possession of Z. A. Enos, Springfield, Illinois. In a convention of surveyors, held at Springfield in 1859, the question was much discussed whether the act of Congress of February 11, 1805, relating to surveys, was intended to control all future surveys and subdivisions of the government lands. It was decided to submit the question to a lawyer for an opinion. Mr. Lincoln was selected, for the reason not only that he was a lawyer of recognized ability, but also because he had been a practical surveyor. A committee having waited upon him, he wrote out the opinion of which a facsimile is here presented. Mr. Enos, who holds the original document, was an active participant in the convention to which this opinion was rendered.

The death of Ann Rutledge plunged Lincoln into the deepest gloom. That abiding melancholy, that painful sense of the incompleteness of life, which had been his mother's dowry to him, asserted itself. It filled and darkened his mind and his imagination, tortured him with its black pictures. One stormy night he was sitting beside William Greene, his head bowed on his hand, while tears trickled through his fingers ; his friend begged him to control his sorrow, to try to forget. "I cannot," moaned Lincoln ; "the thought of the snow and rain on her grave fills me with indescribable grief."

JAMES McGRADY RUTLEDGE, A COUSIN OF ANN RUTLEDGE.

James McGrady Rutledge, son of William Rutledge, is now past eighty-one years of age, having been born in Kentucky, September 29, 1814. He is now a resident of Petersburg. He is active and remarkably free from the infirmities of age. When a boy, with a yoke of oxen, he hauled the logs for the construction of the mill and the dam at New Salem and for some of the cabins of the village. "'Rile' Clary and I carried chain for Lincoln many a time," he says ; "'Rile' going foremost and I following. We became accustomed to it and Lincoln preferred us." Ann Rutledge and her cousin were nearly the same age, and being thoroughly congenial, she made a confidant of him. They were much in each other's company, and Ann often talked to him of Lincoln. "Everybody was happy with Ann," says Mr. Rutledge. "She was of a cheerful disposition, seeming to enjoy life, and helping others enjoy it."

He was found walking alone by the river and through the woods, muttering strange things to himself. He seemed to his friends to be in the shadow of madness. They kept a close watch over him ; and at last Bowling Green, one of the most devoted friends Lincoln then had, took him home to his little log cabin, half a mile north of New Salem, under the brow of a big bluff.

Here, under the loving care of Green and his good wife Nancy, Lincoln remained until he was once more master of himself.

But though he had regained self-control, his grief was deep and bitter. Ann Rutledge was buried in Concord cemetery, a country burying-ground seven miles northwest of New Salem. To this lonely spot Lincoln frequently journeyed to weep over her grave. "My heart is buried there," he said to one of his friends.

When McNamar returned (for McNamar's story was true, and, two months after Ann Rutledge died, he drove into New Salem,

with his widowed mother and his brothers and sisters in the
" prairie schooner " beside him) and learned of Ann's death, he
" saw Lincoln at the post-office," as he afterward said, and " he
seemed desolate and sorely distressed." On himself, apparently,
her death produced no deep impression. Within a year he married another woman ; and his conduct toward Ann Rutledge is
to this day a mystery.

Many years ago a sister of Ann Rutledge, Mrs. Jeane Berry,
told what she knew of Ann's love affairs ; and her statement
has been preserved in a diary kept by the Rev. R. D. Miller, now
Superintendent of Schools of Menard County, with whom she
had the conversation. She declared that Ann's " whole soul
seemed wrapped up in Lincoln," and that they "would have
been married in the fall or early winter" if Ann had lived.
" After Ann died," said Mrs. Berry, " I remember that it was
common talk about how sad Lincoln was ; and I remember myself how sad he looked. They told me that every time he was
in the neighborhood after she died, he would go alone to her
grave and sit there in silence for hours."

In later life, when his sorrow had become a memory, he told
a friend who questioned him : " I really and truly loved the girl
and think often of her now." There was a pause, and then he
added : " And I have loved the name of Rutledge to this day."

CHAPTER XIX.

ABRAHAM LINCOLN AT TWENTY-SIX YEARS OF AGE.

HEN the death of Ann Rutledge came upon
Lincoln, for a time threatening to destroy
his ambition and blast his life, he was in
a most encouraging position. Master of a
profession in which he had an abundance
of work and earned fair wages ; hopeful
of being admitted in a few months to the
bar ; a member of the State Assembly, with
every reason to believe that, if he desired
it, his constituency would return him — few men are as far
advanced at twenty-six as was Abraham Lincoln.

CONCORD CEMETERY.—WHERE ANN RUTLEDGE WAS BURIED.

From a photograph by C. S. McCullough, Petersburg, Illinois. Concord cemetery lies seven miles northwest of the old town of New Salem, in a secluded place, surrounded by woods and pastures, away from the world. In this lonely spot Ann Rutledge was at first laid to rest. Thither Lincoln is said often to have gone alone, and "sat in silence for hours at a time;" and it was to Ann Rutledge's grave here that he pointed and said: "There my heart lies buried." The old cemetery suffered the melancholy fate of New Salem. It became a neglected, deserted spot. The graves were lost in weeds, and a heavy growth of trees kept out the sun and filled the place with gloom. A dozen years ago this picture was taken. It was a blustery day in the autumn, and the weeds and trees were swaying before a furious gale. No other picture of the place, taken while Ann Rutledge was buried there, is known to be in existence. A picture of a cemetery, with the name of Ann Rutledge on a high, flat tombstone, has been published in two or three books; but it is not genuine, the "stone" being nothing more than a board improvised for the occasion. The grave of Ann Rutledge was never honored with a stone until the body was taken up in 1890 and removed to Oakland cemetery, a mile southwest of Petersburg.

Intellectually he was far better equipped than he believed himself to be, better than he has ordinarily been credited with being. True, he had had no conventional college training, but he had by his own efforts attained the chief result of all preparatory study, the ability to take hold of a subject and assimilate it. The fact that in six weeks he had acquired enough of the science of surveying to enable him to serve as deputy surveyor shows how well trained his mind was. The power to grasp a large sub-

JOSEPH DUNCAN, GOVERNOR OF ILLINOIS DURING
LINCOLN'S FIRST TERM IN THE LEGISLATURE.

Joseph Duncan, Governor of Illinois from 1834
to 1838, was born in Kentucky in 1794. The son of
an officer of the regular army, he at nineteen became a soldier in the war of 1812, and did gallant
service. He removed to Illinois in 1818, and soon
became prominent in the State, serving as a major-
general of militia, a State Senator, and from 1826
to 1834 as a member of Congress, resigning from
Congress to take the office of Governor. He was at
first a Democrat, but afterwards became a Whig.
He was a man of the highest character and public
spirit. He died in 1844.

ject quickly and fully is never
an accident. The nights Lincoln spent in Gentryville, lying
on the floor in front of the fire,
figuring on the fire-shovel ; the
hours he passed in poring over
the Statutes of Indiana; the
days he wrestled with Kirkham's Grammar, alone made
the mastery of Flint and Gibson
possible. His struggle with
Flint and Gibson made easier
the volumes he borrowed from
Major Stuart's law library.

Lincoln had a mental trait
which e x p l a i n s his r a p i d
growth in mastering subjects—
seeing clearly was essential to
him. He was unable to put a
question aside until he understood it. It pursued him, irri-
tated him, until solved. Even
in his Gentryville days his comrades noted that he was constantly searching for reasons
and t h a t h e "explained so
clearly." This characteristic
became stronger with years. He was unwilling to pronounce
himself on any subject until he understood it, and he could not
let it alone until he had reached a conclusion which satisfied
him.

This seeing clearly became a splendid force in Lincoln ; because
when he once had reached a conclusion he had the honesty of
soul to suit his actions to it. No consideration could induce him
to abandon the course his reason told him was logical. Not that
he was obstinate, and having taken a position, would not change
it if he saw on further study that he was wrong. In his first
circular to the people of Sangamon County is this characteristic
passage : "Upon the subjects I have treated, I have spoken as I
thought. I may be wrong in any or all of them ; but, holding it
a sound maxim that it is better only sometimes to be right than

at all times to be wrong, so soon as I discover my opinions to be erroneous, I shall be ready to renounce them."

Joined to these strong mental and moral qualities was that power of immediate action which so often explains why one man succeeds in life while another of equal intelligence a n d uprightness fails. As soon as Lincoln saw a thing to do he did it. He wants to know; here is a book—it may be a biography, a volume of dry statutes, a collection of verse; no matter, he reads and ponders it until he has absorbed all it has for him. He is eager to

DR. FRANCIS REGNIER.

From a painting owned by his daughter, Mrs. N. W. Branson, Petersburg, Illinois. Dr. Regnier was one of the New Salem physicians. He lived in the place until most of its inhabitants had deserted it, and then removed to Petersburg. He was for many years a leading citizen in the community. He died in 1858.

see the world; a man offers him a position as a "hand" on a Mississippi flatboat; he takes it without a moment's hesitation over the toil and exposure it demands. John Calhoun is willing to make him a deputy surveyor; he knows nothing of the science; in six weeks he has learned enough to begin his labors. Sangamon County must have representatives; why not he? And his circular goes out. Ambition alone will not explain this power of instantaneous action. It comes largely from that active imagination which, when a new relation or position opens, seizes on all its possibilities and from them creates a situation so real that one enters with confidence upon what seems to the unimaginative the rashest undertaking. Lincoln saw the possibilities in things, and immediately appropriated them.

But the position he filled in Sangamon County in 1835 was not all due to these qualities; much was due to his personal charm. By all accounts he was big, awkward, ill-clad, shy; yet his sterling honor, his unselfish nature, his heart of the true gentleman, inspired respect and confidence. Men might laugh

GRAVE OF ANN RUTLEDGE IN OAKLAND CEMETERY.

From a photograph made for this work by C. S. McCullough, Petersburg, Illinois, in September, 1895. On the 15th of May, 1890, the remains of Ann Rutledge were removed from the long-neglected grave in the Concord graveyard to a new and picturesque burying-ground a mile southwest of Petersburg, called Oakland cemetery. The old grave, though marked by no stone, was easily identified from the fact that Ann was buried by the side of her younger brother, David, who died in 1842, upon the threshold of what promised to be a brilliant career as a lawyer. The removal was made by Samuel Montgomery, a prominent business man of Petersburg. He was accompanied to the grave by James McGrady Rutledge and a few others, who located the grave beyond a doubt. In the new cemetery, the grave occupies a place somewhat apart from others. A young maple tree is growing beside it, and it is marked by an unpolished granite stone bearing the simple inscription, "Ann Rutledge."

at his first appearance, but they were not long in recognizing the real superiority of his nature.

Such was Abraham Lincoln at twenty-six, when the tragic death of Ann Rutledge made all that he had attained, all that he had planned, seem fruitless and empty. He was too sincere and just, too brave a man, to allow a great sorrow permanently to interfere with his activities. He rallied his forces and returned to his law, his surveying, his politics. He brought to his work a new power, that insight and patience which only a great sorrow can give.

APPENDIX.

I.

MEMORANDA FOR LINCOLN'S GENEALOGY.

Prepared especially for this volume by the Hon. L. E. Chittenden, Register of the Treasury under Lincoln, and author of "President Lincoln," etc.

THE Hon. SOLOMON LINCOLN of Hingham, Massachusetts, in an article on the "Lincoln Families of Massachusetts," in the "New England Historical and Genealogical Register," 1865, Volume XIX., page 357, says : "We now come to the family of Samuel Lincoln, in which we find more names than in any other, which leads to the belief that it is in this direction that we must look for the ancestor of Abraham Lincoln. To this family belong the honored names of Levi Lincoln, Attorney-General of the United States, Lieutenant and acting Governor of Massachusetts after the death of Governor Sullivan; also his two distinguished sons, Levi, 1802, who, besides other offices, was by nine elections the popular Governor of Massachusetts; and Enoch Lincoln, Governor of Maine ; and many other able men.

"In a correspondence with the late President, in 1848, when he was in Congress, he stated : 'My father's name is Thomas, my grandfather's was Abraham, the same as my own. He went from Rockingham County, Virginia, to Kentucky, about the year 1782, and two years afterwards was killed by the Indians. We have a vague tradition that my great-grandfather was a Quaker who went from Pennsylvania to Virginia. Further than this I have not heard anything. It may do no harm to say that Abraham and Mordecai are common names in our family.'

"In a subsequent letter in 1848, he wrote : 'I have mentioned that my grandfather's name was Abraham; he had, as I think I have heard, four brothers, Isaac, Jacob, Thomas, and John. He had three sons, Mordecai, Josiah, and Thomas—the last my father. My uncle Mordecai had three sons, Abraham, James, and Mordecai. My uncle Josiah had several daughters and only one son, Thomas. This is all I know certainly on the subject of names. It is, however, my father's understanding that Abraham, Mordecai, and Thomas are old family names of ours.' "

Mr. Solomon Lincoln continues : "We have already mentioned among the sons of the first Samuel—Daniel, Mordecai, and Thomas; and among his grandsons—Mordecai, Isaac, and Abraham.

"It has been stated . . . that about the middle of the last century the great-grandfather of Abraham Lincoln removed from Berks County, Pennsylvania, to Augusta County, Virginia. These facts, from 'Rupp's History of

Berks County,' are furnished by William B. Trask, Esq., of the Genealogical Society."

From the "History of the Town of Hingham, Massachusetts," four volumes, 8vo, 1893, by a committee comprising Ex-Governor Long and two members of the Lincoln family. See Volume I., page 271.

"The Lincolns fill the pages of local and Commonwealth history with the story of their services in the field, the town, the halls of legislation, and the council chamber, from the earliest day to the present time. During the French wars we have seen Benjamin Lincoln, as colonel of his regiment, the historical Third Suffolk, . . . taking an active part. Colonel Lincoln died in March, 1771, leaving, among others, the son Benjamin who so worthily filled the place he long occupied in public estimation and usefulness. The affection that is felt for the great President *Abraham Lincoln, also a descendant from the Hingham family*, has given a national fame to the name in later years."

From "The Lineage of Abraham Lincoln traced from Samuel Lincoln." By Samuel Shackford, Esq., of Chicago, a descendant of Samuel Lincoln. See New England Historical and Genealogical Register, 1887, Volume XLI., page 153.

"Samuel Lincoln came from Norfolk County, England—probably from the town of Hingham—in 1637, at the age of eighteen years, . . . first to Salem, as an apprentice to a weaver; then to Hingham, where his brother Thomas . . . lived. . . . He had ten children. . . . Through his first son, Samuel, came the Governors Levi Lincoln, father and son, and Enoch Lincoln, Governor of Maine. Mordecai, fourth son of Samuel, born at Hingham, June 17, 1767, was a blacksmith ; worked at his trade in Hull ; married Sarah, daughter of Abraham and Sarah (Whitman) Jones. From Hull the family removed to the neighboring town of Scituate, about 1704, where Mordecai established a furnace for smelting iron ore. The children of Mordecai and Sarah (Jones) Lincoln were five in number: Mordecai, born April 1, 1686; Abraham, born January 13, 1689; Isaac, born October 21, 1691; and Sarah, born July 29, 1691—all in Hingham. By a second wife he had Elizabeth and Jacob, born in Scituate.

"The will of Mordecai, dated Scituate, March 3, 1727, is of an unusual character. Isaac and Jacob, the younger sons—Jacob a lad of sixteen years— were named executors; and to them are bequeathed all the testator's lands in Hingham and Scituate, with the saw and grist mill, and all his interest in the iron works. To 'son Mordecai' is left one hundred and ten pounds in money or bills of credit ; to 'son Abraham,' sixty pounds in money or bills, 'besides what he has already had.' To the oldest sons of Mordecai and Abraham, each ten pounds when they come of age; and provision is made for sending three grandsons to college, if they wish a liberal education.

"Shortly before this time the names of Mordecai and Abraham disappear from, and are not after 1727 found on, the records of Massachusetts. They were active men of property ; and this fact, in connection with the will, which gave them only money, and all the immovable property to Isaac and Jacob, raises an almost irresistible inference that Mordecai and Abraham no longer lived in Massachusetts.

"We now turn to New Jersey and Pennsylvania, and find that, in the early part of the last century, the Moores, Hales, Rolfs, Pikes, and other families from eastern Massachusetts, came to Middlesex County, New Jersey, and founded a town which they named, in honor of their old pastor in Newbury, Massachusetts, Woodbridge. At a somewhat later date the names of Mordecai and Abraham Lincoln appear on the records of Monmouth, which adjoins Middlesex County.

"Mordecai Lincoln had married Hannah (Bowne) Salter of Freehold, Monmouth County, New Jersey. Her uncle John Bowne's will, dated September 14, 1714, gives to Hannah Lincoln a bequest of two hundred and fifty pounds. She was the daughter of Richard Salter, a leading lawyer, member of the assembly, and judge. Captain John Bowne was also a leading and influential citizen. The settlement of his estate involved several lawsuits shown by the court records. The first in 1716, by Obadiah Bowne, executor, against the other heirs, Mordecai Lincoln being a defendant. In this a nonsuit was entered, and the second suit ended in the same way. The third, in 1719, also included Mordecai Lincoln as a defendant, but the sheriff returns him *non est*, and in 1720 the suit as to Mordecai was withdrawn.

"These facts are satisfactory proof that Mordecai Lincoln had, before 1720, left Monmouth County."

As further proof of the identity of the New Jersey with the Hingham Mordecai, there is a letter shown to Mr. Shackford by John C. Beekman, Esq., of Monmouth, written by John Bowne, one of the heirs to his uncle Obadiah, in which he calls Mordecai "brother."

A deed on file in the office of the Secretary of State in Trenton, New Jersey, dated February 29, 1720, from Richard Salter to Mordecai Lincoln, both of Freehold, conveys four hundred acres of land, situate on the Machaponix River and Grand Bank, Middlesex County. A like deed, of May 25, 1726, conveys one hundred acres of land in the same locality, and describes Mordecai Lincoln, the grantee, as of Chester County, Pennsylvania.

It appears from these records that Mordecai was in New Jersey in 1720. In 1876 there was unearthed in the old burying-ground near Allentown, New Jersey, a tombstone, bearing this inscription : "To the memory of Deborah Lincoln, who died May 15, 1720, aged three years and four months." As no other Lincolns have been found in the vicinity, it is probable that she was the child of Mordecai and Hannah Lincoln.

A deed on file in the Department of Internal Affairs of Pennsylvania, dated December 24, 1725, from Mordecai Lincoln of Coventry, County of Chester, Pennsylvania, conveys to William Branston, merchant, of Philadelphia, one-third of one hundred and six acres of land, according to an agreement between Samuel Nutt and Mordecai Lincoln, with "the mynes, and minerals, *forges*, buildings, houses, and improvements." This is important, for it shows that Mordecai first resided in Chester County, Pennsylvania, where he made iron, a trade learned at his father's establishment in Scituate.

It is through Mordecai that the pedigree of President Lincoln is traced to Samuel Lincoln. But it is also essential that Abraham of Monmouth County, New Jersey, should be identified as one of the missing sons of Mordecai and Sarah (Jones) Lincoln of eastern Massachusetts.

Abraham, like his father, was a blacksmith, as the next deed shows. By it, on the records of Monmouth County, New Jersey, February 20, 1727, Abraham Lincoln, "blacksmith," conveys to Thomas Williams two hundred and forty acres of land near Creswick, in said county, and two hundred acres conveyed to Abraham Lincoln by Abraham Van Horn. He was probably preparing to follow his brother Mordecai to Pennsylvania.

The will of Abraham Lincoln is dated in Springfield, Chester County, Pennsylvania, April 15, 1745, and was entered for probate on the 29th of the same month. His estate, a plantation in Springfield and two houses in Philadelphia, was divided among his children, viz.: Mordecai, Abraham, Isaac, Jacob, John, Sarah, and Rebecca. Four of his sons bore the same Old Testament names as the four sons of the first Mordecai of Scituate.

Returning to Mordecai, we find in his will, proved June 7, 1736, that he is described as of Amity, Philadelphia County, Pennsylvania. By it he bequeaths to "my sons Mordecai and Thomas all my lands in Amity," etc.; to his daughters Hannah and Mary a piece of land in Machaponix, New Jersey ; and to "my son John three hundred acres of land in the same town ;" and to his daughters Ann and Sarah one hundred acres, also lying in Machaponix, New Jersey.

His oldest son, John, was by his first wife, Hannah Salter, and went with his father to Pennsylvania. A deed from John, on file in the Secretary of State's office in Trenton, New Jersey, describes him as the "son and heir of Mordecai Lincoln, of the town of Carnaervon, County of Lancaster," and the deed conveys to William Dye "three hundred acres in Middlesex County, New Jersey, part of the property conveyed October 20, 1720, by Richard Salter to Mordecai Lincoln, and by him bequeathed to his said son John."

John Lincoln, in 1758, owned a farm in Union township, adjoining Exeter (Pennsylvania ?), which he sold, and went to Virginia, settling in that portion of Augusta County which was organized into Rockingham County in 1779. His will cannot now be found, part of the papers in the probate office at Harrisonburgh having been destroyed by fire. But there is ample proof that he had sons—John, Thomas, Abraham, Isaac, and Jacob—and daughters.

The son Abraham married Mary Shepley in North Carolina, just over the Virginia boundary line, where their sons Mordecai, Josiah, and Thomas were born. In 1782, or about that time, the family removed to Kentucky, where their daughters Mary and Nancy were born. The son THOMAS LINCOLN married Nancy Hanks, September 23, 1806, near Springfield, Kentucky, and ABRAHAM LINCOLN, their son, was born on the twelfth day of February, 1809.

Mr. Shackford continues: "The Lincolns through which the President's genealogy is traced were for six generations, with a single exception, pioneers in the settlement of new countries. I. Samuel, an early settler at Hingham, Massachusetts. II. Mordecai, of Scituate, who lived and died near where he was born. III. Mordecai, settled in Pennsylvania, thirty years before Berks County was organized. IV. John, went to the wilds of Virginia. V. Abraham, went to Kentucky with Boone when it was infested by savages. VI. Thomas, with his son Abraham, pioneers to Indiana."

Mr. Shackford has traced the pedigrees of other members of the Lincoln family, in which the persistence of Scripture names is very marked. We content ourselves with the following, which bears directly on the connection of the Pennsylvania and Virginia families:

"Abraham, the posthumous son of Mordecai and Mary Lincoln of Amity, born in 1736, married Ann Boone, a cousin of Daniel, the Kentucky pioneer. Their grandson, David J. Lincoln of Birdsboro', Pennsylvania, informs me that his father James, who died in 1860, at the age of ninety-four, and his uncle Thomas, who died in 1864, told him that Daniel Boone often visited his friends in Pennsylvania, and always spent part of his time with his cousin Ann, and that his glowing accounts of the South and West induced John Lincoln to remove to Virginia. After his removal he was known as 'Virginia John,' to distinguish him from others of the same name."

A fact which will probably impress the reader is that among the numerous Lincolns mentioned in the six generations from Samuel, the immigrant in 1637, to Abraham, the President, two centuries later, there is not one that does not bear a scriptural name. A coincidence not less remarkable is the identity of names in the successive families.

Among the children of the first Mordecai, 1686, were Mordecai, Abraham, Isaac, Sarah.

Of the second Mordecai, 1727: Mordecai, Abraham, Isaac, Jacob.

Of Abraham, brother of second Mordecai, 1745: Mordecai, Abraham, Isaac, Sarah—identical with the children of the first Mordecai; also John, Jacob, and Rebecca.

Of John of Virginia, or "Virginia John," 1758: Abraham, Isaac, Jacob, Thomas, John.

If there are any doubting Thomases who cannot see in this extraordinary identity of names any blood relationship, no evidence would convince them; neither would they be persuaded though one rose from the dead.

Aside from this identity of names, the foregoing facts, taken from original documents on file, and family papers, prove beyond any reasonable doubt that Samuel Lincoln of Hingham was the ancestor of Abraham Lincoln of Illinois by a line of descent through the first and second Mordecai, "Virginia John," Abraham, and Thomas Lincoln. In genealogical studies it is seldom, indeed, that a pedigree is so clearly established.

II.

CHRISTOPHER COLUMBUS GRAHAM AND HIS REMINISCENCES OF LINCOLN'S PARENTS.

THE most important testimony we have in regard to the character of the parents of Abraham Lincoln, and of the conditions under which they lived, is that of Christopher Columbus Graham. Dr. Graham was born at Worthington's Station, near Danville, Kentucky, in 1784. He lived in the State until his death at Louisville in 1885. This long period was to the very end one of useful activity. A physician by profession, Dr. Graham was, by his love of nature, botanist, geologist, naturalist; and his observations on the flora, fauna, and strata of Kentucky are quoted on both sides of the Atlantic by scientists. For many years Dr. Graham was the owner of the famous Harrodsburg Springs. About 1852 he sold this property to the War Department of the United States as a Retreat for Invalid Military Officers. After the sale of the Springs he spent most of this time in study and in arranging his fine cabinet of Kentucky geology and natural history, before selling it to the Louisville Library Association.

It was only by an accident that Dr. Graham's knowledge of the history of Thomas Lincoln was given to the public. Recluse and student, he heard little or nothing of the stories about the worthlessness of Thomas Lincoln and his wife which were circulated at the time of the election of Abraham Lincoln to the Presidency. To what he did hear he paid little or no attention. One day in the spring of 1882, however, he was visiting at the home of Capt. J. W. Wartmann, Clerk of the United States Court at Evansville, Indiana, and Mr. Wartmann overheard him say that he was present at the marriage of Thomas Lincoln. Realizing at once the historical importance of such a testimony, and thinking that it might lead to the discovery of documentary proofs of the marriage, Mr. Wartmann secured from Mr. Graham the following affidavit :

"I, Christopher C. Graham, now of Louisville, Kentucky, aged ninety-eight years, on my oath say : That I was present at the marriage of Thomas Lincoln and Nancy Hanks, in Washington County, near the town of Springfield, Kentucky ; that one Jesse Head, a Methodist preacher of Springfield, Kentucky, performed the ceremony. I knew the said Thomas Lincoln and Nancy Hanks well, and know the said Nancy Hanks to have been virtuous and respectable, and of good parentage. I do not remember the exact date of the marriage, but was present at the marriage aforesaid ; and I make this affidavit freely, and at the request of J. W. Wartmann, to whom, for the first time, I have this day incidentally stated the fact of my presence at the said wedding of President Lincoln's father and mother. I make this affidavit to vindicate the character of Thomas Lincoln and Nancy Hanks, and to put to rest forever the legitimacy of Abraham Lincoln's birth. I was formerly proprietor of Harrodsburgh Springs ; I am a retired physician, and am now a resident of Louisville, Kentucky. I think Felix Grundy was also present at the marriage of said Thomas Lincoln and Nancy Hanks, the father and mother of Abraham Lincoln. The said Jesse Head, the officiating minister at the marriage aforesaid, afterward removed to Harrodsburgh, Kentucky, and edited a paper there, and died at that place.

"CHRISTOPHER COLUMBUS GRAHAM.

"Subscribed and sworn to before me, this March 20, A.D. 1882. N. C. Butler, Clerk United States Circuit Court, First District, Indiana. By J. W. Wartmann, Deputy Clerk."

This affidavit attracted wide attention, and the "New York Christian Advocate," the leading organ of the Methodist Episcopal Church, in its issue of April 13, 1882, raised several pertinent questions :

1. Was Christopher Columbus Graham, at ninety-eight years of age, in full possession of his faculties ?

2. Why had he not given his precious information before to the public ?

3. Was there a Methodist preacher named Jesse Head ?

These questions called out a large number of answers. The Rev. William M. Grubbs, of the Southwest Indiana Conference, stationed at Castleton,

Marion County, in answer to the editor's first point gave a brief history of Dr. Graham, and explained why he "should never have been heard of before as the possessor of this precious information" :

"The Doctor himself was a man of more than ordinary intelligence, almost a Chesterfield in manners, and a leader for years of the Whig party—a great friend of Henry Clay—and unless he has greatly degenerated, he is now, at ninety-eight years, a good specimen of 'the fine old Kentucky gentleman.' Additional to the fact that he has been quite deaf for many years, he is a great lover of nature in its varied forms. As an evidence of this, at the time I was their guest, in 1855, he had been absent six months in the mountains of Kentucky, pursuing his favorite studies in natural history, geology, etc. Thus, though on good terms with his family, his habits became those of the student and the recluse. The family told us pleasantly that such was his passion for nature in its wildest forms that they did not know when he would think of paying them a visit. The last time I saw him was in Louisville, Kentucky, arranging his large cabinet of natural history, geology, etc., for the Library Association of that city, to which he had sold the same for quite a large sum. Since the death of his wife and the marriage of his daughters, I think he has had no settled home—something of a rover—with ample means and friends everywhere. It is not, therefore, surprising that his habits of indifference to passing events and themes kept him ignorant of the mooted point that he sets to rest by his late statement."

The Rev. John R. Eads, pastor of the Danville, Kentucky, Methodist Episcopal Church, wrote of Dr. Graham : "I have never heard his veracity or his integrity questioned." Of Jesse Head he said : "He is remembered by some of the old people of this community." He added:

"You seem surprised that the testimony of Dr. Graham to the 'precious information' which he communicates should not have been procured earlier. I frankly confess that, while I am a native of central Kentucky, and have spent most of my life here, I never heard before, so far as I can now remember, a question raised as to the legal marriage of Thomas Lincoln and Nancy Hanks. Thinking this might be exceptional in my case, I have taken the pains to-day to ask others if they ever heard such a question raised, and they tell me they have not. I feel quite sure that there must be very few people in central Kentucky who ever heard of a doubt expressed concerning the legal marriage of Thomas Lincoln."

Letters were received from the Rev. R. T. Stephenson of Shelbyville, Kentucky, and others, supplying information as to who the Rev. Jesse Head was and what were his relations to the Methodist Episcopal Church. The facts, however, are all given in condensed shape in the following :

"LAWRENCEBURG, KENTUCKY,
"ANDERSON COUNTY, *May* 3, 1882.
"TO THE REV. J. M. BUCKLEY, D.D.

"*Dear Sir and Brother:*—Your favor reached me on the eve of my leaving Harrodsburg for this place, hence the delay in responding to your request. The Rev. Jesse Head referred to was my grandfather. He was born in Maryland, near Baltimore ; was married to Miss Jane Ramsey, of (what is now) Bedford County, Pennsylvania. He removed to Kentucky, and settled at Springfield, Washington County. He was an ordained minister of the Methodist Episcopal Church, but was never connected with the itinerancy in Kentucky, on account of feeble health. He held several prominent civil offices while living in Springfield, and was actively engaged preaching the gospel of God's grace. He celebrated the rites of matrimony between Thomas Lincoln and Miss Nancy Hanks, father and mother of President Lincoln, in 1806, near

Springfield. He afterwards moved to Harrodsburg, Mercer County, where he lived until his death, which occurred in March, 1842. At Harrodsburg he engaged in merchandising, also owned and edited the county paper for a term of years. He was largely instrumental, if not wholly, in building the first church ever erected in Harrodsburg ; also organized and conducted the first prayer-meeting. In gospel labors he was always abundant. His house was the home for several years of Rev. H. B. Bascom, afterwards Bishop ; also of Bishop McKendree especially, as they were bosom friends. Some time before his death he left the Methodist Episcopal Church, and connected himself with the Radical Methodists, on account of *slavery*, and also some dissatisfaction with the Episcopacy. He then had charge of and preached for a church for years at Lexington, Kentucky. His name at Harrodsburg and through the surrounding country is as ointment poured forth. He was a man of decided and positive character, bold and aggressive, and died loved and honored by all. He died as he lived, in the triumph of the faith of the Gospel of God's Son.

" Fraternally yours,

" E. B. HEAD, P.E.,

" Lawrenceburg Circuit, Kentucky Conference."

The " Christian Advocate," upon receipt of the first letter, requested the Rev. John R. Eads of Danville, Kentucky, to have the marriage record examined, the following reply being returned :

" DANVILLE, KENTUCKY, *April* 25, 1882.

" DR. BUCKLEY.

" *My Dear Brother:*—Your postal card received. I have just received the accompanying paper, which, though somewhat singular in form in some of its parts, will be plain to you in its essential facts. You have received my other two letters, which in connection with this certificate will, I trust, set the whole matter to which they relate in a satisfactory light.

" Fraternally,

" JOHN R. EADS."

Here follows the certificate :

" Clerk's Office, Washington County Court,

" W. F. Booker, Clerk.

" SPRINGFIELD, KENTUCKY, *April* 24, 1882.

" THE REV. JOHN R. EADS.

" *Dear Sir:*—Yours in regard to the marriage certificate of Thomas Lincoln to Nancy Hanks reached here during my absence in Louisville. I now send you a copy of the same :

" I do hereby certify that the following is a true list of the marriage solemnized by me between Thomas Lincoln and Nancy Hanks, September 23, 1806.

" JESSE HEAD, D. N. E. C.

" (Copy attest.)

" W. F. Booker,

" Clerk, Washington County Court.

" Yours respectfully, W. F. B."

The " Christian Advocate," in publishing the letters, said :

" In summing up the whole the following points may be considered as forever settled :

" 1. There was such a man as Jesse Head, a local deacon in the Methodist Episcopal Church, in 1806.

" 2. He married Thomas Lincoln and Nancy Hanks on September 23, 1806,*

---

* The date here given is wrong ; the marriage took place on June 12, 1806. The error arose in copying the record the first time, the date of the marriage following that of Thomas Lincoln being taken instead of the one before his name.

of whom was born the venerated and never-to-be-forgotten Abraham Lincoln.

"3. The fact of the marriage was duly certified by Jesse Head, in the clerk's office of Washington County, Kentucky, where it may now be seen.

"4. The Rev. E. B. Head has spoken of this fact in the family history prior to the publication of this affidavit.

"5. Dr. Graham is a competent witness, and his testimony is confirmed in every point.

"6. In view of these facts, that there should ever have been any doubts raised about the marriage of the parents of Mr. Lincoln, and that it should have been gravely discussed, and never explicitly settled in the various biographies, is remarkable."

Soon after the publication of the above facts a historian of Louisville, Kentucky, Dr. Henry Whitney Cleveland, realizing the importance of Dr. Graham's reminiscences, secured from him, in his hundredth year, an account of what he remembered of Thomas Lincoln. Mr. Cleveland took down word for word what Dr. Graham told him, and we print it in full below. We regard it as in many ways the most important unpublished document we have been able to discover in regard to Thomas Lincoln. As to the mental condition of Dr. Graham in 1884, we have the testimony of some of the leading citizens of Louisville. In the paper read before the Southern Historical Society in 1880, in commemoration of the one hundredth anniversary of Louisville, Dr. Durrett said of Mr. Graham:

"Four years more will make him a centenarian, and yet he moves along the streets every day with the elastic step of manhood's prime, and the eagle eye which made him in youth the finest rifle-shot in the world is shorn but little of its unerring sight. He was a practising physician three-quarters of a century ago, and is the author of several learned books of a professional and philosophical character. His health is yet good, his faculties well preserved, and he seems to-day more like a man of sixty-nine than ninety-six."

In 1884, when Dr. Graham had become a centenarian, a banquet was given him at which all the leading citizens of Louisville were present. Without exception, every one of the persons with whom we have talked of Dr. Graham's condition at this time affirms that he was mentally vigorous and his memory trustworthy. In the face of such testimony the statements in the following document must be accepted:

DR. GRAHAM'S STATEMENT.

The original statement was written out, at Dr. Graham's dictation, by Dr. Henry Whitney Cleveland of Louisville, Kentucky, but was signed by Dr. Graham's own hand.

I, CHRISTOPHER COLUMBUS GRAHAM, now in my hundredth year, and visiting the Southern Exposition in Louisville, where I live, tell this to please my young friend Henry Cleveland, who is nearly half my age. He was often at the Springs Hotel in Harrodsburg, Kentucky, then owned and kept by me for invalids and pleasure-seekers. I am one of the two living men who can prove that Abraham Lincoln, or Linkhorn, as the family was miscalled, was born in lawful wedlock, for I saw Thomas Lincoln marry Nancy Hanks on the twelfth day of June, 1806. He was born at what was then known as the Rock Spring Farm—it is now called the Creal Place—three miles south of Hodgensville, in Larue County, Kentucky.

Kentucky was first a county of Virginia after its settlement, and then was divided into three counties ; and these, again divided, are pretty much the present State. The first historian was Filson, who made and published the first map of the separate territory, with the names of streams and stations as given by Daniel Boone and Squire Boone, James Harrod, and others. I knew all of these, as well as President Lincoln's parents.

I think they lived on the farm four years after he was born. Another boy was born in Hodgensville, or, I should say, buried there. The sister, Sally, was older than Abe, I think. I think the paper now owned by Henry Cleveland is the " marriage lines " written by Rev. Jesse Head, a well-known Methodist preacher. I do not think the old Bible it was found in was that of Tom Lincoln. It would cost too much for him. All of the records in it were those of the father's family—the John M. Hewetts—of the wife of Dr. Theodore S. Bell. Dr. Bell was only about twenty years younger than I am, and probably got the certificate in 1858 or 1860, when assertions were made that Tom Lincoln and Nancy Hanks were not married when Abe was born.

He was reputed to have been born February 12, 1809, and I see no good reason to dispute it. Sally, I am sure, was the first child, and Nancy was a fresh and good-looking girl—I should say past twenty. Nancy lived with the Sparrow family a good bit. It was likely Tom had the family Bible from Virginia, through his father, called Abraham Linkhorn. His brothers, however, were older—if they were brothers, and not uncles, as some say. I was hunting roots for my medicines, and just went to the wedding to get a good supper, and got it.

Bibles cost as much as the spinning-wheel, or loom, or rifle, and were imported in the main. A favorite with the Methodists was Fletcher's, or one he wrote a preface for. Preachers used it, and had no commentaries. A book dedicated to King James or any other king did not take well in Revolutionary times. The Bibles I used to see had no printed records or blanks, but a lot of fine linen hand-made paper would be bound in front or back. On this, family history and land matters were written out fully like a book. Some had fifty pages. The court-houses even were made of logs, and the meeting-houses too, if they had any. No registers were kept as in English parish churches, and are not yet. Before a license could be had, a bond and security was taken of the bridegroom, and the preacher had to return to the court all marriages of the year. This was often a long list, and at times papers were lost or forgotten, but not often. The " marriage lines " given by the preacher to the parties were very important in case the records were burned up by accident. Such is the paper that Henry Cleveland has shown to me. The ring was not often used, as so few had one to use. The Methodist Church discipline forbid " the putting on of gold or costly apparel," and I think a preacher with a gold watch—if not an inherited one—would have been dismissed. A preacher that married was " located," and that ended his itinerancy in the Methodist Church. The Presbyterians were educated and married; Baptists not educated.

Tom Lincoln was a carpenter, and a good one for those days, when a cabin was built mainly with the axe, and not a nail or bolt or hinge in it, only leathers and pins to the door, and no glass, except in watches and spectacles and bottles. Tom had the best set of tools in what was then and now Washington County. Larue County, where the farm was settled, was then Hardin.

Jesse Head, the good Methodist preacher that married them, was also a carpenter or cabinet-maker by trade, and as he was then a neighbor, they were good friends. He had a quarrel with the bishops, and was not an itinerant for several years, but an editor, and county judge afterwards, in Harrodsburg. Mr. Henry Cleveland has his commission from Governor Isaac Shelby.

Many great men of the South and North were then opposed to slavery, mainly because the new negroes were as wild as the Indians, and might prove as dangerous. Few of the whites could read, and yet Pope and Dryden and Shakespeare were as well known as Bunyan's "Pilgrim's Progress" and Baxter's "Saints' Rest." Some were educated in Virginia and North Carolina before they came, and these, when they became teachers, wrote out their school-books entirely by hand.

Thomas Lincoln, like his son after him, had a notion that fortunes could be made by trips to New Orleans by flatboat. This was dangerous, from snags and whirlpools in the rivers, from Indians, and even worse—pirates of the French, Canadians, and half-breeds. Steam was unknown, and the flats had to be sold in New Orleans, as they could not be rowed back against the currents. The neighbors joked Tom for building his boat too high and narrow, from an idea he had about speed, that has since been adopted by ocean steamships. But he lacked in ballast. He loaded her up with deer and bear hams and buffalo, which last was then not so plenty for meat or hides as when the Boone brothers came in. Besides, he had wax, for bees seemed to follow the white people, and he had wolf and coon and mink and beaver skins, gentian root (that folks then called "gensang" or "'sang"), nuts, honey, peach-brandy and whiskey, and jeans woven by his wife and Sally Bush, that he married after Nancy died. Some said she died of heart trouble, from slanders about her and old Abe Enloe, called Inlow, while her Abe, named for the pioneer Abraham Linkhorn, was still little. But I am ahead of my story, for Nancy had just got married where I was telling it, and the flatboat and Sally Bush Lincoln come in before he goes over to what people called "Indiany." I will finish that, and then go back.

He started down Knob Creek when it was flush with rains ; but the leaves held water like a sponge, and the ground was shaded with big trees and papaw and sassafras thickets and "cain," as Bible-read folks spelt the cane, and streams didn't dry up in summer like they do now. When he got to the Ohio it was flush, too, and full of whirlpools and snags. He had his tool-chest along, intending to stop and work in Indiana and take down another boat. But he never got to the Mississippi with that, for it upset, and he only saved his chest and part of his load because he was near to the Indiana shore. He stored what he saved under bark, and came home a-foot, and in debt to neighbors who had helped him. But people never pressed a man that lost by Indians or water.

Now I go back for a spell. Thomas and Nancy both could read and write, and little Abe went to school about a year. He was eight years old at the time of the accident to Tom Lincoln's down-the-river venture. Thomas and Nancy were good common people, not above nor below their neighbors, and I did not take much notice of them, because there was no likelihood that their wedding would mean more than other people's did.

The preacher Jesse Head often talked to me on religion and politics, for I always liked the Methodists. I have thought it might have been as much from his free-spoken opinions as from Henry Clay's American-African colonization scheme in 1817, that I lost a likely negro man, who was leader of my musicians. It is said that Tom Corwin met him in Ohio on his way to Canada, and asked if I was along. The boy said no, he was going for his freedom. Governor Corwin said he was a fool; he had never been whipped or abused, but dressed like a white man, with the best to eat, and that hundreds of white people would be glad of such a good place, with no care, but cared for.

The boy drew himself up and said : "Marse Tom, that situation with all its advantages is open to you, if you want ter go an' fill it."

But Judge Head never encouraged any runaway, nor had any "underground railroad." He only talked freely and boldly, and had plenty of true Southern men with him, such as Clay. The Eli Whitney cotton-gin had now made slavery so valuable that preachers looked in Hebrew and Greek Testaments for scripture for it.

Tom Lincoln and Nancy, and Sally Bush were just steeped full of Jesse Head's notions about the wrong of slavery and the rights of man as explained by Thomas Jefferson and Thomas Paine. Abe Lincoln the Liberator was made in his mother's womb and father's brain and in the prayers of Sally Bush ; by the talks and sermons of Jesse Head, the Methodist circuit rider, assistant county judge, printer-editor, and cabinet-maker. Little Abe grew up to serve as a cabinet-maker himself two Presidential terms.

It was in my trip to Canada after my negro that I met the younger brother of the great chief Tecumseh. A mob wanted to kill me because I was after my property that had legs and a level head. The Indian was one of the finest looking men I ever saw, and in the full uniform of a British officer. He protected me, and we had a talk after the danger was over. He said that history was right about the death of his great brother Tecumseh at the battle of the Thames in 1813. But the story of his skin being taken off by soldiers to make razor-straps was all a lie, as they never had the chance. He was not even slain at the point in the battle indicated by Colonel Richard M. Johnson, whose accession to the Vice-Presidency in 1836 was largely due to the credit which he gained for this supposed exploit. My Indian protector said he was a lad at the time, but [was] there; and that the red men never abandoned their chiefs, dead nor alive.

I come back again to the Lincoln-Hanks wedding of 1806. Rev. or Judge Jesse Head was one of the most prominent men there, as he was able to own slaves, but did not on principle. Next, I reckon, came Mordecai Lincoln, at one time member of the Kentucky legislature. He was a good Indian fighter ; and although some say he was the elder brother of Tom Lincoln, I understood he was his uncle, or father's brother. The story of his killing the Indian who killed old Abraham Linkhorn is all "my eye and Betty Martin."

My acceptance of this whole pedigree is on hearsay, and none of it from the locality of Tom Lincoln's home. There is a Virginia land warrant, No. 3,334, of March 4, 1780, for four hundred acres of land, cost one hundred and sixty pounds, located in Jefferson County, Kentucky, on Long Run ; and [there is a report of survey for the same tract (see pages 22 and 23)] signed by William Shanon, D. S. J. C., and William May, S. J. C., witnessed by Ana- niah Lincoln and Josiah Lincoln, C. C. (chain-carriers), and Abraham Link- horn, Marker, dated May 7, 1785, five years later. "Mordecai Lincoln, Gentleman," is the title given one who died in Berks County, Pennsylvania, in 1735, and his will is recorded in the Register's office in Philadelphia. New Jersey, Virginia, and Tennessee also have the name correctly, in the last century. The fame of General Benjamin Lincoln of the Revolution was on every tongue at that time. In the field-book of Daniel Boone, owned by Lyman C. Draper, five hundred acres of land was entered for Abraham Lincoln on treasury warrant No. 5,994, December 11, 1782. The officers of the land-office of Virginia could spell, and so could the surveyor and deputy sur- veyor (Record " B," p. 60 of Jefferson County in 1785). The two chain-car- riers spelled the name correctly. Why not also think that the third man spelled his correctly ? A very illiterate man could pronounce what he could not spell, and Abraham Linkhorn, who had money and could write, knew his own name. President Lincoln told James Speed : "I don't know who my grandfather was, and am more concerned to know what his grandson will be." I am not sure that we know, either, perfectly yet.*

While you pin me down to facts I will say that I saw Nancy Hanks Lincoln at her wedding, a fresh-looking girl, I should say over twenty. Tom was a respectable mechanic and could choose, and she was treated with respect. . . .

I was at the infare, too, given by John H. Parrott, her guardian, and only girls with money had guardians appointed by the court. We had bear-meat (that you can eat the grease of, and it not rise like other fats) ; venison ; wild turkey and ducks ; eggs, wild and tame (so common that you could buy them at two bits a bushel) ; maple sugar, swung on a string, to bite off for coffee or whiskey ; syrup in big gourds ; peach-and-honey ; a sheep that the two families barbecued whole over coals of wood burned in a pit, and covered with green boughs to keep the juices in ; and a race for the whiskey bottle. The sheep cost the most, and corn was early raised in what is now Boyle County, at the Isaac Shelby place. I don't know who stamped in the first peach-seed, but they grew before the apples. Our table was of the puncheons cut from solid logs, and on the next day they were the floor of the new cabin.

It is all stuff about Tom Lincoln keeping his wife in an open shed in a winter when the wild animals left the woods and stood in the corners next the stick-and-clay chimneys, so as not to freeze to death ; or, if climbers, got on the roof. The Lincolns had a cow and calf, milk and butter, a good feather bed, for I have slept in it (while they took the buffalo robes on the floor, be- cause I was a doctor). They had home-woven "kiverlids," big and little pots, a loom and wheel ; and William Hardesty, who was there too, can say with me that Tom Lincoln was a man and took care of his wife.

* The memoranda for Lincoln's genealogy (page 223), and the introduction to this work, as well as the first chapter, show that we do know now, beyond a doubt, who and what Lincoln's ancestors were.

I have been in bark camps with Daniel and Squire Boone and James Harrod. We have had to wade in the " crick," as Daniel spelt it, to get our scent lost in the water, and the Indian dogs off our trail. When trailed and there was no water handy, I have seen Daniel cut a big grapevine loose at the bottom, with his tomahawk, from the ground. Then, with a run and swing from the tree it hung to, swing and jump forty feet clear, to break the scent on the ground. I have done it too, but not so far. He could beat any man on the run and jump, but it took more than two Indians or one bear to make him do it. If no dog barked in the silent woods, we could run backward very fast, and make Mr. Indian think we had gone the way we came. They went that way, and we the other for dear scalps and hair. Squirrels barking or chattering at Indians, or dogs, often told us of our danger. I wanted to have a pioneer exhibit at the great Louisville Southern Expositions of 1883 and 1884. I wanted the dense laurel and the papaw thickets planted in rich soil ; the bear climbing the bee-tree, and beaten by the swinging log hung by the hunter in his way ; the creeping Indian with his tomahawk, and the hunter with the old flint-and-steel rifle, just as I had seen them. Then I wanted to have women from the mountains and the counties that railroads and turnpikes have not opened, and have them in real life, to spin and weave, or bead and fringe the moccasin and hunting-shirt and leggings as they did when I was a boy. This, by the side of the industries and arts of the new era, and the wool and cotton machinery in its present perfection, would indeed tell to the eyes of the changes seen by an old man who has lived a hundred years. As they did not listen to me, I have asked Henry Cleveland, who was a boy and played with my little children at the Harrodsburg Springs in the forties, to write it as I talked to him. I am very deaf, but can see and talk, and will now write my autograph to what he has written and copied off, and will take up James Harrod at another time.

Christopher Columbus Graham

in my 100th year

III.

A LEAF FROM LINCOLN'S EXERCISE-BOOK, USED IN 1824. HITHERTO UNPUBLISHED. (See page 78.)

From the Collection of Mr. William H. Lambert of Philadelphia.

MR. LAMBERT's collection of Lincolniana has been made most intelligently. Primarily it consists of the literature directly relating to Lincoln, and includes a large number of books and pamphlets, the list of biographies and eulogies being very full. It also comprises a large number of engravings of Lincoln, and a number of autograph letters and documents, chief among which are a leaf from Lincoln's sum-book, 1824; the precipe in his first lawsuit; letter to William H. Herndon, relative to General Taylor and the Mexican War; letter to his step-brother, John D. Johnston, refusing assent to the latter's proposition to dispose of the mother's interest in property; printed copy of the Emancipation Proclamation, signed by Lincoln, attested by Mr. Seward, and certified by Mr. Nicolay, being one of the twenty copies made for the great Sanitary Fair in Philadelphia, 1864; and a series of autograph letters of William H. Herndon, written in 1866 and 1867, relative to his lectures on Lincoln and the biography which he proposed writing. Among the books are a copy of Paley's works, from Lincoln's private library; "Angel on Limitations," from his law library; and "Webster's Dictionary," used by Lincoln at the White House.

The office table, bookcase, revolving chair, and wooden inkstand owned and used by Lincoln in his law office at Springfield, with certificates from Mr. Herndon and others as to the genuineness of these articles, are in the collection. From the inkstand, Mr. Herndon states, the "house-divided-against-itself" speech was written.

The Volk life-mask and casts of hands, the Clark-Mills life-mask, and an original ambrotype of Lincoln, made in August, 1860, are also owned by Mr. Lambert.

IV.

THE OLDROYD LINCOLN COLLECTION.

THE oldest and probably the largest collection of Lincolniana which has been made is known as the Oldroyd collection, and is at present in the house in Washington, D. C., where Lincoln died, April 15, 1865. The collection takes its name from its owner, Colonel O. H. Oldroyd. The germ of the collection was a campaign badge which excited the possessor's desire to have others. In the days of 1860 in Ohio—Mr. Oldroyd lived in Ohio—it was easy to get badges adorned with Mr. Lincoln's face, or with a section of the rail fence and the flat-boat which had been adopted by the people as his armorial bearings. The campaign badges which young Oldroyd saved naturally drew other things to them; pictures off tomato cans, tobacco pouches, soap and chewing-gum wrappers, and what not; cuts from the newspapers, campaign pictures.

If Mr. Oldroyd had not been born with the collecting spirit all this would probably have amounted to nothing. It would have been relegated to the garret and one day have been burned. But he had that itching for possession, and the more he had the more he wanted. He spent all he could earn in buying new treasures, and he began a general exchange with other collectors, until by the close of the war he probably had the finest lot of Lincolniana in the United States.

It was the possession of this collection which induced Mr. Oldroyd to go to Springfield, Ill. Here he hoped to add easily to what he had already gathered, much concerning Lincoln's early life, and to find a permanent home for his whole collection. Few people appreciated the value of Lincoln souvenirs in those days, and many curious pieces came into Mr. Oldroyd's hands for the asking. As the collection became larger and the public began to show interest in it, Mr. Oldroyd determined to put it in a place where he could exhibit it freely. The old Lincoln homestead, bought by Mr. Lincoln in 1846, the house where he was living when elected to the Presidency, was standing. It had been sadly neglected for many years, and now was vacant. Mr. Oldroyd rented it, and put his collection into the double parlors of the house. The place became soon one of the "monuments" of Springfield, and visitors went out of their way to see it. It became the headquarters for old soldiers and the starting point for all kinds of patriotic gatherings. Mr. Robert Lincoln, seeing the interest which the public took in his father's old home, and appreciating the efforts of Mr. Oldroyd to make a complete collection, turned over the Lincoln homestead in 1887 to the State as a perpetual memorial to Abraham Lincoln. The legislature of Illinois formally accepted the gift, and installed Mr. Oldroyd as guardian of the house, it being understood that his collection was to remain with him.

The undertaking proved a success, and matters went well until in 1893 the administration changed. For some reason which only those initiated into the mysteries of party government can understand, it was deemed unwise by the party rulers to allow Mr. Oldroyd, who happened to be of the opposing faith, to remain in charge of the Lincoln Home; so he was relieved of his functions as guardian, and a new incumbent selected. One result of the change, which the new administration had probably not counted on, was that, as the collection in the house belonged to Mr. Oldroyd, and not to the State, when he went out that went out too. The intelligent people of Springfield of both parties regretted exceedingly this ludicrous application of party principles to so non-partisan a subject as a collection of Lincoln relics; but nothing was done to save the museum, and Mr. Oldroyd was obliged to leave the town where he had struggled with pathetic patience for so many years to get a permanent home for his Lincolniana.

After some casting about he finally determined to remove to Washington, and he was encouraged to this step by several men of the city and government—prominent among whom were Chief Justice Fuller, Dr. Hamlin, a leading clergyman, General Schofield, and the Hon. G. G. Hubbard. These gentlemen had founded a Lincoln Memorial Association; and, renting the house on Tenth Street where Lincoln had died on April 15, 1865, they installed Mr. Oldroyd in it. Their plan was to petition Congress to buy the house and collection, and to appropriate enough for the guardian's salary. Considerable interest was awakened in the enterprise, and the association, on the strength of this, felt justified in keeping the house open for several months. The appropriation did not come, however, and the gentlemen decided that the expenses could not be kept up indefinitely, and that it would be necessary to close up the exhibit until the heart of Congress could be converted.

The situation was a difficult one for Mr. Oldroyd. He had made the change from Springfield to Washington at large expense to himself, and now he could ill afford to carry on the enterprise alone. But with a pluck and a devotion to his cause which has characterized all his movements he decided to take the burden on himself, rent the house, keep open the museum, and trust to the public to support it. To aid in the undertaking, he compiled and published a small volume—" The Words of Lincoln." The profits from the sale of this book, together with the small fee charged to enter the museum, are all that now support the undertaking.

The collection whose history has been here sketched is full of curious and interesting articles. Among the personal effects of Mr. Lincoln which Mr. Oldroyd has collected, the most valuable is undoubtedly the tall silk hat which was worn by Lincoln on the night of his assassination. There are several specimens of the plain and homely garments used by Mr. Lincoln in his early days in Illinois. Of household furniture there are many examples. The most touching is, undoubtedly, the simple, old-fashioned cradle in which Mrs. Lincoln, and, if tradition is correct, Mr. Lincoln also, rocked " Tad " and Willie. A wooden settee which stood for years on the veranda of the Springfield house, is exhibited, as well as the cooking-stove which stood in the Lincoln kitchen at the time when the family moved to Washington. Mr. Oldroyd says that he has been offered extravagant sums by stove dealers for this stove, they wanting it presumably to use as an advertisement. Another valuable piece of furniture is the wooden office chair which Mr. Lincoln used when he first began to practise law in 1837. A chair of still greater interest is an old-fashioned hair-cloth rocker in which he sat in Ford's Theatre on the night on which he received his death-wound.

Several autograph letters from Mr. Lincoln are owned by Mr. Oldroyd. By far the most interesting specimen of his writing is the short autobiography which he prepared for his friend Jesse Fell before the campaign of 1860. This autobiography was the foundation of all the histories which were issued in such great numbers just before and after his first election.

In Lincoln portraiture the collection is very full, though it is rather from a historical point of view than from an artistic that it is valuable. Mr. Oldroyd has copies of nearly all of the engravings and lithographs issued in Mr. Lincoln's lifetime. He has also a splendid lot of wood-cuts gathered from newspapers, magazines, and pamphlets. In this collection of prints there are numbers of views of the Lincoln family and of various scenes connected with Mr. Lincoln's public career. From the spring of 1860 until after the funeral, in 1865, there were few issues of the illustrated papers in this country which did not contain something on the President. Mr. Oldroyd has succeeded in getting nearly all of these prints, among them a great many caricatures. He has a full set of " Vanity Fair," and many of the Currier and Ives lithographs, now so rare. An interesting feature of the collection is the number of curios it contains—campaign documents of various kinds, such as badges, medals, pins, letter paper and envelopes, flags, etc.

The use that was made by advertisers of Lincoln's face during his Presidency is shown by a case of common articles ; there are tomato cans, soap, washing fluid, tobacco pouches, cigarette cases, spruce gum, and many other trivial articles, all enclosed in highly-colored papers bearing portraits of Mr. Lincoln, surrounded by a rail fence or some popular campaign legend.

The only complete collection of the portraits of Lincoln issued by the government which we have ever seen, Mr. Oldroyd owns. Among them is a revenue stamp calling for five pounds of tobacco ; another is good for seventy gallons of distilled spirits, a third for four ounces of snuff, and a fourth

calls for cigarettes.   Lincoln's head appears on a variety of postage stamps ;
the four, six, fifteen, and ninety-cent stamps all bear his face.   The six-cent
stamp of each of the Departments has a head of Lincoln.   The old fifty-cent
" shin plaster " is exhibited.   It was the only one of our scrip issue which bore
a head of Lincoln.   His picture is also to be found on a ten-dollar greenback,
a one-hundred-dollar United States note, and a one-hundred-dollar government
bond.

     The most valuable portion of the Oldroyd collection is undoubtedly its
books, pamphlets, and clippings.   The library contains almost all of the
biographies which have been issued, a large number of memoirs by con-
temporaries of Lincoln, and many war records.   There are copies of some
three hundred different sermons delivered at the time of Lincoln's death,
as well as a great number of the pieces of music composed in his honor.

     A precious book in Mr. Oldroyd's Lincoln library is the Bible owned by
Thomas Lincoln, the father of the President.   This Bible bears the date of
1798 ; it undoubtedly went with the Lincolns from Kentucky to Indiana, and
was carried from there by them when they moved into Illinois.   It was kept
in the family of Thomas Lincoln's step-children until 1892, when it was sold
to be exhibited at the World's Fair.   It afterward passed to Mr. Oldroyd.

     At present it is not known what will be done with the Oldroyd collection.
The owner has made heroic efforts to keep it together, and it is to be hoped
that some way will open by which he can realize his ambition.

*A series of articles on the middle and later periods of Lincoln's life will be found
in the* McClure's Magazine, *beginning with the number for March,* 1896.   *These
articles are prepared by the authors of the present volume, assisted by many persons
who were in close personal association with Lincoln, and possess important facts and
reminiscences never before published.   The articles are very fully illustrated with
numerous portraits of Lincoln, his friends and associates, and with pictures, specially
drawn or photographed for the Magazine, of all important places and scenes with
which he was connected.*